THE WORLD'S BEST-LOVED POEMS

THE WORLD'S BEST-LOVED POEMS

Compiled by
JAMES GILCHRIST LAWSON

Editor of
"THE WORLD'S BEST HUMOROUS ANECDOTES"
"THE WORLD'S BEST EPIGRAMS"
"THE WORLD'S BEST CONUNDRUMS"
"THE WORLD'S BEST PROVERBS AND MAXIMS"
Etc., Etc.

HARPER & ROW, PUBLISHERS
NEW YORK, EVANSTON, AND LONDON

Introduction

It has been the purpose of the compiler and publishers of *The World's Best-Loved Poems* to gather into one volume the choicest of the world's most helpful short religious and popular poems and brief prose selections, including famous old-time favorites and the best of current popular verse; the masterpieces of renowned poets and gems of anonymous writers.

Many of the pieces were selected not from the standpoint of highest literary merit, but because of their appeal to the human heart. It is confidently believed the compilation as a whole will add a quota of cheer and inspiration to all of us—world pilgrims that we are!

The compiler has endeavored to include no copyrighted poem without the consent of the owner. He is grateful to those who have generously granted this favor: without this co-operation the anthology could not have been so comprehensive.

J. Gilchrist Lawson

Contents

ix

xv

xviii

xxiii

The Death of the Flowers [1]

THE melancholy days are come, the saddest of the
  year—
Of wailing winds and naked woods and meadows brown
  and sear.
Heaped in the hollows of the grove, the autumn leaves
  lie dead;
They rustle to the eddying gust, and to the rabbit's tread.
The robin and the wren are flown, and from the shrubs
  the jay,
And from the wood-top calls the crow through all the
  gloomy day.

Where are the flowers, the fair young flowers, that lately
  sprang and stood
In brighter light and softer airs, a beauteous sisterhood?
Alas! they all are in their graves; the gentle race of
  flowers
Are lying in their lowly beds with the fair and good of
  ours.
The rain is falling where they lie, but the cold November
  rain
Calls not from out the gloomy earth the lovely ones again.

The wind-flower and the violet, they perished long ago,
And the briar-rose and the orchis died amid the summer
  glow;

[1] From "Poetical Works of William Cullen Bryant." By special permission of
D. Appleton & Co.

But on the hill the golden-rod, and the aster in the wood,
And the yellow sunflower by the brook, in autumn beauty
stood,
Till fell the frost from the clear cold heaven, as falls the
plague on men,
And the brightness of their smile has gone from upland,
glade, and glen.

And now, when comes the calm mild day, as still such
days will come,
To call the squirrel and the bee from out their winter
home;
When the sound of dropping nuts is heard, though all the
trees are still,
And twinkle in the smoky light the waters of the rill;
The south-wind searches for the flowers whose fragrance
late he bore,
And sighs to find them in the wood and by the stream
no more.

And then I think of one who in her youthful beauty died,
The fair meek blossom that grew up and faded by my
side,
In the cold moist earth we laid her, when the forests cast
the leaf,
And we wept that one so lovely should have a life so brief;
Yet not unmeet it was that one, like that young friend of
ours,
So gentle and so beautiful, should perish with the flowers.

—William Cullen Bryant

Beautiful Things

BEAUTIFUL faces are those that wear—
It matters little if dark or fair—
Whole-souled honesty printed there.

Beautiful eyes are those that show,
Like crystal panes where heart-fires glow,
Beautiful thoughts that burn below.

Beautiful lips are those whose words
Leap from the heart like songs of birds,
Yet whose utterance prudence girds.

Beautiful hands are those that do
Work that is earnest and brave and true,
Moment by moment the long day through.

Beautiful feet are those that go
On kindly ministries to and fro—
Down lowliest way, if God wills it so.

Beautiful shoulders are those that bear
Ceaseless burdens of homely care
With patient grace and daily prayer.

Beautiful lives are those that bless—
Silent rivers of happiness
Whose hidden fountains but few may guess.

—Ellen P. Allerton

Beautiful

BEAUTIFUL sun that giveth us light,
Beautiful moon that shineth by night,
Beautiful planets in the heaven so far,
Beautiful twinkle of each little star.

Beautiful waters so blue and so clear,
Beautiful sound of the surges we hear,
Beautiful brooklet, its ripples so sweet,
Beautiful flowers that bloom at our feet.

Beautiful springtime when all is delight;
Beautiful summer, so warm and so bright;
Beautiful autumn, with fruits and with grain;
Beautiful winter, with snowflakes again.

—*W. A. Bixler*

BELLS

The Bells

HEAR the sledges with the bells—
Silver bells!
What a world of merriment their melody foretells!
How they tinkle, tinkle, tinkle,
In the icy air of night!
While the stars that oversprinkle

All the heavens, seem to twinkle
With a crystalline delight;
Keeping time, time, time,
In a sort of Runic rhyme,
To the tintinnabulation that so musically wells
From the bells, bells, bells, bells,
Bells, bells, bells,—
From the jingling and the tinkling of the bells.

Hear the mellow wedding bells,
Golden bells!
What a world of happiness their harmony foretells!
Through the balmy air of night
How they ring out their delight!
From the molten-golden notes,
And all in tune,
What a liquid ditty floats
To the turtle dove that listens, while she gloats
On the moon!
Oh, from out the sounding cells,
What a gush of euphony voluminously wells!
How it swells!
How it dwells
On the Future! how it tells
Of the rapture that impels
To the swinging and the ringing
Of the bells, bells, bells,
Of the bells, bells, bells, bells,
Bells, bells, bells,—
To the rhyming and the chiming of the bells!

Hear the loud alarum bells—
Brazen bells!
What a tale of terror now their turbulency tells!
In the startled ear of night
How they scream out their affright!
Too much horrified to speak
They can only shriek, shriek,
Out of tune,
In a clamorous appealing to the mercy of the fire,
In a mad expostulation with the deaf and frantic fire,
Leaping higher, higher, higher,
With a desperate desire,
And a resolute endeavor,
Now—now to sit or never,
By the side of the pale-faced moon.
Oh, the bells, bells, bells!
What a tale their terror tells
Of despair!
How they clang, and clash, and roar!
What a horror they outpour
On the bosom of the palpitating air!
Yet the ear it fully knows,
By the twanging,
And the clanging,
How the danger ebbs and flows;
Yet the ear distinctly tells,
In the jangling,
And the wrangling,
How the danger sinks and swells,
By the sinking or the swelling in the anger of the bells—
Of the bells—

Of the bells, bells, bells, bells,
Bells, bells, bells,—
In the clamor and the clangor of the bells!

Hear the tolling of the bells—
Iron bells!
What a world of solemn thought their monody compels!
In the silence of the night,
How we shiver with affright
At the melancholy menace of their tone!
For every sound that floats
From the rust within their throats
Is a groan.
And the people—ah, the people—
They that dwell up in the steeple,
All alone,
And who tolling, tolling, tolling,
In that muffled monotone,
Feel a glory in so rolling
On the human heart a stone—
They are neither man nor woman—
They are neither brute nor human—
They are Ghouls:
And their king it is who tolls;
And he rolls, rolls, rolls,
Rolls
A paean from the bells!
And his merry bosom swells
With the paean of the bells!
And he dances, and he yells;
Keeping time, time, time,
In a sort of Runic rhyme,

To the paean of the bells—
Of the bells:
Keeping time, time, time,
In a sort of Runic rhyme,
To the throbbing of the bells—
Of the bells, bells, bells—
To the sobbing of the bells;
Keeping time, time, time,
As he knells, knells, knells,
In a happy Runic rhyme,
To the rolling of the bells—
Of the bells, bells, bells—
To the tolling of the bells,
Of the bells, bells, bells, bells—
Bells, bells, bells—
To the moaning and the groaning of the bells!

—*Edgar Allan Poe*

THE BIBLE

Holy Bible, Book Divine

HOLY Bible, book divine,
Precious treasure, thou art mine;
Mine to tell me whence I came,
Mine to teach me what I am.

Mine to chide me when I rove,
Mine to show a Saviour's love;
Mine art thou to guide my feet,
Mine to judge, condemn, acquit.

8

Mine to comfort in distress,
If the Holy Spirit bless;
Mine to show by living faith
Man can triumph over death.

Mine to tell of joys to come,
And the rebel sinner's doom;
Holy Bible, book divine,
Precious treasure, thou art mine.

—*John Burton*

Sir Walter Scott's Tribute

The great *Sir Walter Scott* wrote:

"WITHIN this awful volume lies
The mystery of mysteries:
Happiest they of human race,
To whom their God has given grace
To read, to fear, to hope, to pray,
To lift the latch, to force the way;
But better had they ne'er been born,
Who read to doubt, or read to scorn."

My Mother's Bible

THIS Book is all that's left me now—
Tears will unbidden start;
With faltering lip and throbbing brow
I press it to my heart.

For many generations past
　Here is our family tree:
My mother's hands this Bible clasped,
　She, dying, gave it me.

Ah! well do I remember those
　Whose names these records bear;
Who round the hearthstone used to close
　After the evening prayer,
And speak of what these pages said
　In tones my heart would thrill!
Though they are with the silent dead,
　Here are they living still!

My father read this holy Book
　To brothers, sisters, dear:
How calm was my poor mother's look,
　Who loved God's Word to hear!
Her angel face—I see it yet!
　What thronging memories come!
Again the little group is met
　Within the halls of home!

The truest friend man ever knew,
　Thy constancy I've tried;
When all were false, I found thee true,
　My counselor and guide.
The mines of earth no treasures give
　That could this volume buy;
In teaching me the way to live,
　It taught me how to die!

　　　　　　　　　　—George P. Morris

A Home Without a Bible [1]

(Abridged)

WHAT is home without a Bible?
　　'Tis a home where day is night,
Starless night, for o'er life's pathway
Heaven can shed no kindly light.

What is home without a Bible?
　　'Tis a home where daily bread
For *the body* is provided,
　　But *the soul* is never fed.

What is home without a Bible?
　　'Tis a family out at sea,
Compass lost and rudder broken,
　　Drifting, drifting, *thoughtlessly.*

—*C. D. Meigs*

BIRDS

Robert of Lincoln [2]

(Abridged)

MERRILY swinging on brier and weed,
　　Near to the nest of his little dame,
Over the mountain-side or mead,

---

[1] Copyright by Charles D. Meigs.　Used by permission of Meigs Publishing Co., Indianapolis.
[2] From "Poetical Works of William Cullen Bryant." By special permission of D. Appleton & Company.

Robert of Lincoln is telling his name:
    Bob-o'-link, bob-o'-link,
    Spink, spank, spink;
Snug and safe is that nest of ours,
Hidden among the summer flowers.
            Chee, chee, chee.

Robert of Lincoln is gaily dressed,
    Wearing a bright black wedding-coat;
White are his shoulders and white his crest.
    Hear him call in his merry note:
        Bob-o'-link, bob-o'-link,
        Spink, spank, spink;
Look, what a nice new coat is mine,
Sure there was never a bird so fine.
            Chee, chee, chee.

Robert of Lincoln's Quaker wife,
    Pretty and quiet, with plain brown wings,
Passing at home a patient life,
    Broods in the grass while her husband sings:
        Bob-o'-link, bob-o'-link,
        Spink, spank, spink;
Brood, kind creature; you need not fear
Thieves and robbers while I am here.
            Chee, chee, chee.
                        —*William Cullen Bryant*

The Sand-Piper

ACROSS the narrow beach we flit,
  One little sand-piper and I;
And fast I gather, bit by bit,
  The scattered drift-wood, bleached and dry.
The wild waves reach their hands for it,
  The wild wind raves, the tide runs high,
As up and down the beach we flit—
  One little sand-piper and I.

Above our heads the sullen clouds
  Scud black and swift across the sky;
Like silent ghosts, in misty shrouds
  Stand out the white light-houses nigh.
Almost as far as eye can reach,
  I see the close-reefed vessels fly,
As fast we flit along the beach—
  One little sand-piper and I.

I watch him as he skims along,
  Uttering his sweet and mournful cry;
He starts not at my fitful song,
  Or flash of fluttering drapery:
He has no thought of any wrong,
  He scans me with a fearless eye;
Staunch friends are we, well-tried and strong,
  This little sand-piper and I.

Comrade, where wilt thou be to-night,
  When the loosed storm breaks furiously?
My drift-wood fire will burn so bright!

To what warm shelter canst thou fly?
I do not fear for thee, though wroth
    The tempest rushes through the sky,
For are we not God's children both,
    Thou little sand-piper and I?

—*Celia Thaxter*

From "The Birds of Killingsworth"

DO you ne'er think what wondrous beings these?
    Do you ne'er think who made them, and who taught
The dialect they speak, where melodies alone are the
    interpreters of thought
Whose household words are songs in many keys,
Sweeter than instrument of men e'er caught!
Whose habitations in the tree-tops even
Are half-way houses on the road to heaven!

Think, every morning when the sun peeps through
The dim, leaf-latticed windows of the grove,
How jubilant the happy birds renew
Their old, melodious madrigals of love!
And when you think of this, remember too,
'Tis always morning somewhere, and above
The awakening continents, from shore to shore,
Somewhere the birds are singing evermore.

—*H. W. Longfellow*

To a Waterfowl [1]

WHITHER, 'midst falling dew,
  While glow the heavens with the last steps of day,
Far, through their rosy depths, dost thou pursue
  Thy solitary way?

Vainly the fowler's eye
  Might mark thy distant flight to do thee wrong,
As, darkly painted on the crimson sky,
  Thy figure floats along.

Seek'st thou the plashy brink
  Of weedy lake, or marge of river wide,
Or where the rocking billows rise and sink
  On the chafed ocean's side?

There is a Power whose care
  Teaches thy way along that pathless coast—
The desert and illimitable air—
  Lone wandering, but not lost.

All day thy wings have fanned,
  At that far height, the cold, thin atmosphere,
Yet stoop not weary, to the welcome land,
  Though the dark night is near.

And soon that toil shall end;
  Soon shalt thou find a summer home, and rest,
And scream among thy fellows; reeds shall bend,
  Soon, o'er thy sheltered nest.

[1] From "Poetical Works of William Cullen Bryant." By special permission
of D. Appleton & Company.

Thou'rt gone! the abyss of heaven
Hath swallowed up thy form; yet on my heart
Deeply hath sunk the lesson thou hast given,
And shall not soon depart.

He who, from zone to zone,
Guides through the boundless sky thy certain flight,
In the long way that I must tread alone
Will lead my steps aright.

—*William Cullen Bryant*

BLACKSMITHS

The Village Blacksmith

UNDER a spreading chestnut tree
The village smithy stands;
The smith, a mighty man is he,
With large and sinewy hands;
And the muscles of his brawny arms
Are strong as iron bands.

His hair is crisp, and black, and long,
His face is like the tan;
His brow is wet with honest sweat,
He earns whate'er he can,
And looks the whole world in the face,
For he owes not any man.

Week in, week out, from morn till night,
You can hear his bellows blow;

You can hear him swing his heavy sledge,
　　With measured beat and slow,
Like a sexton ringing the village bell,
　　When the evening sun is low.

And children coming home from school
　　Look in at the open door:
They love to see the flaming forge,
　　And hear the bellows roar,
And catch the burning sparks that fly
　　Like chaff from a threshing floor.

He goes on Sunday to the church,
　　And sits among the boys;
He hears the parson pray and preach,
　　He hears his daughter's voice
Singing in the village choir,
　　And makes his heart rejoice.

It sounds to him like her mother's voice,
　　Singing in Paradise!
He needs must think of her once more,
　　How in the grave she lies;
And with his hard, rough hand he wipes
　　A tear out of his eyes.

Toiling,—rejoicing,—sorrowing,
　　Onward through life he goes;
Each morning sees some task begun,
　　Each evening sees it close;
Something attempted, something done,
　　Has earned a night's repose.

17

Thanks, thanks to thee, my worthy friend,
  For the lesson thou hast taught!
Thus at the flaming forge of life
  Our fortunes must be wrought;
Thus on its sounding anvil shaped
  Each burning deed and thought!

—H. W. Longfellow

BOYS

The Boy We Want

A BOY that is truthful and honest
    And faithful and willing to work;
But we have not a place that we care to disgrace
  With a boy that is ready to shirk.

Wanted—a boy you can tie to,
  A boy that is trusty and true,
A boy that is good to old people,
  And kind to the little ones too.

A boy that is nice to the home folks,
  And pleasant to sister and brother,
A boy who will try when things go awry
  To be helpful to father and mother.

These are the boys we depend on—
  Our hope for the future, and then
Grave problems of state and the world's work await
  Such boys when they grow to be men.

—Anon.

The Barefoot Boy

(Abridged)

BLESSINGS on thee, little man,
Barefoot boy, with cheek of tan!
With thy turned-up pantaloons,
And thy merry whistled tunes;
With thy red lip, redder still,
Kissed by strawberries on the hill;
With the sunshine on thy face,
Through thy torn brim's jaunty grace,
From my heart I give thee joy,—
I was once a barefoot boy.
Prince thou art,—the grown-up man
Only is republican,
Let the million-dollared ride!
Barefoot, trudging at his side,
Thou hast more than he can buy,
In the reach of ear and eye—
Outward sunshine, inward joy;
Blessings on thee, barefoot boy!

Oh, for boyhood's time of June.
Crowding years in one brief moon,
When all things I heard or saw,
Me, their master, waited for.
I was rich in flowers and trees,
Humming-birds and honeybees,
For my sport the squirrel played,
Plied the snouted mole his spade;
For my task the blackberry cone

Purpled over hedge and stone;
Laughed the brook for my delight
Through the day and through the night,—
Whispering at the garden wall,
Talked with me from fall to fall;
Mine the sand-rimmed pickerel pond,
Mine the walnut slopes beyond,
Mine, on bending orchard trees,
Apples of Hesperides!
Still, as my horizon grew,
Larger grew my riches too;
All the world I saw or knew
Seemed a complex Chinese toy
Fashioned for a barefoot boy.

Cheerily, then, my little man,
Live and laugh as boyhood can!
Though the flinty slopes be hard,
Stubble-speared the new-mown sward,
Every morn shall lead thee through
Fresh baptisms of the dew;
Every evening from thy feet
Shall the cool wind kiss the heat;
All too soon these feet must hide
In the prison cells of pride,
Lose the freedom of the sod,
Like a colt's for work be shod,
Made to tread the mills of toil,
Up and down in ceaseless moil;
Happy if their track be found
Never on forbidden ground;
Happy if they sink not in

Quick and treacherous sands of sin,
Ah! that thou couldst know thy joy,
Ere it passes, barefoot boy!

—*John Greenleaf Whittier*

Honest, Wouldn't You?

DID you ever think you'd like to
Back up just a little ways,
And enjoy again the pleasures
Of your happy boyhood days?

Would you trade your patent leathers
And your made-to-order clothes
For an hour of runnin' barefoot,
Squeezin' mud between your toes?

How'd you swap your old dyspepsia
And your job of findin' fault
For a hatful of green apples
And a pocketful of salt?

Would you give your fancy tackle
For a nice long willow pole,
An old can full of fishworms
And a little sunfish hole?

Oh! we knew you'd say you wouldn't,
But we're all just grown-up boys,
And it's only pride that robs us
Of the fun the kid enjoys.

—*Anon.*

21

Business Is Business [1]

"BUSINESS is Business," the Little Man said,
  "A battle where 'everything goes,'
Where the only gospel is 'get ahead,'
  And never spare friends or foes.
'Slay or be slain,' is the slogan cold;
  You must struggle and slash and tear,
For Business is Business, a fight for gold,
  Where all that you do is fair!"

"Business is Business," the Big Man said,
  "A battle to make of earth
A place to yield us more clothes and bread,
  More pleasure and joy and mirth;
There are still some bandits and buccaneers
  Who are jungle-bred beasts of trade,
But their number dwindles with passing years
  And dead is the code they made!"

"Business is Business," the Big Man said,
  "But it's something that's more, far more;
For it makes sweet gardens of deserts dead,
  And cities it built now roar
Where once the deer and gray wolf ran
  From the pioneer's swift advance;
Business is Magic that toils for man,
  Business is True Romance.

[1] Used by permission of the author.

"And those who make it a ruthless fight
   Have only themselves to blame
If they feel no whit of the keen delight
   In playing the Bigger Game,
The game that calls on the heart and head,
   The best of man's strength and nerve;
'Business is Business,' " the Big Man said,
   "And that Business is to serve!"

                                    —*Berton Braley*

CHARACTER

The Choir Invisible

OH, may I join the choir invisible
   Of those immortal dead who live again
In minds made better by their presence; live
In pulses stirred to generosity,
In deeds of daring rectitude, in scorn
For miserable aims that end with self,
In thoughts sublime that pierce the night like stars,
And with their mild persistence urge men's search
To vaster issues. So to live is heaven:
To make undying music in the world,
Breathing a beauteous order that controls
With growing sway the growing life of man.
So we inherit that sweet purity
For which we struggled, failed, and agonized
With widening retrospect that bred despair.
Rebellious flesh that would not be subdued,
A vicious parent shaming still its child,

Poor anxious penitence, is quick dissolved;
Its discords, quenched by meeting harmonies,
Die in the large and charitable air.
And all our rarer, better, truer self,
That sobbed religiously in yearning song,
That watched to ease the burden of the world,
Laboriously tracing what must be,
And what may yet be better,—saw within
A worthier image for the sanctuary,
And shaped it forth before the multitude,
Divinely human, raising worship so
To higher reverence more mixed with love,—
That better self shall live till human Time
Shall fold its eyelids, and the human sky
Be gathered like a scroll within the tomb
Unread forever. This is life to come,—
Which martyred men have made more glorious
For us who strive to follow. May I reach
That purest heaven,—be to other souls
That cup of strength in some great agony,
Enkindle generous ardor, feed pure love,
Beget the smiles that have no cruelty,
Be the sweet presence of a good diffused,
And in diffusion ever more intense!
So shall I join the choir invisible
Whose music is the gladness of the world.

                    —*George Eliot (Mary Ann Evans)*

Life Sculpture

CHISEL in hand stood a sculptor boy
　　With his marble block before him,
And his eyes lit up with a smile of joy,
　　As an angel-dream passed o'er him.

He carved the dream on that shapeless stone,
　　With many a sharp incision;
With heaven's own light the sculpture shone,—
　　He'd caught that angel-vision.

Children of life are we, as we stand
　　With our lives uncarved before us,
Waiting the hour when, at God's command,
　　Our life-dream shall pass o'er us.

If we carve it then on the yielding stone,
　　With many a sharp incision,
Its heavenly beauty shall be our own,—
　　Our lives, that angel-vision.

—George Washington Doane

Just Try to be the Fellow That Your Mother Thinks You Are

WHILST walking a crowded city street the other day,
　　I heard a little urchin to a comrade turn and say:
"Say, Chimmey, let me tell youse, I'd be happy as a clam,
If I only was de fellar dat me Mudder tinks I am.

25

"She tinks I am a wonder, an' she knows her little lad
Could never mix wit' nuttin' dat was ugly, mean or bad.
Oh! lots of times I sit and tink how nice t'would be, gee
  whiz!
If a fellar was de fellar dat his Mudder tinks he is."

My friend, be yours a life of toil or undiluted joy,
You still can learn a lesson from this small, unlettered boy.
Don't aim to be an earthly Saint, with eyes fixed on a star,
Just try to be the fellow that your Mother thinks you are.

—Will S. Adkin

CHEERFULNESS

Just Be Glad

O HEART of mine, we shouldn't worry so!
  What we've missed of sun, we couldn't have, you
    know;
  What we've met of stormy pain and of sorrow's driv-
    ing rain,
We can better meet again, if it blow.
We have erred in that dark hour we have known,
When our tears fell with a shower, all alone;
  Were not shine and shadow blent as the gracious Master
    meant?
Let us temper our content with his own.
For we know, not every morrow can be sad;
So forgetting all the trouble we have had,
Let us fold away our tears, and put by our foolish fears,
And through all the coming years, just be glad!

—James Whitcomb Riley

Was It You?

SOME one started the whole day wrong—was it you?
Some one robbed the day of its song—was it you?
Early this morning some one frowned;
Some one sulked until others scowled,
And soon harsh words were passed around—was it you?

Some one started the day aright—was it you?
Some one made it happy and bright—was it you?
Early this morning, we are told,
Some one smiled, and all through the day
This smile encouraged young and old—was it you?

—Stewart I. Long

Get a Transfer

IF you are on the Gloomy Line,
Get a transfer.
If you're inclined to fret and pine,
Get a transfer.
Get off the track of doubt and gloom,
Get on the Sunshine Track—there's room—
Get a transfer.

If you're on the Worry Train,
Get a transfer.
You must not stay there and complain,
Get a transfer.
The Cheerful Cars are passing through,
And there's lots of room for you—
Get a transfer.

27

If you're on the Grouchy Track,
    Get a transfer.
Just take a Happy Special back,
    Get a transfer.
Jump on the train and pull the rope,
That lands you at the Station Hope—
    Get a transfer.

—*Anon.*

The Zest of Life

LET me but live from year to year,
    With forward face and unreluctant soul.
  Not hastening to, nor turning from the goal;
Not mourning for the things that disappear
In the dim past, nor holding back in fear
  From what the future veils; but with a whole
  And happy heart, that pays its toll
To youth and age, and travels on with cheer.
So let the way wind up the hill or down,
  Through rough or smooth, the journey will be joy;
  Still seeking what I sought when but a boy,
New friendship, high adventure, and a crown,
  I shall grow old, but never lose life's zest,
  Because the road's last turn will be the best.

—*Henry Van Dyke*

"Ain't It Fine Today!"

SURE, this world is full of trouble—
  I ain't said it ain't.
Lord! I've had enough, an' double,
  Reason for complaint.
Rain an' storm have come to fret me,
  Skies were often gray;
Thorns an' brambles have beset me
  On the road, but say,
  Ain't it fine today!

What's the use of always weepin',
  Makin' trouble last?
What's the use of always keepin'
  Thinkin' of the past?
Each must have his tribulation,
  Water with his wine.
Life it ain't no celebration.
  Trouble? I've had mine—
  But today is fine.

It's today that I am livin',
  Not a month ago,
Havin', losin', takin', givin'
  As time wills it so.
Yesterday a cloud of sorrow
  Fell across the way;
It may rain again tomorrow,
  It may rain—but, say,
  Ain't it fine today!—

—Douglas Malloch

CHILDHOOD MEMORIES

Rock Me To Sleep

BACKWARD, turn backward, O time, in your flight,
Make me a child again just for to-night!
Mother, come back from the echoless shore,
Take me again to your heart as of yore;
Kiss from my forehead the furrows of care,
Smooth the few silver threads out of my hair;
Over my slumbers your loving watch keep;—
Rock me to sleep, mother—rock me to sleep!

Backward, flow backward, oh, tide of the years!
I am so weary of toil and of tears—
Toil without recompense, tears all in vain—
Take them, and give me my childhood again!
I have grown weary of dust and decay—
Weary of flinging my soul-wealth away;
Weary of sowing for others to reap;—
Rock me to sleep, mother—rock me to sleep!

Tired of the hollow, the base, the untrue,
Mother, O mother, my heart calls for you!
Many a summer the grass has grown green,
Blossomed and faded, our faces between:
Yet, with strong yearning and passionate pain,
Long I to-night for your presence again.
Come from the silence so long and so deep;—
Rock me to sleep, mother—rock me to sleep!

Over my heart, in the days that are flown,
No love like mother-love ever has shone;
No other worship abides and endures—
Faithful, unselfish, and patient like yours:
None like a mother can charm away pain
From the sick soul and the world-weary brain.
Slumber's soft calms o'er my heavy lips creep;—
Rock me to sleep, mother—rock me to sleep!

Come, let your brown hair, just lighted with gold,
Fall on your shoulders again as of old;
Let it drop over my forehead to-night,
Shading my faint eyes away from the light;
For with its sunny-edged shadows once more
Haply will throng the sweet visions of yore;
Lovingly, softly, its bright billows sweep:—
Rock me to sleep, mother—rock me to sleep!

Mother, dear mother, the years have been long
Since I last listened your lullaby song:
Sing, then, and unto my soul it shall seem
Womanhood's years have been only a dream.
Clasped to your heart in a loving embrace,
With your light lashes just sweeping my face,
Never hereafter to wake or to weep;—
Rock me to sleep, mother—rock me to sleep!

—Elizabeth A. Allen

Memory

[*We are not accustomed to think of Abraham Lincoln as a poet, but he wrote several compositions in verse. This poem was written in 1846, when the author was thirty-seven years of age.*]

MY childhood's home I see again,
    And sadden with the view;
And still, as memory crowds my brain,
    There's pleasure in it, too.

O memory! thou midway world
    'Twixt earth and paradise,
Where things decayed and loved ones lost
    In dreamy shadows rise,

And, freed from all that's earthly, vile,
    Seem hallowed, pure and bright,
Like scenes in some enchanted isle
    All bathed in liquid light.

As dusky mountains please the eye
    When twilight chases day;
As bugle notes that, passing by,
    In distance die away;

As leaving some grand waterfall,
    We, lingering, list its roar—
So memory will hallow all
    We've known but know no more.

Near twenty years have passed away
    Since here I bid farewell

To woods and fields, and scenes of play,
    And playmates loved so well.

Where many were, but few remain
    Of old familiar things,
But seeing them to mind again
    The lost and absent brings.

The friends I left that parting day,
    How changed, as time has sped!
Young childhood grown, strong manhood gray;
    And half of all are dead.

I hear the loved survivors tell
    How nought from death could save,
Till every sound appears a knell
    And every spot a grave.

I range the fields with pensive tread,
    And pace the hollow rooms,
And feel (companion of the dead)
    I'm living in the tombs.

—Abraham Lincoln

The Old Oaken Bucket

HOW dear to my heart are the scenes of my childhood,
    When fond recollection presents them to view!
The orchard, the meadow, the deep-tangled wildwood,
    And every loved spot which my infancy knew;

The wide-spreading pond, and the mill which stood by it,
    The bridge, and the rock where the cataract fell;
The cot of my father, the dairy-house nigh it,
    And e'en the rude bucket which hung in the well—
The old oaken bucket, the iron-bound bucket,
The moss-covered bucket which hung in the well.

That moss-covered vessel I hail as a treasure;
    For often, at noon, when returned from the field,
I found it the source of an exquisite pleasure,
    The purest and sweetest that nature can yield.
How ardent I seized it, with hands that were glowing!
    How quick to the white-pebbled bottom it fell;
Then soon, with the emblem of truth over-flowing,
    And dripping with coolness, it rose from the well—
The old oaken bucket, the iron-bound bucket,
The moss-covered bucket arose from the well.

How sweet from the green mossy brim to receive it,
    As, poised on the curb, it inclined to my lips!
Not a full blushing goblet could tempt me to leave it,
    Though filled with the nectar that Jupiter sips.
And now, far removed from the loved situation,
    The tear of regret will intrusively swell,
As fancy reverts to my father's plantation,
    And sighs for the bucket which hangs in the well—
The old oaken bucket, the iron-bound bucket,
The moss-covered bucket which hangs in the well.

—Samuel Woodworth

The Old Oaken Bucket

(As censored by the Board of Health)

WITH what anguish of mind I remember my child-
hood,
  Recalled in the light of knowledge since gained,
The malarious farm, the wet fungus-grown wildwood,
  The chills then contracted that since have remained;
The scum-covered duck-pond, the pig-sty close by it,
  The ditch where the sour-smelling house drainage fell,
The damp, shaded dwelling, the foul barnyard nigh it—
  But worse than all else was that terrible well,
And the old oaken bucket, the mold-crusted bucket,
  The moss-covered bucket that hung in the well.

Just think of it! Moss on the vessel that lifted
  The water I drank in the days called to mind;
Ere I knew what professors and scientists gifted
  In the waters of wells by analysis find;
The rotting wood-fiber, the oxide of iron,
  The algae, the frog of unusual size,
The water as clear as the verses of Byron,
  Are things I remember with tears in my eyes.

Oh, had I but realized in time to avoid them—
  The dangers that lurked in that pestilent draft—
I'd have tested for organic germs and destroyed them—
  With potassic permanganate ere I had quaffed.
Or perchance I'd have boiled it, and afterward strained it
  Through filters of charcoal and gravel combined;
Or, after distilling, condensed and regained it
  In potable form with its filth left behind.

How little I knew of the enteric fever
   Which lurked in the water I ventured to drink,
But since I've become a devoted believer
   In the teachings of science, I shudder to think.
And now, far removed from the scenes I'm describing,
   The story of warning to others I tell,
As memory reverts to my youthful imbibing
   And I gag at the thought of that horrible well,
And the old oaken bucket, the fungus-grown bucket—
   In fact, the slop-bucket—that hung in the well.

                                              —*Anon.*

CHILDREN

The Children's Hour

BETWEEN the dark and the daylight,
   When night is beginning to lower,
Comes a pause in the day's occupations,
   That is known as the children's hour.

I hear in the chamber above me
   The patter of little feet,
The sound of a door that is opened,
   And voices soft and sweet.

From my study I see in the lamplight,
   Descending the broad hall stair,
Grave Alice and laughing Allegra,
   And Edith with golden hair.

A whisper and then a silence;
  Yet I know by their merry eyes
They are plotting and planning together
  To take me by surprise.

A sudden rush from the stairway,
  A sudden raid from the hall,—
By three doors left unguarded,
  They enter my castle wall.

They climb up into my turret,
  O'er the arms and back of my chair;
If I try to escape, they surround me:
  They seem to be everywhere.

They almost devour me with kisses,
  Their arms about me entwine,
Till I think of the Bishop of Bingen,
  In his Mouse-Tower on the Rhine.

Do you think, O blue-eyed banditti,
  Because you have scaled the wall,
Such an old mustache as I am
  Is not a match for you all?

I have you fast in my fortress,
  And will not let you depart,
But put you into the dungeon
  In the round-tower of my heart.

And there will I keep you forever,
  Yes, forever and a day,

Till the walls shall crumble to ruin,
And moulder in dust away.

—H. W. Longfellow.

CHRIST

O Little Town of Bethlehem! [1]

O LITTLE town of Bethlehem,
    How still we see thee lie!
Above thy deep and dreamless sleep
    The silent stars go by:
Yet in thy dark streets shineth
    The everlasting Light;
The hopes and fears of all the years
    Are met in thee to-night.

For Christ is born of Mary;
    And gathered all above,
While mortals sleep, the angels keep
    Their watch of wondering love.
O morning stars together
    Proclaim the holy birth;
And praises sing to God the King,
    And peace to men on earth.

How silently, how silently,
    The wondrous Gift is given!
So God imparts to human hearts
    The blessings of His Heaven.

[1] From "Christmas Songs and Easter Carols," by Phillips Brooks. Copyright
1903, by E. P. Dutton & Co.

No ear may hear His coming,
　　But in this world of sin,
Where meek souls will receive Him still,
　　The dear Christ enters in.

O holy Child of Bethlehem,
　　Descend to us, we pray;
Cast out our sins, and enter in,
　　Be born in us to-day.
We hear the Christmas angels
　　The great glad tidings tell;
O come to us, abide with us,
　　Our Lord Emmanuel.

—*Phillips Brooks*

Bethlehem Town

AS I was going to Bethlehem town
　　Upon the earth I cast me down
All underneath a tree,
That whispered in this wise to me:
"Oh! I shall stand on Calvary
And bear what burthen saveth thee!"

As up I fared to Bethlehem town
I met a shepherd coming down,
And thus he quoth: "A wondrous sight
Hath spread before mine eyes this night.
An angel host most fair to see,
That sang full sweetly of a tree
That shall uplift on Calvary
What burthen saveth you and me."

And as I got to Bethlehem town,
Lo, Wise Men came and brought the crown,
And while the Infant smiling slept
Upon their knees they fell and wept;
But with her Babe upon her knee
Naught recked that mother of the tree
That should uplift on Calvary
What burthen saveth all and me.

Again I walk in Bethlehem town,
And think on Him that wears the crown.
I may not kiss His feet again,
Nor worship Him as I did then;
My King hath died upon the tree
And hath outpoured on Calvary
What Blood redeemeth you and me!

—*Eugene Field*

CHRISTMAS

The Night Before Christmas

T'WAS the night before Christmas, when all through the house
Not a creature was stirring, not even a mouse;
The stockings were hung by the chimney with care,
In hopes that St. Nicholas soon would be there;
The children were nestled all snug in their beds,
While visions of sugar-plums danced in their heads;
And Mamma in her kerchief, and I in my cap,
Had just settled our brains for a long winter's nap,

When out on the lawn there arose such a clatter,
I sprang from my bed to see what was the matter.
Away to the window I flew like a flash,
Tore open the shutters and threw up the sash.
The moon, on the breast of the new-fallen snow,
Gave a luster of mid-day to objects below;
When, what to my wandering eyes should appear,
But a miniature sleigh, and eight tiny reindeer,
With a little old driver, so lively and quick,
I knew in a moment it must be St. Nick.
More rapid than eagles his coursers they came,
And he whistled, and shouted, and called them by name:
"Now Dasher! now, Dancer! now, Prancer and Vixen!
On, Comet! on, Cupid! on, Donder and Blitzen!
To the top of the porch, to the top of the wall!
Now, dash away, dash away, dash away, all!"
As dry leaves that before the wild hurricane fly,
When they meet with an obstacle, mount to the sky,
So, up to the house-top the coursers they flew,
With the sleigh full of toys—and St. Nicholas, too.
And then in a twinkling I heard on the roof
The prancing and pawing of each little hoof.
As I drew in my head, and was turning around,
Down the chimney St. Nicholas came with a bound.
He was dressed all in fur from his head to his foot,
And his clothes were all tarnished with ashes and soot;
A bundle of toys he had flung on his back,
And he looked like a peddler just opening his pack.
His eyes how they twinkled! his dimples how merry!
His cheeks were like roses, his nose like a cherry;
His droll little mouth was drawn up like a bow,
And the beard on his chin was as white as the snow.

The stump of a pipe he held tight in his teeth,
And the smoke it encircled his head like a wreath;
He had a broad face and a little round belly
That shook, when he laughed, like a bowlful of jelly.
He was chubby and plump—a right jolly old elf;
And I laughed when I saw him, in spite of myself.
A wink of his eye, and a twist of his head,
Soon gave me to know I had nothing to dread.
He spoke not a word, but went straight to his work,
And filled all the stockings; then turned with a jerk,
And laying his finger aside of his nose,
And giving a nod, up the chimney he rose.
He sprang to his sleigh, to his team gave a whistle,
And away they all flew like the down of a thistle;
But I heard him exclaim, ere he drove out of sight,
"Happy Christmas to all, and to all a good-night!"

—Clement Clarke Moore

Christmas Everywhere [1]

EVERYWHERE, everywhere, Christmas tonight!
Christmas in lands of the fir-tree and pine,
Christmas in lands of the palm-tree and vine,
Christmas where snow peaks stand solemn and white,
Christmas where cornfields stand sunny and bright.
Christmas where children are hopeful and gay,
Christmas where old men are patient and gray,
Christmas where peace, like a dove in his flight,
Broods o'er brave men in the thick of the fight;
Everywhere, everywhere, Christmas tonight!

[1] Taken from "Christmas Songs and Easter Carols," by Phillips Brooks. Copyright 1903, by E. P. Dutton & Co.

For the Christ-child who comes is the Master of all;
No palace too great, no cottage too small.

—*Phillips Brooks*

CHURCH

It Isn't the Church—It's You

IF you want to have the kind of a church
　Like the kind of a church you like,
You needn't slip your clothes in a grip
　And start on a long, long hike.
You'll only find what you left behind,
　For there's nothing really new.
It's a knock at yourself when you knock your church;
　It isn't the church—it's *you*.

When everything seems to be going wrong,
　And trouble seems everywhere brewing;
When prayer-meeting, Young People's meeting, and all,
　Seem simmering slowly—stewing,
Just take a look at yourself and say,
　"What's the use of being blue?"
Are you doing your "bit" to make things "hit"?
　It isn't the church—it's *you*.

It's really strange sometimes, don't you know,
　That things go as well as they do,
When we think of the little—the very small mite—
　We add to the work of the few.

We sit, and stand round, and complain of what's done,
  And do very little but fuss.
Are we bearing our share of the burdens to bear?
  It isn't the church—it's *us*.

So, if you want to have the kind of a church
  Like the kind of a church you like,
Put off your guile, and put on your best smile,
  And hike, my brother, just hike,
To the work in hand that has to be done—
  The work of saving a few.
It isn't the church that is wrong, my boy;
  It isn't the church—it's *you*.

—Anon.

Some Who Do Not Go to Church

MR. SPEEDS will clean his auto,
  Mr. Spurrs will groom his horse,
Mr. Gadds will go to Coney,
  With the little Gadds, of course.
Mr. Flite will put carbolic
  On his homing pigeon's perch,
Mr. Weeds will mow his bluegrass,
  Mr. Jones will go to church.

Mr. Cleet will drive a golf ball,
  Mr. Tiller steer his boat,
Mr. Popper on his cycle,
  Round and round the State will mote.

44

Mr. Swatt will watch a ball game,
  Mr. Stake and son will search
Through the bosky wood for mushrooms,
  Mr. Wilks will go to church.

Do you ask me what's the matter?
  Do you wonder what is wrong?
When the nation turns from worship,
  Sermon, prayer, and sacred song?
Why do people rush for pleasure,
  Leave religion in the lurch?
Why prefer a padded auto
  To the cushioned pew in church?

Reader, well I know the answer,
  But if I should speak aloud,
What I think is the real reason,
  It would queer me with the crowd.
You'll be popular, dear reader,
  When you wield the critic's birch,
You'll be safely in the fashion
  If you blame things on the church.

                                        —*Anon.*

That Radio Religion

NOW whether folks are Methodists,
  Or Baptists, it's the same;
Or whether they profess to faiths
  Of any other name—

If they elect to stay at home,
  To churches never go,
Whatever be the creed they own,
  They've swapped for—Radio.

It's nice to loll in easy chairs,
  In comfort when it rains,
And listen in to cheerful songs
  And distant organ strains;
And not be worried by the fact—
  The passing plate is due
To pause a second at your place
  For "sustenance" from you.

This Radio Religion may
  For shut-ins do a heap;
But for those well enough to go—
  There's little good to reap;
And whether folks are Methodists,
  Or Baptists, here or there,
No church on earth can be replaced
  By "service"—on the air!

                              —*William Ludlum*

The Ten Commandments

I

Thou shalt have no other gods before me.

II

Thou shalt not make unto thee any graven image, or any likeness of any thing that is in heaven above, or that is in the earth beneath, or that is in the water under the earth:

Thou shalt not bow down thyself to them, nor serve them: for I the Lord thy God am a jealous God, visiting the iniquity of the fathers upon the children unto the third and fourth generation of them that hate me;

And shewing mercy unto thousands of them that love me, and keep my commandments.

III

Thou shalt not take the name of the Lord thy God in vain; for the Lord will not hold him guiltless that taketh his name in vain.

IV

Remember the Sabbath day to keep it holy.

Six days shalt thou labor, and do all thy work:

But the seventh day is the Sabbath of the Lord thy God: in it thou shalt not do any work, thou, nor thy son, nor thy daughter, thy man-servant, nor thy maid-servant, nor thy cattle, nor thy stranger that is within thy gates:

For in six days the Lord made heaven and earth, the

sea, and all that in them is, and rested the seventh day: wherefore the Lord blessed the sabbath day, and hallowed it.

V

Honour thy father and thy mother: that thy days may be long upon the land which the Lord thy God giveth thee.

VI

Thou shalt not kill.

VII

Thou shalt not commit adultery.

VIII

Thou shalt not steal.

IX

Thou shalt not bear false witness against thy neighbor.

X

Thou shalt not covet thy neighbor's house, thou shalt not covet thy neighbor's wife, nor his man-servant, nor his maid-servant, nor his ox, nor his ass, nor any thing that is thy neighbor's.

—*The Bible* (Exodus 20:3-17)

Life's Common Things

THE things of every day are all so sweet—
The morning meadows wet with dew,
The dance of daisies in the noon; the blue
Of far-off hills where twilight shadows lie;
The night, with all its tender mystery of sound
And silence, and God's starry sky!
Oh, life—the whole of life—is far too fleet.
The things of every day are all so sweet.

The common things of life are all so dear—
The waking in the warm half gloom
To find again the old familiar room,
The scents and sights and sounds that never tire;
The homely work, the plans, the lilt of baby's laugh,
The crackle of the open fire;
The waiting, then the footsteps coming near,
The opening door, your hand-clasp—and your kiss—
Is Heaven not after all the Now and Here?
The common things of life are all so dear.

—Alice E. Allen

Life's Common Duties

DREAM not of noble service elsewhere wrought,
The simple duty that awaits thy hand
Is God's voice uttering a divine command;
Life's common duties build what saints have thought.

In wonder-workings of some bush aflame
Men look for God, and fancy Him concealed;
But in earth's common things He stands revealed,
While grass and stars and flowers spell out His name.

—Minot J. Savage

CONTRITION

Recessional

GOD of our fathers, known of old—
Lord of our far-flung battle line—
Beneath Whose awful hand we hold
Dominion over palm and pine—
Lord God of Hosts, be with us yet,
Lest we forget—lest we forget!

The tumult and the shouting dies;
The captains and the kings depart:
Still stands Thine ancient Sacrifice,
An humble and a contrite heart.
Lord God of Hosts, be with us yet,
Lest we forget—lest we forget!

Far-called, our navies melt away;
On dune and headland sinks the fire:
Lo, all our pomp of yesterday
Is one with Nineveh and Tyre!
Judge of the Nations, spare us yet,
Lest we forget—lest we forget!

If, drunk with sight of power, we loose
  Wild tongues that have not Thee in awe—
Such boasting as the Gentiles use
  Or lesser breeds without the Law—
Lord God of Hosts, be with us yet,
  Lest we forget—lest we forget!

For heathen heart that puts her trust
  In reeking tube and iron shard—
All valiant dust that builds on dust,
  And guarding, calls not on Thee to guard—
For frantic boast and foolish word,
  Thy mercy on Thy people, Lord!
Amen.

—Rudyard Kipling

Recessional

O GOD, our Help in ages past,
  Our Hope for years to come,
Our Shelter from the stormy blast,
  And our Eternal Home!

Before the hills in order stood,
  Or earth received her frame,
From everlasting Thou art God,
  To endless years the same.

A thousand ages in Thy sight
  Are like an evening gone;
Short as the watch that ends the night
  Before the rising sun.

51

Time, like an ever-rolling stream,
    Bears all its sons away;
They fly, forgotten, as a dream
    Dies at the opening day.

O God, our Help in ages past,
    Our Hope for years to come,
Be Thou our Guard while life shall last,
    And our Eternal Home.

                 —Isaac Watts

Oh, If They Only Knew!

SOME people think I think I'm good.
  Oh, if they only understood!
Could they but draw aside the screen
Of shielding clay that stands between,
And see the penitent within
That craves so oft release from sin;

If some kind angel could reveal
The sense of guilt and shame I feel
Because my heart will ope to things
Whose very entrance blights and stings;
Oh, if they only, only knew
The grace it takes to just ring true!

If they could understand my need,
And hear what I confess and plead,
And know how fully I depend
Upon my precious Lord and Friend;

52

I wonder, would they call such dress
The mantle of self-righteousness?

—Edith L. Mapes

The Bird with a Broken Wing

I WALKED through the woodland meadows,
   Where sweet the thrushes sing,
And found on a bed of mosses
   A bird with a broken wing.
I healed its wound, and each morning
   It sang its old sweet strain;
But the bird with a broken pinion
   Never soared as high again.

I found a young life broken
   By sin's seductive art;
And, touched with a Christlike pity,
   I took him to my heart.
He lived with a noble purpose,
   And struggled not in vain;
But the life that sin had stricken
   Never soared as high again.

But the bird with a broken pinion
   Kept another from the snare,
And the life that sin had stricken
   Raised another from despair.
Each loss has its compensation,
   There is healing for every pain;

But the bird with a broken pinion
  Never soars as high again.

—Hezekiah Butterworth

The Fool's Prayer

THE royal feast was done; the King
  Sought some new sport to banish care,
And to his jester cried: "Sir Fool,
  Kneel now, and make for us a prayer!"

The jester doffed his cap and bells,
  And stood the mocking court before;
They could not see the bitter smile
  Behind the painted grin he wore.

He bowed his head, and bent his knee
  Upon the monarch's silken stool;
His pleading voice arose: "O Lord,
  Be merciful to me, a fool!

"No pity, Lord, could change the heart
  From red with wrong to white as wool;
The rod must heal the sin: but, Lord,
  Be merciful to me, a fool!

" 'Tis not by guilt the onward sweep
  Of truth and right, O Lord, we stay;
'Tis by our follies that so long
  We hold the earth from heaven away.

54

"These clumsy feet, still in the mire,
  Go crushing blossoms without end;
These hard, well-meaning hands we thrust
  Among the heart-strings of a friend.

"The ill-timed truth we might have kept—
  Who knows how sharp it pierced and stung?
The word we had not sense to say—
  Who knows how grandly it had rung?

"Our faults no tenderness should ask,
  The chastening stripes must cleanse them all;
But for our blunders—oh, in shame
  Before the eyes of heaven we fall.

"Earth bears no balsam for mistakes;
  Men crown the knave, and scourge the tool
That did his will; but Thou, O Lord,
  Be merciful to me, a fool!"

The room was hushed; in silence rose
  The King, and sought his gardens cool,
And walked apart, and murmured low,
  "Be merciful to me, a fool!"

                              —*Edward R. Sill*

CONVERSATION

Our Lips and Ears

IF you your lips would keep from slips,
  Five things observe with care:
Of whom you speak, to whom you speak,
  And how and when and where.

If you your ears would save from jeers,
  These things keep meekly hid:
Myself and I, and mine and my,
  And how I do and did.

                                    —*Anon.*

THE COUNTRY

Thank God for the Country!

THANK God for the country, the vast stretch of land,
  Sun-kissed and by Heaven's sweet breath ever
    fanned;
Blue skies overlooking the grass and the trees,
The singing of birds and the humming of bees.

'Twas man made the skyscrapers, towering so high,
That shut out the sunshine from all who pass by;
The fields and green pastures, the brooks and the flowers,
Were fashioned alike by omnipotent powers.

56

'Twas man built the tenements, crowding the poor,
Where women and children foul air must endure;
But God gave the open, the fresh country breeze,
Where children may frolic and play as they please.

'Twas man made the city, apartment and street,
Where riches and poverty closely now meet;
But God gave the country, the rich fertile soil,
And the fat of the land for all who will toil.

Thank God for the country, the quiet and rest,
The peace and the plenty with which it is blest,
The ground and the grass for our pavement-tired feet,
The honey and cream and the good things to eat.

Thank God for the country, thrice blessed are they
Who bathe in its glories and beauties to-day,
Oh, short is our span in the city's fast life!
But hoary heads crowneth the farmer and wife.

—*Mrs. Major Arnold*

Vacation

IT seems to me I'd like to go
Where bells don't ring, nor whistles blow,
Nor clocks don't strike, nor gongs don't sound,
And I'd have stillness all around.
No real stillness, but just the tree's
Low whispering, or the hum of bees,
Or brooks' faint babbling over stones
In strangely, softly tangled tones,

Or maybe a cricket or katydid,
Or the song of birds in hedges hid,
Or just such sweet sounds as these
To. fill the tired heart with ease,
If 'tweren't for sight and sound and smell
I'd like a city pretty well,
But when it comes to getting rest
I like the country lots the best.
Sometimes it seems to me I must
Just quit the city's din and dust
And get out where the sky is blue;
And say, how does it seem to you?

—*Eugene Field*

COURAGE

Landing of the Pilgrim Fathers

THE breaking waves dashed high
   On a stern and rock-bound coast;
And the woods against a stormy sky,
   Their giant branches tossed;
And the heavy night hung dark
   The hills and waters o'er—
When a band of exiles moored their bark
   On a wild New England shore.

Not as the conqueror comes,
   They, the true-hearted, came;—
Not with the roll of the stirring drums,
   And the trumpet that sings of fame;—

Not as the flying come,
  In silence and in fear;
They shook the depths of the desert's gloom
  With their hymns of lofty cheer.

Amidst the storm they sang,
  And the stars heard, and the sea!
And the sounding aisles of the dim woods rang
  To the anthem of the free;
The ocean eagle soared
  From his nest by the white waves' foam,
And the rocking pines of the forest roared:—
  This was their welcome home!

There were men with hoary hair
  Amidst that pilgrim band;
Why had they come to wither there,
  Away from their childhood's land?
There was woman's fearless eye,
  Lit by her deep love's truth;
There was manhood's brow serenely high,
  And the fiery heart of youth.

What sought they thus afar?
  Bright jewels of the mine?
The wealth of seas? the spoils of war?
  They sought a faith's pure shrine!
Ay, call it holy ground,
  The soil where first they trod!
They left unstained what there they found
  Freedom to worship God!

—*Mrs. Felicia Dorothea Hemans*

59

The Glove and the Lions

KING FRANCIS was a hearty king, and loved a royal
    sport,
And one day, as his lions fought, sat looking on the court;
The nobles filled the benches, with the ladies in their pride,
And 'mongst them sat the Count de Lorge with one for
    whom he sighed:
And truly 't was a gallant thing to see that crowning
    show,—
Valor and love, and a king above, and the royal beasts
    below.

Ramped and roared the lions, with horrid laughing jaws:
They bit, they glared, gave blows like beams, a wind
    went with their paws;
With wallowing might and stifled roar they rolled on one
    another,
Till all the pit, with sand and mane, was in a thunderous
    smother;
The bloody foam above the bars came whisking through
    the air:
Said Francis then, "Faith gentlemen, we're better here
    than there!"

De Lorge's love o'erheard the king,—a beauteous, lively
    dame,
With smiling lips and sharp, bright eyes, which always
    seemed the same:
She thought, "The Count, my lover, is brave as brave
    can be,—

He surely would do wondrous things to show his love of
 me.
King, ladies, lovers, all look on; the occasion is divine;
I'll drop my glove to prove his love; great glory will be
 mine."

She dropped her glove to prove his love, then looked at
 him and smiled;
He bowed, and in a moment leaped among the lions wild:
The leap was quick, return was quick, he has regained
 his place,
Then threw the glove, but not with love, right in the
 lady's face.
"In faith," cried Francis, "rightly done!" and he rose
 from where he sat;
"No love," quoth he, "but vanity, sets love a task like
 that."

—James Henry Leigh Hunt

Death of Gaudentis

*[Gaudentis was the architect of the Coliseum. Upon his tomb
in the Catacombs was found this inscription: "Thus thou keepest thy
promises, O Vespasian! The rewarding with death of him, the
crown of thy glory in Rome. Do rejoice, O Gaudentis! the cruel
tyrant promised much, but Christ gave thee all, who prepared thee
such a mansion."]*

BEFORE Vespasian's regal throne
 Skilful Gaudentis stood;
"Build me," the haughty monarch cried,
 "A theater for blood.

I know thou'rt skilled in mason's work;
    Thine is the power to frame
Rome's Coliseum vast and wide,
    And honor to thy name.

"Over seven acres spread thy work,
    And by the gods of Rome,
Thou shalt hereafter by my side
    Have thy resplendent home.
A citizen of Roman rights,
    Silver and golden store,
These shall be thine; let Christian blood
    But stain the marble floor."

So rose the Amphitheater,
    Tower and arch and tier;
There dawned a day when martyrs stood
    Within that ring of fear.
But strong their quenchless trust in God,
    And strong their human love;
Their eyes of faith, undimmed, were fixed
    On temples far above.

And thousands gazed, in brutal joy,
    To watch those Christians die;
But one beside Vespasian leaned,
    With a strange light in his eye.
What thoughts welled up within his breast
    As on that group he gazed!
What gleams of holy light from heaven
    Upon his dark soul blazed!

Had he by password gained access
  To the dark Catacomb,
And learned the hope of Christ's beloved,
  Beyond the rack, the tomb?
The proud Vespasian o'er him bends—
  "My priceless architect,
Today I will announce to all
  Thy privilege elect—

A free-made citizen of Rome."
  Calmly, Gaudentis rose,
And folding, o'er his breast, his arms,
  Turned to the Savior's foes;
And in a strength not all his own,
  With life and death in view,
The fearless architect exclaimed,
  "I am a Christian too."

Only a few brief moments passed,
  And brave Gaudentis lay
Within the Amphitheater,
  A lifeless mass of clay.
Vespasian promised him the rights
  Of proud Imperial Rome,
But Christ with martyrs crowned him king,
  Beneath heaven's cloudless dome.
                    —"Harriet Annie"

63

Be Strong

BE strong!
We are not here to play, to dream, to drift;
We have hard work to do, and loads to lift;
Shun not the struggle—face it; 'tis God's gift.

Be strong!
Say not, "The days are evil. Who's to blame?"
And fold the hands and acquiesce—oh shame!
Stand up, speak out, and bravely, in God's name.

Be strong!
It matters not how deep intrenched the wrong,
How hard the battle goes, the day how long;
Faint not—fight on! To-morrow comes the song.

—Maltbie Davenport Babcock

Slaves

THEY are slaves who fear to speak,
For the fallen and the weak;
They are slaves who will not choose,
Hatred, scoffing and abuse;
Rather than in silence shrink,
From the truth they needs must think;
They are slaves who dare not be,
In the right with two or three.

—James Russell Lowell

CRITICISM

People Will Talk

YOU may get through the world, but 'twill be very slow,
If you listen to all that is said as you go;
You'll be worried and fretted and kept in a stew,
For meddlesome tongues will have something to do;
　　　For people will talk.

If quiet and modest, you'll have it presumed
That your humble position is only assumed;
You're a wolf in sheep's clothing, or else you're a fool,
But don't get excited, keep perfectly cool;
　　　For people will talk.

If generous and noble, they'll vent out their spleen.
You'll hear some loud hints that you're selfish and mean;
If upright and honest and fair as the day,
They'll call you a rogue in a sly, sneaking way!
　　　For people will talk.

And then if you show any boldness of heart,
Or a slight inclination to take your own part,
They will call you an upstart, conceited and vain;
But keep straight ahead, don't stop and explain;
　　　For people will talk.

If threadbare your dress, or old-fashioned your hat,
Some one will surely take notice of that,
And hint rather strong that you can't pay your way;
But don't get excited whatever they say,
　　　For people will talk.

If you dress in the fashion, don't think to escape,
For they criticize then in a different shape;
You're ahead of your means, or your tailor's unpaid
But mind your own business, don't mind what is said;
   For people will talk.

Now, the best way to do is to do as you please,
For your mind, if you have one, will then be at ease.
Of course you will meet with all sorts of abuse,
But don't think to stop it, it is of no use,
   For people will talk.

      —*Samuel Dodge*

"They Say" [1]

HAVE you heard of the terrible family They,
 And the dreadful venomous things They say?
Why, half the gossip under the sun,
If you trace it back, you will find begun
 In that wretched House of They.

A numerous family, so I am told,
And its genealogical tree is old;
For ever since Adam and Eve began
To build up the curious race of man,
 Has existed the House of They.

Gossip-mongers and spreaders of lies,
Horrid people whom all despise!
And yet the best of us now and then,

[1] Used by permission of the W. B. Conkey Co., Hammond, Ind

Repeat queer tales about women and men
   And quote the House of They.

They live like lords, and never labor;
A They's one task is to watch his neighbor,
And tell his business and private affairs
To the world at large; they are sowers of tares—
   These folks in the House of They.

It is wholly useless to follow a They
With a whip or a gun, for he slips away
And into his house, where you can not go;
It is locked and bolted and guarded so—
   This horrible House of They.

Though you can not get in, yet they get out,
And spread their villainous tales about;
Of all the rascals under the sun
Who have come to punishment, never one
   Belonged to the House of They.

                        —*Ella Wheeler Wilcox*

The Three Wise Monkeys

IN a temple at Kioto in far-away Japan,
   The little Apes of Nikko are sitting, wondrous wise;
And one they call Mizaru—he's a funny little man!
   Mizaru sees no evil with his eyes.

The next is Kikazaru—quite funny, too, is he;
   But ah! the people tell me he is wise beyond his years;

As fine a little gentleman as any ape could be;
  Kikazaru hears no evil with his ears.

The third one is Mazaru, and, like the other two,
  His way is often quoted by the folk he dwells among;
And that which makes him famous is a simple thing to
  do—
  Mazaru speaks no evil with his tongue.

Now the temple at Kioto few of us may ever see,
  Or the Little Apes of Nikko, they're so very far away,
But if we would do as they do, I think you'll all agree,
  We might in time become as wise as they.

—*Florence Boyce Davis*

The Tongue

"THE boneless tongue, so small and weak,
  Can crush and kill," declared the Greek.

"The tongue destroys a greater horde,"
The Turk asserts, "than does the sword."

A Persian proverb wisely saith,
"A lengthy tongue—an early death";

Or sometimes takes this form instead,
"Don't let your tongue cut off your head."

"The tongue can speak a word whose speed,"
Says the Chinese, "outstrips the steed";

68

While Arab sages this impart,
"The tongue's great storehouse is the heart."

From Hebrew wit the maxim sprung,
"Though feet should slip, ne'er let the tongue."

The sacred writer crowns the whole:
"Who keeps the tongue doth keep his soul."

—*Philip B. Strong*

Forget It

IF you see a tall fellow ahead of a crowd,
A leader of men marching fearless and proud,
And you know of a tale whose mere telling aloud
Would mean that his head must in anguish be bowed,
  It's a pretty good plan to forget it.

If you know of a skeleton hidden away
In a closet, and guarded and kept from the day
In the dark; and whose showing, whose sudden display,
Would cause grief and sorrow and life-long dismay,
  It's a pretty good plan to forget it.

If you know of a thing that will darken the joy
Of a man or a woman, a girl or a boy,
That will wipe out a smile, or the least way annoy
A fellow, or cause any gladness to cloy,
  It's a pretty good plan to forget it.

—*Anon.*

A Chip on His Shoulder

HE always has something to grumble about,
  Has the man with a chip on his shoulder;
The world to the dogs is going, no doubt,
  To the man with a chip on his shoulder;
The clouds are too dark, the sun is too bright.
No matter what happens, it is never right;
When peace is prevailing, he is spoiling to fight,
  The man with a chip on his shoulder.

—Anon.

If

IF you were busy being kind,
  Before you knew it, you would find
You'd soon forget to think 'twas true
That someone was unkind to you.

If you were busy being glad,
And cheering people who are sad,
Although your heart might ache a bit,
You'd soon forget to notice it.

If you were busy being good,
And doing just the best you could,
You'd not have time to blame some man
Who's doing just the best he can.

If you were busy being true
To what you know you ought to do,
You'd be so busy you'd forget
The blunders of the folks you've met.

If you were busy being right,
You'd find yourself too busy quite
To criticise your neighbor long,
Because he's busy being wrong.

—Rebecca Foresman

"The Question"

WERE the whole world good as you—not an atom
better—
Were it just as pure and true,
Just as pure and true as you;
Just as strong in faith and works;
Just as free from crafty quirks;
All extortion, all deceit;
Schemes its neighbors to defeat;
Schemes its neighbors to defraud;
Schemes some culprit to applaud—
Would this world be better?

If the whole world followed you—followed to the letter—
Would it be a nobler world,
All deceit and falsehood hurled
From it altogether;
Malice, selfishness, and lust,
Banished from beneath the crust,
Covering human hearts from view—
Tell me, if it followed you,
Would the world be better?

—Anon.

Folks and Me

IT is a funny thing, but true,
  That folks you don't like don't like you.
I don't know why this should be so,
But just the same I allus know
If I am "sour," friends are few;
If I am friendly, folks are too.

Sometimes I get up in the morn
A-wishin' I was never born.
I make of cross remarks a few,
And then my family wishes too
That I had gone some other place
Instead of showin' them my face.

But let me change my little tune
And sing and smile, then pretty soon
The folks around me sing and smile
(I guess 'twas catchin' all the while).
Yes, 'tis a funny thing, but true,
That folks you like will sure like you.

—*Lucile Crites*

The Blind Men and the Elephant

IT was six men of Indostan
  To learning much inclined,
Who went to see the elephant
  (Though all of them were blind),

72

That each by observation
  Might satisfy his mind.

The first approached the elephant,
  And, happening to fall
Against his broad and sturdy side,
  At once began to bawl,
"God bless me! but the elephant
  Is very like a wall!"

The second, feeling of the tusk
  Cried: "Ho! what have we here
So very round and smooth and sharp?
  To me 'tis mighty clear
This wonder of an elephant
  Is very like a spear!"

The third approached the animal,
  And, happening to take
The squirming trunk within his hands,
  Thus boldly up and spake:
"I see," quoth he, "the elephant,
  Is very like a snake!"

The fourth reached out his eager hand,
  And felt about the knee;
"What most this wondrous beast is like
  Is mighty plain," quoth he;
"'Tis clear enough the elephant
  Is very like a tree."

73

The fifth, who chanced to touch the ear,
　　Said: "E'en the blindest man
Can tell what this resembles most.
　　Deny the fact who can,
This marvel of an elephant
　　Is very like a fan!"

The sixth no sooner had begun
　　About the beast to grope,
Than, seizing on the swinging tail
　　That fell within his scope,
"I see," quoth he, "the elephant
　　Is very like a rope!"

And so these men of Indostan
　　Disputed loud and long,
Each in his own opinion
　　Exceeding stiff and strong,
Though each was partly in the right,
　　And all were in the wrong!

So, oft in theologic wars
　　The disputants, I ween,
Rail on in utter ignorance
　　Of what each other mean,
And prate about an elephant
　　Not one of them has seen!

—John G. Saxe

Horse Sense

A HORSE can't pull while kicking.
This fact I merely mention.
And he can't kick while pulling.
Which is my chief contention.

Let's imitate the good old horse
And lead a life that's fitting;
Just pull an honest load, and then
There'll be no time for kicking.

—Anon.

The Owl Critic

(A Lesson to Fault Finders)

"WHO stuffed that owl?" No one spoke in the shop;
The barber was busy, and he could not stop;
The customers, waiting their turns, were all reading
The different dailies, and so, little heeding
The young man who blurted out such a blunt question
Not one raised his head, or even made a suggestion:
And the barber kept on shaving.

"Don't you see, Mr. Brown?"
Cried the youth with a frown,
"How wrong the whole thing is?
How preposterous each wing is?
How flattened the head is? how jammed down the neck is?
In short, the whole owl, what an ignorant wreck 'tis!

75

I make no apology;
I've learned owl-eology.
I've passed days and nights in a hundred collections,
And cannot be blinded to any deflections
Arising from unskilled fingers that fail
To stuff a bird right, from his beak to his tail.
Mister Brown! Mister Brown!
Do take that bird down;
Or you'll be the laughing stock all over town!"
      And the barber kept on shaving.

"I've *studied* owls,
And other night fowls;
And I tell you
What I know to be true:
An owl cannot roost
With his limbs so unloosed;
No owl in this world
Ever had his claws curled,
Ever had his legs slanted,
Ever had his bill canted,
Ever had his neck screwed
Into that attitude.
He can't *do* it, because
'Tis against all bird laws.
Anatomy teaches,
Ornithology preaches,
An owl has a toe
That *can't* turn out so!
I've made the white owl my study for years,
And to see such a job almost moves me to tears!
Mr. Brown! I'm amazed

76

You should be so gone crazed
As to put up a bird
In that posture absurd!
To *look* at the owl really brings on a dizziness;
The man who stuffed him don't half know his business!"
        And the barber kept on shaving.

"Examine those eyes!
I'm filled with surprise
Taxidermists should pass
Off on you such poor glass!
So unnatural they seem
They'd make Audubon scream,
And John Burroughs laugh
To encounter such chaff.
Do take that bird down!
Have him stuffed again, Brown!"
        And the barber kept on shaving.

"With some sawdust and bark,
I could stuff in the dark
An owl better than that;
I could make an old hat
Look more like an owl,
Than that horrid fowl,
Stuck up there so stiff like a side of coarse leather;
In fact, about *him,* there's not one natural feather."
Just then, with a wink and a sly normal lurch,
The owl very gravely got down from his perch,
Walked around, and regarded his fault-finding critic
(Who thought he was stuffed) with a glance analytic;
And then fairly hooted, as if he would say:

"Your learning's at fault this time, anyway;
I'm an owl; you're another. Sir Critic, good-day!"
      And the barber kept on shaving.

With a face very red,
Not another word said
That knowing young man,
But from the shop ran,
As if with a desire
To go look for a fire;
And when at last he looked in a glass,
He said to the image, "Don't you see you're an ass?
I'm a judge of a beast, if not of a fowl,
And I say you're an ass for mistaking that owl!"
And the figure in the glass
Repeated "You're an ass!"
      And the barber kept on shaving.
                —*James T. Fields*

A Cure for Fault-Finding

"JUST stand aside, and watch yourself go by;
   Think of yourself, as 'he' instead of 'I.'
  Pick flaws, find fault, forget the man is you,
  And strive to make your estimate ring true.
The faults of others then will dwarf and shrink.
Love's chain grows stronger by one mighty link,
  When you with 'he' as substitute for 'I,'
  Have stood aside, and watched yourself go by."
         —*Abridged from Strickland W. Gillilan*

Boosting the Booster

BOOST your city, boost your friend;
 Boost the church that you attend.
Boost the street on which you're dwelling,
Boost the goods that you are selling.
Boost the people 'round about you,
They can get along without you.
But success will quicker find them
If they know that you're behind them.
Boost for every forward movement;
Boost for every new improvement;
Boost the man for whom you labor;
Boost the stranger and the neighbor.
Cease to be a chronic knocker;
Cease to be a progress-blocker;
If you'd make your city better
Boost it to the final letter.

—*Anon.*

The Quarrelsome Trio

WHEN you hark to the voice of the knocker,
 As you list to his hammer fall,
  Remember the fact
  That the knocking act
Requires no brains at all.

When you list to the growl of the growler,
As you list to his ceaseless growl,

You will please recall
That a dog is all
It takes for an endless howl.

As you watch for the kick of the kicker,
As you notice his strenuous kick,
You'll observe the rule
That a stubborn mule
Is great at the same old trick.

The knocker, the growler, the kicker,
Fault-finders, large and small,
What do they need
For each day's deed?
No brains, no sense—just gall.

—*L. G.*

Get Into the Boosting Business

DO you know there's lots of people
Sitting round most every town,
Growling like a broody chicken,
Knocking every good thing down?
Don't be that kind of cattle,
'Cause they ain't no use on earth,
But just be a booster rooster,
Crow and boost for all you're worth.

If your town needs boostin' boost her;
Don't hold her back and wait to see

If some other fellow's willin';
   Sail right in, this country's free.
No one's got a mortgage on it,
   It's just yours as much as his;
If your town is shy of boosters,
   You get in the boostin' biz.

If things don't seem to suit you
   An' the world seems kinder wrong,
What's the matter with a boostin'
   Just to help the thing along?
'Cause if things should stop again,
   We'd be in a sorry plight,
You just keep the horn a-blowin',
   Boost her up with all your might.

If you see some fellow tryin'
   For to make some project go.
An' you can boost it up a trifle,
   That's your clew to let him know
That you're not going to knock it,
   Just because it ain't your shout,
But that you're going to boost a little
   'Cause he's got the best thing out.

—Anon.

DEATH

Oh! Why Should the Spirit of Mortal be Proud?

(Well-known as a favorite poem of President Lincoln)

OH! why should the spirit of mortal be proud?
Like a swift-fleeting meteor, a fast-flying cloud,
A flash of the lightning, a break of the wave,
He passes from life to his rest in the grave.

The leaves of the oak and the willow shall fade,
Be scattered around, and together be laid;
And the young, and the old, and the low and the high,
Shall moulder to dust, and together shall lie.

The infant a mother attended and loved,
The mother that infant's affection who proved,
The husband that infant and mother who blessed,
Each, all are away to their dwelling of rest.

The maid on whose cheek, on whose brow, in whose eye
Shone beauty and pleasure, her triumphs are by;
And the memory of those that beloved her and praised
Are alike from the minds of the living erased.

The hand of the king that the scepter hath borne,
The brow of the priest that the miter hath worn,
The eye of the sage, and the heart of the brave
Are hidden and lost in the depths of the grave.

The peasant, whose lot was to sow and to reap,
The herdsman, who climbed with his goats to the steep,
The beggar, who wandered in search of his bread,
Have faded away like the grass that we tread.

The saint, who enjoyed the communion of heaven,
The sinner, who dared to remain unforgiven,
The wise and the foolish, the guilty and just,
Have quietly mingled their bones in the dust.

So the multitude goes, like the flower and the weed,
That wither away, to let others succeed;
So the multitude comes, even those we behold,
To repeat every tale that hath often been told.

For we are the same that our fathers have been,
We see the same sights that our fathers have seen;
We drink the same stream, and we feel the same sun
And run the same course that our fathers have run.

The thoughts we are thinking our fathers would think,
From the death we are shrinking our fathers would shrink,
To the life we are clinging our fathers would cling,
But it speeds from the earth like a bird on the wing.

They loved, but the story we cannot unfold,
They scorned, but the heart of the haughty is cold;
They grieved, but no voice from their slumbers may come;
They joyed, but the voice of their gladness is dumb.

They died; aye, they died; and we, things that are now,
Who walk on the turf that lies over their brow,

Who make in their dwelling a transient abode,
Meet the changes they met on their pilgrimage road.

Yea! hope and despondency, pleasure and pain,
Are mingled together like sunshine and rain;
And the smile and the tear, and the song and the dirge
Still follow each other, like surge upon surge.

'Tis the twink of an eye, 'tis the draught of a breath,
From the blossom of health to the paleness of death,
From the gilded saloon to the bier and the shroud,
Oh, why should the spirit of mortal be proud?

—William Knox

There Is No Death

THERE is no death! The stars go down
  To rise upon some fairer shore;
And bright, in heaven's jeweled crown,
  They shine for evermore.

There is no death! The dust we tread
  Shall change beneath the summer showers
To golden grain or mellow fruit,
  Or rainbow-tinted flowers.

The granite rocks disorganize,
  And feed the hungry moss they bear;
The forest-leaves drink daily life
  From out the viewless air.

There is no death! The leaves may fall,
   And flowers may fade and pass away;
They only wait through wintry hours
   The coming of May-day.

There is no death! An angel-form
   Walks o'er the earth with silent tread;
And bears our best-loved things away,
   And then we call them "dead."

He leaves our hearts all desolate,
   He plucks our fairest, sweetest flowers;
Transplanted into bliss, they now
   Adorn immortal bowers.

The bird-like voice, whose joyous tones
   Made glad the scenes of sin and strife,
Sings now an everlasting song
   Around the tree of life.

Where'er he sees a smile too bright,
   Or heart too pure for taint and vice,
He bears it to that world of light,
   To dwell in Paradise.

Born unto that undying life,
   They leave us but to come again;
With joy we welcome them the same,
   Except their sin and pain.

And ever near us, though unseen,
   The dear immortal spirits tread;

For all the boundless universe
Is life—there is no dead!

Thanatopsis [1]

TO him who, in the love of Nature, holds
   Communion with her visible forms, she speaks
A various language: for his gayer hours
She has a voice of gladness, and a smile
And eloquence of beauty; and she glides
Into his darker musings, with a mild
And healing sympathy, that steals away
Their sharpness, ere he is aware. When thoughts
Of the last bitter hour come like a blight
Over thy spirit, and sad images
Of the stern agony, and shroud, and pall,
And breathless darkness, and the narrow house,
Make thee to shudder, and grow sick at heart,—
Go forth under the open sky, and list
To Nature's teachings, while from all around—
Earth and her waters, and the depths of air—
Comes a still voice:—Yet a few days, and thee
The all-beholding sun shall see no more
In all his course; nor yet in the cold ground,
Where thy pale form was laid, with many tears,
Nor in the embrace of ocean, shall exist
Thy image. Earth, that nourished thee, shall claim
Thy growth, to be resolved to earth again;

[1] From "Poetical Works of William Cullen Bryant." By special permission of
D. Appleton & Company.

And, lost each human trace, surrendering up
Thine individual being, shalt thou go
To mix forever with the elements;
To be a brother to the insensible rock,
And to the sluggish clod, which the rude swain
Turns with his share, and treads upon. The oak
Shall send his roots abroad, and pierce thy mold.
Yet not to thine eternal resting place
Shalt thou retire alone—nor couldst thou wish
Couch more magnificent. Thou shalt lie down
With patriarchs of the infant world—with kings,
The powerful of the earth—the wise, the good,
Fair forms, and hoary seers of ages past,
All in one mighty sepulcher. The hills,
Rock-ribbed, and ancient as the sun; the vales
Stretching in pensive quietness between;
The venerable woods; rivers that move
In majesty, and the complaining brooks,
That make the meadows green; and, poured round all,
Old ocean's gray and melancholy waste—
Are but the solemn decorations all
Of the great tomb of man! The golden sun,
The planets, all the infinite host of heaven,
Are shining on the sad abodes of death,
Through the still lapse of ages. All that tread
The globe are but a handful to the tribes
That slumber in its bosom. Take the wings
Of morning, pierce the Barcan wilderness,
Or lose thyself in the continuous woods
Where rolls the Oregon and hears no sound
Save his own dashings—yet the dead are there;
And millions in those solitudes, since first

The flight of years began, have laid them down
In their last sleep—the dead reign there alone!
So shalt thou rest, and what if thou withdraw
In silence from the living; and no friend
Take note of thy departure? All that breathe
Will share thy destiny. The gay will laugh
When thou art gone, the solemn brood of care
Plod on, and each one as before shall chase
His favorite phantom; yet all these shall leave
Their mirth and their employments, and shall come
And make their bed with thee. As the long train
Of ages glides away, the sons of men—
The youth in life's green spring, and he who goes
In the full strength of years, matron and maid,
And the sweet babe, and the gray-headed man—
Shall one by one be gathered to thy side,
By those, who in their turn shall follow them.

    So live that when thy summons comes to join
The innumerable caravan that moves
To that mysterious realm, where each shall take
His chamber in the silent halls of death,
Thou go not, like the quarry-slave at night,
Scourged to his dungeon, but, sustained and soothed
By an unfaltering trust, approach thy grave
Like one who wraps the drapery of his couch
About him, and lies down to pleasant dreams.

—*William Cullen Bryant*

Elegy Written in a Country Church-Yard

THE curfew tolls the knell of parting day,
    The lowing herd winds slowly o'er the lea,
The ploughman homeward plods his weary way,
    And leaves the world to darkness and to me.

Now fades the glimmering landscape on the sight,
    And all the air a solemn stillness holds,
Save where the beetle wheels his droning flight,
    And drowsy tinklings lull the distant folds;

Save that, from yonder ivy-mantled tower,
    The moping owl does to the moon complain
Of such as, wandering near her secret bower,
    Molest her ancient, solitary reign.

Beneath those rugged elms, that yew-tree's shade,
    Where heaves the turf in many a mould'ring heap,
Each is his narrow cell forever laid,
    The rude forefathers of the hamlet sleep.

The breezy call of incense-breathing morn,
    The swallow twittering from the straw-built shed,
The cock's shrill clarion, or the echoing horn,
    No more shall rouse them from their lowly bed.

For them no more the blazing hearth shall burn,
    Or busy housewife ply her evening care;
No children run to lisp their sire's return,
    Or climb his knees the envied kiss to share.

Oft did the harvest to their sickle yield,
　　Their furrow oft the stubborn glebe has broke;
How jocund did they drive their team afield!
　　How bowed the woods beneath their sturdy stroke!

Let not ambition mock their useful toil,
　　Their homely joys, and destiny obscure;
Nor grandeur hear with a disdainful smile
　　The short and simple annals of the poor.

The boast of heraldry, the pomp of power,
　　And all that beauty, all that wealth e'er gave,
Awaits alike the inevitable hour:
　　The paths of glory lead but to the grave.

Nor you, ye proud, impute to these the fault,
　　If memory o'er their tomb no trophies raise
Where through the long-drawn aisle and fretted vault
　　The pealing anthem swells the note of praise.

Can storied urn or animated bust
　　Back to its mansion call the fleeting breath?
Can Honor's voice provoke the silent dust
　　Or Flattery soothe the dull cold ear of Death?

Perhaps in this neglected spot is laid
　　Some heart once pregnant with celestial fire;
Hands that the rod of empire might have swayed,
　　Or wak'd to ecstasy the living lyre;

But Knowledge to their eyes her ample page,
　　Rich with the spoils of time, did ne'er unroll;

Chill Penury repressed their noble rage,
　And froze the genial current of the soul.

Full many a gem of purest ray serene
　The dark, unfathomed caves of ocean bear:
Full many a flower is born to blush unseen,
　And waste its sweetness on the desert air.

Some village Hampden, that, with dauntless breast,
　The little tyrant of his fields withstood,
Some mute, inglorious Milton, here may rest;
　Some Cromwell guiltless of his country's blood.

The applause of list'ning senates to command,
　The threats of pain and ruin to despise,
To scatter plenty o'er a smiling land,
　And read their history in a nation's eyes,

Their lot forbade; nor circumscribed alone
　Their growing virtues, but their crimes confined;
Forbade to wade thro' slaughter to a throne,
　And shut the gates of mercy on mankind;

The struggling pangs of conscious truth to hide,
　To quench the blushes of ingenuous shame,
Or heap the shrine of Luxury and Pride
　With incense kindled at the Muse's flame.

Far from the madding crowd's ignoble strife,
　Their sober wishes never learned to stray;
Along the cool sequestered vale of life
　They kept the noiseless tenor of their way.

Yet even these bones from insult to protect,
  Some frail memorial still erected nigh,
With uncouth rhymes and shapeless sculpture decked,
  Implores the passing tribute of a sigh.

Their names, their years, spelt by the unlettered Muse,
  The place of fame and elegy supply:
And many a holy text around she strews
  That teach the rustic moralist to die.

For who, to dumb forgetfulness a prey,
  This pleasing anxious being e'er resigned,
Left the warm precincts of the cheerful day,
  Nor cast one longing, lingering look behind?

On some fond breast the parting soul relies,
  Some pious drops the closing eye requires;
Ev'n from the tomb the voice of Nature cries,
  Ev'n in our ashes live their wonted fires.

For thee who, mindful of the unhonor'd dead,
  Dost in these lines their artless tale relate;
If chance, by lonely contemplation led,
  Some kindred spirit shall inquire thy fate,—

Haply some hoary-headed swain may say:
  "Oft have we seen him, at the peep of dawn,
Brushing with hasty steps the dews away,
  To meet the sun upon the upland lawn.

"There at the foot of yonder nodding beech,
  That wreathes its old fantastic roots so high,

His listless length at noontide would he stretch,
  And pore upon the brook that babbles by.

"Hard by yon wood, now smiling as in scorn,
  Mutt'ring his wayward fancies, he would rove;
Now drooping, woeful-wan, like one forlorn,
  Or craz'd with care, or cross'd in hopeless love.

"One morn I missed him on the custom'd hill,
  Along the heath, and near his favorite tree;
Another came,—nor yet beside the rill,
  Nor up the lawn, nor at the wood was he:

"The next, with dirges due, in sad array,
  Slow through the church-way path we saw him borne;—
Approach and read (for thou canst read) the lay
  Grav'd on the stone beneath yon aged thorn."

THE EPITAPH

Here rests his head upon the lap of earth,
  A youth to fortune and to fame unknown;
Fair Science frown'd not on his humble birth,
  And Melancholy mark'd him for her own.

Large was his bounty, and his soul sincere;
  Heaven did a recompense as largely send:
He give to misery all he had, a tear;
  He gained from heaven ('twas all he wished) a friend.

No farther seek his merits to disclose,
  Or draw his frailties from their dread abode,—

(There they alike in trembling hope repose,)
The bosom of his Father and his God.

—Thomas Gray

They Never Quite Leave Us

THEY never quite leave us, our friends who have passed
   Through the shadows of death to the sunlight
      above;
A thousand sweet memories are holding them fast
   To the places they blessed with their presence and love.
The work which they left and the books which they read
   Speak mutely, though still with an eloquence rare,
And the songs that they sang, the words that they said,
   Yet linger and sigh on the desolate air.
And oft when alone, and oft in the throng,
   Or when evil allures us, or sin draweth nigh,
A whisper comes gently, "Nay, do not the wrong,"
   And we feel that our weakness is pitied on high.

—Margaret E. Sangster

The Graves of a Household

THEY grew in beauty side by side,
   They filled one home with glee,
Their graves are severed far and wide,
   By mount, and stream, and sea.
The same fond mother bent at night
   O'er each fair sleeping brow,

94

She had each folded flower in sight—
  Where are those dreamers now?

One midst the forests of the West,
  By a dark stream, is laid;
The Indian knows his place of rest
  Far in the cedar shade.
The sea, the blue lone sea, hath one,
  He lies where pearls lie deep,
He was the loved of all, yet none
  O'er his low bed may weep.

One sleeps where southern vines are drest
  Above the noble slain;
He wrapt his colours round his breast
  On a blood-red field of Spain.
And one—o'er her the myrtle showers
  Its leaves, by soft winds fanned;
She faded midst Italian flowers,
  The last of that bright band.

And, parted thus, they rest—who played
  Beneath the same green tree,
Whose voices mingled as they prayed
  Around one parent knee!
They that with smiles lit up the hall,
  And cheered with song the hearth,—
Alas for love, if thou wert all,
  And nought beyond, oh earth!

                    —*Mrs. Felicia Dorothea Hemans*

Not Lost, But Gone Before

HOW mournful seems, in broken dreams,
    The memory of the day,
When icy Death hath sealed the breath
    Of some dear form of clay.

When pale, unmoved, the face we loved,
    The face we thought so fair,
And the hand lies cold, whose fervent hold
    Once charmed away despair.

Oh, what could heal the grief we feel
    For hopes that come no more,
Had we ne'er heard the Scripture word,
    "Not lost, but gone before."

Oh sadly yet with vain regret
    The widowed heart must yearn;
And mothers weep their babes asleep
    In the sunlight's vain return.

The brother's heart shall rue to part
    From the one through childhood known;
And the orphan's tears lament for years
    A friend and father gone.

For death and life, with ceaseless strife,
    Beat wild on this world's shore,
And all our calm is in that balm,
    "Not lost, but gone before."

Oh! world wherein nor death, nor sin,
  Nor weary warfare dwells;
Their blessed home we parted from
  With sobs and sad farewells.

Where eyes awake, for whose dear sake
  Our own with tears grow dim,
And faint accords of dying words
  Are changed for heaven's sweet hymn;

Oh! there at last, life's trials past,
  We'll meet our loved once more,
Whose feet have trod the path to God—
  "Not lost, but gone before."

                    —*Hon. Mrs. Norton*

The Burial of Moses

BY Nebo's lonely mountain,
  On this side Jordan's wave,
In a vale in the land of Moab,
  There lies a lonely grave.
And no one knows that sepulchre,
  And no man saw it e'er;
For the angels of God upturned the sod,
  And laid the dead man there.

That was the grandest funeral
  That ever passed on earth;
But no man heard the trampling,
  Or saw the train go forth:

Noiselessly as the daylight
  Comes back when the night is done,
And the crimson streak on ocean's cheek,
  Grows into the great sun.

Noiselessly as the springtime
  Her crown of verdure weaves,
And all the trees on all the hills
  Open their thousand leaves;
So without sound of music
  Or voice of them that wept,
Silently down from the mountain's crown
  The great procession swept.

Perchance the bald old eagle
  On gray Beth-Peor's height,
Out of his lonely eyrie
  Looked on the wondrous sight;
Perchance the lion stalking
  Still shuns that hallowed spot;
For beast and bird have seen and heard
  That which man knoweth not.

But when the warrior dieth,
  His comrades in the war,
With arms reversed and muffled drum,
  Follow his funeral car;
They show the banners taken,
  They tell his battles won,
And after him lead his masterless steed,
  While peals the minute-gun.

Amid the noblest of the land
  We lay the sage to rest,
And give the bard an honored place,
  With costly marble drest;
In the great minster transept,
  Where lights like glories fall,
And the organ rings and the sweet choir sings
  Along the emblazoned wall.

This was the truest warrior
  That ever buckled sword;
This the most gifted poet
  That ever breathed a word;
And never earth's philosopher
  Traced with his golden pen
On the deathless page, truths half so sage
  As he wrote down for men.

And had he not high honor?
  The hillside for a pall;
To lie in state while angels wait,
  With stars for tapers tall,
And the dark rock-pines like tossing plumes
  Over his bier to wave;
And God's own hand, in that lonely land,
  To lay him in the grave.

In that strange grave, without a name,
  Whence his uncoffined clay
Shall break again—oh, wondrous thought!
  Before the judgment day;
And stand with glory wrapped around

On the hills he never trod,
And speak of the strife that won our life
With th' Incarnate Son of God.

O lonely tomb in Moab's land!
O dark Beth-peor's hill!
Speak to these curious hearts of ours,
And teach them to be still.
God hath His mysteries of grace,
Ways that we cannot tell,
He hides them deep, like the secret sleep
Of him he loved so well.

—*Cecil Frances Alexander*

We Are Seven

A SIMPLE child
That lightly draws its breath,
And feels its life in every limb,
What should it know of death?

I met a little cottage girl:
She was eight years old, she said;
Her hair was thick with many a curl
That clustered round her head.

She had a rustic, woodland air,
And she was wildly clad;
Her eyes were fair, and very fair;
—Her beauty made me glad.

"Sisters and brothers, little maid,
How many may you be?"
"How many? Seven in all," she said,
And wondering looked at me.

"And where are they? I pray you tell."
She answered, "Seven are we;
And two of us at Conway dwell,
And two are gone to sea.

"Two of us in the churchyard lie,
My sister and my brother;
And, in the churchyard cottage, I
Dwell near them with my mother."

"You run about, my little maid,
Your limbs they are alive;
If two are in the churchyard laid,
Then ye are only five."

"Their graves are green, they may be seen,"
The little maid replied,
"Twelve steps or more from my mother's door,
And they are side by side.

"My stockings there I often knit,
My kerchief there I hem;
And there upon the ground I sit—
I sit and sing to them.

"And often after sunset, Sir,
When it is light and fair,

I take my little porringer,
And eat my supper there.

"The first that died was little Jane;
In bed she moaning lay,
Till God released her of her pain:
And then she went away.

"So in the churchyard she was laid;
And all the summer dry,
Together round her grave we played,
My brother John and I.

"And when the ground was white with snow,
And I could run and slide,
My brother John was forced to go,
And he lies by her side."

"How many are you, then," said I,
"If they two are in heaven?"
The little maiden did reply,
"O master! we are seven."

"But they are dead: those two are dead!
Their spirits are in heaven!"
'Twas throwing words away: for still
The little maid would have her will,
And said, "Nay, we are seven!"

—*William Wordsworth*

Emancipation

WHY be afraid of death
　　As though your life were breath?

　　　　　　Death but anoints your eyes
　　　　　　With clay, O glad surprise!

Why should you be forlorn?
Death only husks the corn.

　　　　　　Why should you fear to meet
　　　　　　The Thresher of the wheat?

Is sleep a thing to dread?
Yet, sleeping you are dead

　　　　　　Till you awake and rise,
　　　　　　Here, or beyond the skies.

Why should it be a wrench
To leave your wooden bench?

　　　　　　Why not, with happy shout,
　　　　　　Run home when school is out?

The dear ones left behind?
O foolish one and blind,

　　　　　　A day, and you will meet;
　　　　　　A night, and you will greet.

This is the death of death:
To breathe away a breath,

　　　　　　And know the end of strife,
　　　　　　And taste the deathless life,

And joy without a fear,
And smile without a tear,

　　　　　　And work, not care nor rest,
　　　　　　And find the last the best.

　　　　　　　　　　—Maltbie D. Babcock

'Tis the Last Rose of Summer

'TIS the last rose of Summer,
    Left blooming alone;
All her lovely companions
    Are faded and gone;
No flower of her kindred,
    No rosebud is nigh,
To reflect back her blushes,
    Or give sigh for sigh!

I'll not leave thee, thou lone one,
    To pine on the stem;
Since the lovely are sleeping,
    Go sleep thou with them.
Thus kindly I scatter
    Thy leaves o'er the bed
Where thy mates of the garden
    Lie scentless and dead.

So soon may I follow,
    When friendships decay,
And from Love's shining circle
    The gems drop away!
When true hearts lie withered,
    And fond ones are flown,
Oh! who would inhabit
    This bleak world alone?

—Thomas Moore

Memorial Day

A DAY of tender memory,
　　A day of sacred hours,
Of little bands of marching men,
　　Of drums and flags and flowers.

A day when a great nation halts
　　Its mighty, throbbing pace,
And pays its meed of gratitude
　　And love with willing grace.

A day when battles are retold,
　　And eulogies are said,
When dirges sound, and chaplains read
　　The office for the dead.

A day when fairest, sweetest blooms
　　Are laid upon each grave,
And wreaths are hung on monuments,
　　And banners, half-mast, wave.

A day to keep from year to year
　　In memory of the dead;
Let music sound, and flowers be laid
　　Upon each resting-bed.

—Emma A. Lent

A Dead Past (?)

NOT so, for living yet are those
    Who long since passed away;
They live within our memories
    Yes, there they live alway.

Their look of love yet still remains,
    The words they spoke, we hear,
And in a corner of our heart
    Their face and form appear.

Not only those we know and love
    But others passed along,
Who yet are living by their deeds,
    And lead a mighty throng.

A Dead Past? No that cannot be,
    A past lives through the years,
Gives hope and comfort day by day
    By faith, gives hopes to fears.

The Mighty Prince of Peace yet lives
    We feel Him close at hand,
His Word controls the universe
    It yields to His command.

I cannot think of a Dead Past,
    It often speaks to me
And in my soul I hear its words,
    Hence alive the Past must be.

                    —*C. C. Munson*

Break, Break, Break

BREAK, break, break,
   On thy cold, gray stones, O sea!
And I would that my tongue could utter
   The thoughts that arise in me.

Oh, well for the fisherman's boy
   That he shouts with his sister at play!
Oh, well for the sailor lad
   That he sings in his boat on the bay!

And the stately ships go on
   To the haven under the hill;
But oh, for the touch of a vanished hand,
   And the sound of a voice that is still!

Break, break, break,
   At the foot of thy crags, O sea!
But the tender grace of a day that is dead
   Will never come back to me.

—Alfred Tennyson

Crossing the Bar

SUNSET and evening star,
   And one clear call for me,
And may there be no moaning of the bar,
   When I put out to sea.

But such a tide as moving seems asleep,
　　Too full for sound and foam,
When that which drew from out the boundless deep
　　Turns again home.

Twilight and evening bell,
　　And after that the dark!
And may there be no sadness of farewell,
　　When I embark;

For tho' from out our bourne of time and place
　　The flood may bear me far,
I hope to see my Pilot face to face
　　When I have crossed the bar.

　　　　　　　　　　　　　—*Alfred Tennyson*

DELAY

What Have We Done Today?

WE shall do much in the years to come,
　　But what have we done today?
We shall give our gold in a princely sum,
　　But what did we give today?
We shall lift the heart and dry the tear,
We shall plant a hope in the place of fear,
We shall speak the words of love and cheer,
　　But what did we speak today?

We shall be so kind in the after while,
　　But have we been today?

We shall bring to each lonely life a smile,
  But what have we brought today?
We shall give to truth a grander birth,
And to steadfast faith a deeper worth,
We shall feed the hungering souls of earth,
  But whom have we fed today?

We shall reap such joys in the by and by,
  But what have we sown today?
We shall build us mansions in the sky,
  But what have we built today?
'Tis sweet in the idle dreams to bask;
But here and now, do we our task?
Yet, this is the thing our souls must ask,
  What have we done today?

                              —*Nixon Waterman*

Do It Now!

IF you've got a job to do,
                  Do it now!
If it's one you wish were through
                  Do it now!
If you're sure the job's your own,
Don't hem and haw and groan—
                  Do it now!
Don't put off a bit of work,
                  Do it now!
It doesn't pay to shirk,
                  Do it now!
If you want to fill a place
And be useful to the race,

Just get up and take a brace—
                    Do it now!
Don't linger by the way,
                    Do it now!
You'll lose if you delay,
                    Do it now!

If the other fellows wait,
Or postpone until it's late,
You hit up a faster gait—
                    Do it now!
                              —*Anon.*

The Dreamer

HE used to dream of things he'd do
    When grown to be a man,
Beguiling boyhood years away
    With many an idle plan.
And now, when grown to be a man,
    He knows no greater joy
Than dreaming of the things he'd do
    If still he were a boy.

                    —*Thomas Nunan*

Mr. Meant-To

MR. MEANT-TO has a comrade,
    And his name is Didn't Do;
Have you ever chanced to meet them?
    Did they ever call on you?

These two fellows live together
In the house of Never-Win,
And I'm told that it is haunted
By the ghost of Might-Have-Been.

—Anon.

DISCONTENT

The Other Fellow's Job

THERE'S a craze among us mortals that is cruel hard
  to name;
Whereso'er you find a human you will find the case the
  same;
You may seek among the worst of men or seek among the
  best,
And you'll find that every person is precisely like the rest:
Each believes his real calling is along some other line
Than the one at which he's working—take for instance
  yours and mine.
From the meanest "me-too" creature to the leader of the
  mob,
There's a universal craving for "the other fellow's job."

There are millions of professions in the busy world to-day
Each a drudge to him who holds it, but to him who doesn't,
  play;
Every farmer's broken-hearted that in youth he missed his
  call,
While that same unhappy farmer is the envy of us all.
Any task you care to mention seems a vastly better lot

Than the one special something which you happen to
    have got.
There's but one sure way to smother envy's heartache and
    her sob;
Keep too busy at your own to want "the other fellow's
    job."

—Strickland Gillilan

DISCOURAGEMENT

The Bridge of Sighs

ONE more unfortunate,
    Weary of breath,
Rashly importunate,
    Gone to her death!

Take her up tenderly,
    Lift her with care;
Fashioned so slenderly,
    Young, and so fair.

Look at her garments
    Clinging like cerements;
Whilst the wave constantly
    Drips from her clothing;
Take her up instantly,
    Loving, not loathing.

Touch her not scornfully;
Think of her mournfully;
    Gently and humanly;

Not of the stains of her;
All that remains of her
    Now is pure womanly.

Make no deep scrutiny
Into her mutiny
    Rash and undutiful;
Past all dishonour,
Death has left on her
    Only the beautiful.

Still, for all slips of hers,
    One of Eve's family,
Wipe those poor lips of hers
    Oozing so clammily.

Loop up her tresses
    Escaped from the comb,
Her fair auburn tresses;
Whilst wonderment guesses
    Where was her home?

Who was her father?
    Who was her mother?
Had she a sister?
    Had she a brother?
Or was there a dearer one
Still, and a nearer one
    Yet, than all other?

Alas! for the rarity
Of Christian charity
    Under the sun!

Oh, it was pitiful!
Near a whole city full,
　　Home she had none!

Sisterly, brotherly,
Fatherly, motherly
　　Feelings had changed;
Love, by harsh evidence,
Thrown from its eminence;
Even God's providence
　　Seeming estranged.

Where the lamps quiver
So far in the river,
　　With many a light
From window and casement,
From garret to basement,
She stood with amazement,
　　Houseless by night.

The bleak wind of March
　　Made her tremble and shiver;
But not the dark arch,
　　Or the black flowing river;
Mad from life's history,
Glad to death's mystery,
　　Swift to be hurled—
Anywhere, anywhere,
　　Out of the world.

In she plunged boldly,
No matter how coldly
　　The rough river ran—

Over the brink of it—
Picture it, think of it,
    Dissolute man!
Lave in it, drink of it,
    Then, if you can!

Take her up tenderly,
    Lift her with care;
Fashioned so slenderly,
    Young, and so fair!

Ere her limbs frigidly
Stiffen too rigidly,
    Decently, kindly
Smooth and compose them;
And her eyes, close them,
    Staring so blindly!

Dreadfully staring
    Through muddy impurity,
As when with the daring
Last look of despairing
    Fixed on futurity.

Perishing gloomily,
Spurred by contumely,
Cold inhumanity,
Burning insanity,
    Into her rest.

Cross her hands humbly,
As if praying dumbly,
    Over her breast!

Owning her weakness,
    Her evil behavior;
And leaving with meekness,
    Her sins to her Savior!

                            —*Thomas Hood*

Thinking

IF you think you are beaten, you are;
    If you think you dare not, you don't.
If you'd like to win but you think you can't,
    It's almost a cinch you won't.

If you think you'll lose, you're lost,
    For out of the world we find
Success begins with a fellow's will—
    It's all in the state of mind.

If you think you're outclassed, you are;
    You've got to think high to rise;
You've got to be sure of yourself before
    You can ever win a prize.

Life's battle don't always go
    To stronger or faster man;
But soon or late the man who wins,
    Is the one who *thinks he can*.

                            —*Walter D. Wintle*

Try This Once

WHEN you are discouraged
    Don't let your courage fade
When you get a lemon
    Just make some lemonade.

DOGS

The Dog

I'VE never known a dog to wag
    His tail in glee he did not feel,
Nor quit his old-time friend to tag
    At some more influential heel.
The yellowest cur I ever knew
Was to the boy who loved him true.

I've never known a dog to show
    Half-way devotion to his friend;
To seek a kinder man to know,
    Or richer; but unto the end
The humblest dog I ever knew
Was to the man that loved him true.

I've never known a dog to fake
    Affection for a present gain,
A false display of love to make
    Some little favor to attain.
I've never known a Prince or Spot
That seemed to be what he was not.

117

And I have known a dog to bear
　　Starvation's pangs from day to day,
With him who had been glad to share
　　His bread and meat along the way.
No dog, however mean or rude,
Is guilty of ingratitude.

—Anon.

Eulogy of the Dog

GENTLEMEN of the jury, the best friend a man has in this world may turn against him and become his enemy. His son or daughter whom he has reared with loving care may prove ungrateful. Those who are nearest and dearest to us—those whom we trust with our happiness and our good name—may become traitors to their faith. The money that a man has he may lose. It flies away from him, perhaps when he needs it most. A man's reputation may be sacrificed in a moment of ill-considered action. The people who are prone to fall on their knees to do us honor when success is with us may be the first to throw the stone of malice when failure settles its cloud upon our heads. The one absolute, unselfish friend that man can have in this selfish world—the one that never deserts him, the one that never proves ungrateful or treacherous—is his dog.

Gentlemen of the jury, a man's dog stands by him in prosperity and in poverty, in health and in sickness. He will sleep on the cold ground, where the wintry winds blow and the snow drives fiercely, if only he can be near his master's side. He will kiss the hand that has no food to offer, he will lick the wounds and sores that come in encounter with the roughness of the world. He guards the sleep of his pauper master as if he were a prince. When all other friends desert, he remains. When riches take wings and reputation falls to pieces he is as constant in his love as the sun in its journey through the heavens. If fortune drives the master forth an outcast in the world, friendless and homeless, the faithful dog asks no higher privilege than that of accompanying him to guard against danger, to fight against his enemies. And when the last scene of all comes, and death takes the master in its embrace, and his body is laid away in the cold ground, no matter if all other friends pursue their way, there by his graveside will the noble dog be found, his head between his paws, his eyes sad but open in alert watchfulness, faithful and true even to death.

—Hon. George G. Vest

DUTY

Just Keep On

JUST keep on a-livin' an' keep on a-givin',
 An' keep on a-tryin' to smile;
Just keep on a-singin', a-trustin' an' a-clingin'
 To the promise of an after while.

For the sun comes up and the sun goes down,
 An' the morning follows night.
There's a place to rest like a mother's breast,
 An' a time when things come right.

Just keep on believin' an' a-hidin' all your grievin',
    An' keep on a-tryin' to cheer.
Just keep on a-prayin', a-lovin' an' a-sayin'
    The things that we love to hear.

For the tide comes in an' the tide goes out,
    An' the dark will all turn bright;
There's a rest from the load an' an end to the road,
    An' a place where things come right.
                                        —*Clifton Abbott*

"Too Busy"

THE Lord had a job for me, but I had so much to do.
    I said: "You get somebody else—or wait till I get
    through."
I don't know how the Lord came out, but He seemed to
    get along,
But I felt kind o' sneakin' like—knowed I'd done God
    wrong.

One day I needed the Lord, needed him right away—
And he never answered me at all, but I could hear him say
Down in my accusin' heart—"Nigger, I's got too much
    to do.
You get somebody else or wait till I get through."

Now, when the Lord has a job for me, I never tries to
    shirk;
I drops what I have on hand and does the good Lord's
    work;

And my affairs can run along, or wait till I get through.
Nobody else can do the work that God's marked out for
you.

—Paul Laurence Dunbar

The Three Fishers

THREE fishers went sailing out into the west—
　　Out into the west as the sun went down;
Each thought of the woman who loved him the best,
　　And the children stood watching them out of the town;
For men must work, and women must weep;
And there's little to earn, and many to keep,
　　Though the harbor bar be moaning.

Three wives sat up in the light-house tower,
　　And trimmed the lamps as the sun went down;
They looked at the squall, and they looked at the shower,
　　And the night-rack came rolling up, ragged and brown;
But men must work, and women must weep,
Though storms be sudden and waters deep,
　　And the harbor bar be moaning.

Three corpses lay out on the shining sands
　　In the morning gleam as the tide went down,
And the women are weeping and wringing their hands,
　　For those who will never come back to the town;
For men must work, and women must weep,—
And the sooner it's over, the sooner to sleep,—
　　And good-by to the bar and its moaning.

—Charles Kingsley

Just Try This

IF the day looks kinder gloomy,
  And your chances purty slim,
If the situation's puzzlin'
  An' the prospects awful grim,
An' perplexities keep pressin',
  Till all hope is nearly gone,
Just bristle up and grit your teeth,
  An' keep on keepin' on.

—Anon.

The Sands of Dee

OH, Mary, go and call the cattle home.
  And call the cattle home,
  And call the cattle home,
Across the sands of Dee."
The western wind was wild and dark with foam,
  And all alone went she.

The western tide crept up along the sand,
  And o'er and o'er the sand,
  And round and round the sand,
As far as eye could see.
The rolling mist came down and hid the land:
  And never home came she.

"Oh! is it weed, or fish, or floating hair—
  A tress of golden hair,
  A drowned maiden's hair,
Above the nets at sea?"

Was never salmon yet that shone so fair
   Among the stakes of Dee.

They rowed her in across the rolling foam,
   The cruel crawling foam,
   The cruel hungry foam,
To her grave beside the sea.
But still the boatmen hear her call the cattle home,
   Across the sands of Dee.

—*Charles Kingsley*

Things That Endure

HONOR and truth and manhood—
   These are the things that stand,
Though the sneer and jibe of the cynic tribe
   Are loud through the width of the land.
The scoffer may lord it an hour on earth,
   And a lie may live for a day,
But truth and honor and manly worth
   Are things that endure alway.

Courage and toil and service,
   Old, yet forever new—
These are the rock that abides the shock
   And holds through the storm, flint-true.
Fad and folly, the whims of an hour,
   May bicker and rant and shrill:
But the living granite of truth will tower
   Long after their rage is still.

123

Labor and love and virtue—
　Time does not dim their glow;
Though the smart may say, in their languid way,
　"Oh, we've outgrown all that, you know!"
But a lie, whatever the guise it wears,
　Is a lie, as it was of yore.
And a truth that has lasted a million years
　Is good for a million more!

—Ted Olson

God's Will For Us

JUST to be tender, just to be true;
　Just to be glad the whole day through;
Just to be merciful, just to be mild;
Just to be trustful as a child;
Just to be gentle and kind and sweet;
Just to be helpful with willing feet;
Just to be cheery when things go wrong;
Just to drive sadness away with a song,
Whether the hour is dark or bright;
Just to be loyal to God and right;
Just to believe that God knows best;
Just in His promise ever to rest;
Just to let love be our daily key:
This is God's will, for you and me.

—Anon.

The Average Man

WHEN it comes to a question of trusting
    Yourself to the risks of the road,
When the thing is the sharing of burdens,
    The lifting the heft of the load,
In the hour of peril or trial,
    In the hour you meet as you can,
You may safely depend on the wisdom
    And skill of the average man.

'Tis the average man, and no other,
    Who does his plain duty each day,
The small thing his wage is for doing,
    On the commonplace bit of the way.
'Tis the average man, may God bless him,
    Who pilots us still in the van,
Over land, over sea, as we travel,
    Just the plain, hardy, average man.

So, on through the days of existence,
    All mingling in shadows and shine,
We may count on the every-day hero,
    Whom haply the gods may divine.
But who wears the swart grime of his calling,
    And labors and earns as he can,
And stands at the last with the noblest,
    The commonplace, average man.

                     —*Margaret E. Sangster*

Better, Wiser and Happier [1]

DO you wish the world were better?
 Let me tell you what to do;
Set a watch upon your actions,
 Keep them always straight and true;
Rid your mind of selfish motives;
 Let your thoughts be clean and high,
You can make a little Eden
 Of the sphere you occupy.

Do you wish the world were wiser?
 Well, suppose you make a start,
By accumulating wisdom
 In the scrapbook of your heart;
Do not waste one page on folly;
 Live to learn, and learn to live.
If you want to give men knowledge
 You must get it, ere you give.

Do you wish the world were happy?
 Then remember day by day
Just to scatter seeds of kindness
 As you pass along the way;
For the pleasures of the many
 May be ofttimes traced to one,
As the hand that plants an acorn
 Shelters armies from the sun.

                    —*Ella Wheeler Wilcox*

[1] Used by permission of the W. B. Conkey Co., Hammond, Ind.

Four Things To Do

FOUR things a man must learn to do
If he would keep his record true:
To think, without confusion, clearly;
To love his fellow-man sincerely;
To act from honest motives purely;
To trust in God and Heaven securely.

—Henry Van Dyke

FAITH

Jericho's Blind Beggar

BLIND Bartimaeus at the gates
Of Jericho in darkness waits:
He hears the crowd:—He hears a breath
Say, "It is Christ of Nazareth!"
And calls in tones of agony,
"Iesou, eleeson Me!"

The thronging multitudes increase:
"Blind Bartimaeus, hold thy peace."
But still, above the noisy crowd,
The beggar's cry is shrill and loud;
Until they say, "He calleth thee!"
"Tharsei! egeirai! phonei se."

Then saith the Christ, as silent stands
The crowd, "What wilt thou at My hands?"
And he replies, "O give me light!

Rabbi, restore the blind man's sight."
And Jesus answers, "Hupage:
He pistis sou sesoke se."

Ye that have eyes, yet cannot see,
In darkness and in misery,
Recall these mighty voices three,
"Iesou, eleeson me!"
"Tharsei, egeirai!"   "Hupage;
He pistis sou sesoke se."

—Henry W. Longfellow

FASHION

"A Dresscessional"

GIRL of the Future, feared of all,
  Chasing the far-flung Fashion line,
What awful things may yet appall,
  Hung on your human form divine!
Girl of To-day, stay with us yet,
Lest we regret! Lest we regret!

The tunic and the peplum dies,
  The plaiting and the flare depart;
Oh, what must we next sacrifice
  To future of a fearful art?
Girl of To-day, stay with us all,
Lest worse befall! Lest worse befall!

The blouse and bodice melt away,
  Forever fades the silhouette;

Lo! all the mode of yesterday
    Is one with puff and pantalette.
Girl of To-day, stay with us, do!
Lest worse ensue! Lest worse ensue!

If drunk with mad designs we loose
    Wild styles that hold no art in awe,—
Such clothing as the Fijis use,
    Or lesser breeds without the law,—
Girl of To-day, stay here with we,
Lest worse may be! Lest worse may be!

For foolish maid who puts her trust
    In French tailleur or smart modiste,
In valiant men of mien august,
    Without discernment in the least—
For frantic fads of Fashion's whirl,
Have mercy on us, Future Girl!

                —*Carolyn Wells, in Harper's Magazine*

FLOWERS

The Daffodils

I WANDERED lonely as a cloud
    That floats on high o'er vales and hills,
When all at once I saw a crowd,
    A host of golden daffodils,
Besides the lake, beside the trees,
Fluttering and dancing in the breeze.

Continuous as the stars that shine
  And twinkle on the milky way,
They stretched in never-ending line
  Along the margin of a bay;
Ten thousand saw I at a glance,
Tossing their heads in sprightly dance.

The waves beside them danced, but they
  Outdid the sparkling waves in glee;—
A poet could not but be gay,
  In such a jocund company;
I gazed, and gazed, but little thought
What wealth that show to me had brought

For oft when on my couch I lie,
  In vacant or in pensive mood,
They flash upon that inward eye
  Which is the bliss of solitude;
And then my heart with pleasure fills,
And dances with the daffodils.

—William Wordsworth

To a Mountain Daisy

(On Turning One Down With the Plough, in April, 1786)

WEE, modest, crimson-tippèd flow'r,
    Thou's met me in an evil hour;
For I maun crush amang the stoure
      Thy slender stem:
To spare thee now is past my pow'r,
      Thou bonnie gem.

Alas! it's no thy neebor sweet,
The bonnie Lark, companion meet!
Bending thee 'mang the dewy weet!
      Wi' spreckl'd breast,
When upward-springing, blythe, to greet
      The purpling east.

Cauld blew the bitter-biting north
Upon thy early, humble birth;
Yet cheerfully thou glinted forth
      Amid the storm,
Scarce rear'd above the parent-earth
      Thy tender form.

The flaunting flow'rs our gardens yield,
High shelt'ring woods and wa's maun shield,
But thou, beneath the random bield *
      O' clod, or stane,
Adorns the histie † stibble-field,
      Unseen, alane.

There, in thy scanty mantle clad,
Thy snawy bosom sunward spread,
Thou lifts thy unassuming head
      In humble guise;
But now the share uptears thy bed,
      And low thou lies!

Such is the fate of artless Maid,
Sweet flow'ret of the rural shade!
By love's simplicity betray'd,
      And guileless trust,

* Shelter.   † Dry.

131

Till she, like thee, all soil'd, is laid
        Low i' the dust.

Such is the fate of simple Bard,
On life's rough ocean luckless starr'd:
Unskilful he to note the card
        Of prudent lore,
Till billows rage, and gales blow hard,
        And whelm him o'er!

Such fate to suffering worth is giv'n,
Who long with wants and woes has striv'n,
By human pride or cunning driv'n
        To mis'ry's brink,
Till, wrench'd of ev'ry stay but Heav'n,
        He, ruin'd, sink!

Ev'n thou who mourn'st the Daisy's fate,
That fate is thine—no distant date;
Stern Ruin's ploughshare drives, elate,
        Full on thy bloom,
Till crush'd beneath the furrow's weight,
        Shall be thy doom.

                —*Robert Burns*

Just Forget

FORGET the slander you have heard,
Forget the hasty unkind word,
Forget the quarrel and the cause,
Forget the whole affair because
Forget it is the only way;
Forget the storm of yesterday.
Forget those with the sour face,
Forget and smile in any place.
Forget the trials you have had,
Forget the weather if it's bad.
Forget the knocker, he's a freak,
Forget him seven days a week,
Forget you're not a millionaire,
Forget the gray streaks in your hair,
Forget wherever you may roam,
Forget when traveling or at home.

—Myrtle May Dryden

On File

IF an unkind word appears,
File the thing away,
If some novelty in jeers,
File the thing away.

If some clever little bit,
Of a sharp and pointed wit,

Carrying a sting with it,
File the thing away.

If some bit of gossip come,
File the thing away.
Scandalously spicy crumb,
File the thing away.

If suspicion come to you,
That your neighbor isn't true,
Let me tell you what to do—
File the thing away.

Do this for a little while
Then go out and burn the file.

—*John Kendrick Bangs*

GARDENS

My Garden

A GARDEN is a lovesome thing, God wot!
   Rose plot,
      Fringed pool
Fern'd grot—
      The veriest school
      Of peace; and yet the fool
Contends that God is not—
Not God! in gardens! when the eve is cool?
      Nay, but I have a sign;
      'Tis very sure God walks in mine.

—*Thomas Edward Brown*

The Isolation of Genius

HE who ascends to mountain-tops shall find
　　The loftiest peaks most wrapt in clouds and snow;
He who surpasses or subdues mankind,
Must look down on the hate of those below.
Though high above the sun of glory glow,
And far beneath the earth and ocean spread,
Round him are icy rocks, and loudly blow
Contending tempests on his naked head.
And thus reward the toils which to those summits led.

—Lord Byron

GOD

Each in His Own Tongue [1]

A FIRE-MIST and a planet,
　　A crystal and a cell,
A jelly-fish and a saurian,
　　And caves where the cave-men dwell;
Then a sense of law and beauty
　　And a face turned from the clod—
Some call it Evolution,
　　And others call it God.

A haze on the far horizon,
　　The infinite, tender sky,

[1] From "Each in His Own Tongue and Other Poems." G. P. Putnam's Sons
New York.

135

The ripe rich tint of the cornfields,
　　And the wild geese sailing high—
And all over upland and lowland
　　The charm of the golden-rod—
Some of us call it Autumn
　　And others call it God.

Like tides on a crescent sea-beach,
　　When the moon is new and thin,
Into our hearts high yearnings
　　Come welling and surging in—
Come from the mystic ocean,
　　Whose rim no foot has trod,—
Some of us call it Longing,
　　And others call it God.

A picket frozen on duty,
　　A mother starved for her brood,
Socrates drinking the hemlock,
　　And Jesus on the rood;
And millions who, humble and nameless,
　　The straight, hard pathway plod,—
Some call it Consecration,
　　And others call it God.

—William Herbert Carruth

The Nineteenth Psalm

THE heavens declare the glory of God;
　And the firmament sheweth his handywork.

Day unto day uttereth speech,
And night unto night sheweth knowledge.

There is no speech nor language;
Their voice can not be heard.

Their line is gone out through all the earth,
And their words to the end of the world.
In them hath he set a tabernacle for the sun,

Which is as a bridegroom coming out of his chamber,
And rejoiceth as a strong man to run his course.

His going forth is from the end of the heaven,
And his circuit unto the ends of it:
And there is nothing hid from the heat thereof.

The law of the LORD is perfect, restoring the soul:
The testimony of the LORD is sure, making wise the
    simple.

The precepts of the LORD are right, rejoicing the heart:
The commandment of the LORD is pure, enlightening the
    eyes.

The fear of the LORD is clean, enduring for ever;
The judgments of the LORD are true, and righteous alto-
    gether.

More to be desired are they than gold, yea, than much
    fine gold:
Sweeter also than honey and the honeycomb.

Moreover by them is thy servant warned:
In keeping of them there is great reward.

Who can discern his errors?
Clear thou me from hidden faults.

Keep back thy servant also from presumptuous sins;
Let them not have dominion over me: then shall I be
    perfect,
And I shall be clear from great trangression.

Let the words of my mouth and the meditation of my
    heart be acceptable in thy sight,
O Lord, my rock, and my redeemer.

                                        —*The Bible*

Nearer, My God, To Thee

NEARER, my God, to Thee,
    Nearer to Thee!
E'en though it be a cross
    That raiseth me;
Still all my song shall be,
Nearer, my God, to Thee,
    Nearer to Thee!

Though like the wanderer,
    The sun gone down,
Darkness be over me,
    My rest a stone;
Yet in my dreams I'd be

Nearer, my God, to Thee,
    Nearer to Thee!

There let the way appear
    Steps unto Heaven,
All that Thou sendest me
    In mercy given;
Angels to beckon me
Nearer, my God, to Thee,
    Nearer to Thee!

Then with my waking thoughts
    Bright with Thy praise,
Out of my stony griefs,
    Bethel I'll raise;
So by my woes to be
Nearer, my God, to Thee,
    Nearer to Thee!

Or if, on joyful wing,
    Cleaving the sky,
Sun, moon and stars forgot,
    Upward I fly,
Still all my song shall be,
Nearer, my God, to Thee,
    Nearer to Thee!

—*Sarah Flower Adams*

God in the Nation's Life

PUTTING God in the Nation's life,
  Bringing us back to the ideal thing—
There's something fine in a creed like that,
  Something true in those words that ring.
Sneer as you will at the "preacher air,"
  Scoff as you will at the Bible tang,
It's putting God in the Nation's life
  That will keep it clear of the crooked "gang."

We've kept Him out of its life too long,
  We've been afraid—to our utter shame—
To put Him into our speech and song,
  To stand on the hustings and speak His name.
We've put all things in that life but Him,
  We've put our selfishness, pride and show;
It is time for the true ideal to come,
  And time for the low desire to go.

Putting God in the Nation's life,
  Helping us think of the higher thing
That is the kind of speech to make
  That is the kind of song to sing.
Upward and forward and let us try,
  The new ideal in the forthright way—
Putting God in the Nation's life,
  And putting it there in a style to stay.

—Anon.

Just the Same Today

WHEN Moses and his people
   From Egypt's land did flee,
Their enemies behind them,
   And in front of them the sea,
God raised the waters like a wall
   And opened up the way,
And the God that lived in Moses' time
   Is just the same to-day.

When David and Goliath met,
   The wrong against the right—
The giant armed with human power
   And David with God's might;
God's power with David's sling and stone
   The giant low did lay,
And the God that lived in David's time
   Is just the same to-day.

When Pentecost had fully come,
   And the fire from Heaven did fall,
As a mighty wind the Holy Ghost
   Baptized them one and all;
Three thousand got converted,
   And were workers right away
And the God that lived at Pentecost,
   Is just the same to-day.

—Anon.

The Heart's Proof

DO you ask me how I prove
    That our Father, God, is love?
By this world which he hath made,
By the songs of grove and blade,
By the brooks that singing run,
By the shining of the sun,
By the breeze that cools my brow,
By fresh odors from the plow,
By the daisy's golden head,
Shining in the fields I tread,
By the chorus of the bees
In the flowering willow trees,
By the gentle dews and rain,
By the farmer's springing grain,
By the light of golden eyes,
By the sheen of forest leaves,
By the sweets of woodland springs,
By the joy right-doing brings—
By a thousand, thousand things!

                —*James Buckham*

Convinced by Sorrow

"THERE is no God," the foolish saith,
    But none, "There is no sorrow."
And nature oft the cry of faith,
    In bitter need will borrow:
Eyes which the preacher could not school,
    By wayside graves are raised,

And lips say, "God be pitiful,"
  Who ne'er said, "God be praised."
    Be pitiful, O God!

—*Elizabeth Barrett Browning*

The Voice of God

YOU'VE never heard the voice of God?
  Look at the stars above,
Their luminous orbs of many rays,
Speak of infinite love.

The universe to you doth speak
You need not know her laws
The grass the flowers all growing things,
In them there are no flaws.

The seasons as they come and go
The wind, the sun, the rain;
The voice is there and every where,
It speaks and speaks again.

So lift your eyes to the starry sky,
And feel the voice of God.
Oh fainting heart, oh weary soul,
And His great works applaud.

—*Katherine R. Barnard*

Revelation

ALL things burn with the fire of God—
　Violets bursting from the sod;
The hill-top, tip-toe cherry tree,
Shouting with silver ecstacy;
Wild birds blowing down the wind;
Blue-brook music far and thinned;
Many-hued roses; rains that beat
On spreading fields of yellow wheat;
Sun-flame, moon-flame, flame of star;
Opal-walled heaven where bright clouds are;
Dreams, and pain, and love's desire . . .
All things burn with God's white fire.

—Verne Bright

GOD'S LOVE

The Little Black Sheep

PO' lil' brack sheep dat strayed away,
　Done los' in de win' an' de rain—
An' de Shepherd He say, "O, hirelin',
　Go fin' my sheep again."
An' de hirelin' say, "O, Shepherd,
　Dat sheep am brack an' bad."
But de Shepherd He smile, like dat lil' brack sheep
　Wuz de onliest lamb He had.

An' de Shepherd go out in de darkness
　Where de night wuz col' an' bleak,

144

An' dat lil' brack sheep, He fin' it.
    An' lay it agains' His cheek.
An' de hirelin' frown; "O, Shepherd,
    Don' bring dat sheep to me!"
But de Shepherd He smile, an' He hol' it close.
    An'—dat lil' brack sheep—wuz—me!

—Paul Laurence Dunbar

He Giveth More

He giveth more grace (Jas. 4:6). He increaseth strength (Isa. 40: 29). Mercy unto you, and peace, and love, be multiplied (Jude 21).

HE giveth more grace when the burdens grow greater,
    He sendeth more strength when the labors increase;
To added affliction He addeth his mercy,
    To multiplied trials, His multiplied peace.

When we have exhausted our store of endurance,
    When our strength has failed ere the day is half done,
When we reach the end of our hoarded resources,
    Our Father's full giving is only begun.

His love has no limit, His grace has no measure,
    His power no boundary known unto men;
For out of his infinite riches in Jesus
    He giveth and giveth and giveth again.

—Annie Johnson Flint

There's a Wideness

FOR the love of God is broader
   Than the measure of man's mind,
And the heart of the Eternal
   Is most wonderfully kind.
If our love were but more simple,
   We should take Him at His word;
And our lives would be all sunshine
   In the sweetness of our Lord.

            —*Frederick W. Faber*

GOODNESS

"I Shall Not Pass Again This Way"

THE bread that bringeth strength I want to give
   The water pure that bids the thirsty live;
I want to help the fainting day by day;
I'm sure I shall not pass again this way.

I want to give the oil of joy for tears,
The faith to conquer crowding doubts and fears,
Beauty for ashes may I give always;
I'm sure I shall not pass again this way.

I want to give good measure running o'er
And into angry hearts I want to pour
The answer soft that turneth wrath away;
I'm sure I shall not pass again this way.

I want to give to others hope and faith;
I want to do all that the Master saith;
I want to live aright from day to day;
I'm sure I shall not pass again this way.

—Anon.

I Shall Not Pass This Way Again [1]

(A Symphony)

I SHALL not pass this way again—
    Although it bordered be with flowers,
  Although I rest in fragrant bowers,
      And hear the singing
      Of song-birds winging
To highest heaven their gladsome flight;
Though moons are full and stars are bright,
And winds and waves are softly sighing,
While leafy trees make low replying;
Though voices clear in joyous strain
Repeat a jubilant refrain;
Though rising suns their radiance throw
On summer's green and winter's snow,
In such rare splendor that my heart
Would ache from scenes like these to part;
      Though beauties heighten,
      And life-lights brighten,
And joys proceed from every pain,—
I shall not pass this way again.

[1] Taken by permission from "A Treasury of Canadian Verse." Published by E. P. Dutton & Co.

Then let me pluck the flowers that blow,
And let me listen as I go
        To music rare
        That fills the air;
        And let hereafter
        Songs and laughter
Fill every pause along the way;
And to my spirit let me say:
"O soul, be happy; soon 'tis trod,
The path made thus for thee by God.
Be happy, thou, and bless His name
By whom such marvellous beauty came."
And let no chance by me be lost
To kindness show at any cost.
I shall not pass this way again;
Then let me now relieve some pain,
Remove some barrier from the road,
Or brighten some one's heavy load;
A helping hand to this one lend,
Then turn some other to befriend.

        O God, forgive
        That now I live
As if I might, sometime, return
To bless the weary ones that yearn
For help and comfort every day—
For there be such along the way.
O God, forgive that I have seen
The beauty only, have not been
Awake to sorrow such as this;
That I have drunk the cup of bliss

Remembering not that those there be
Who drink the dregs of misery.

I love the beauty of the scene,
Would roam again o'er fields so green;
But since I may not, let me spend
My strength for others to the end,—
For those who tread on rock and stone,
And bear their burdens all alone,
Who loiter not in leafy bowers,
Nor hear the birds nor pluck the flowers.
A larger kindness give to me,
A deeper love and sympathy;
    Then, oh, one day
    May someone say—
Remembering a lessened pain—
"Would she could pass this way again."

        —*Eva Rose York*

My Aim

I LIVE for those who love me, whose hearts are kind and
   true,
For the heaven that smiles above me, and awaits my
   spirit, too;
For all human ties that bind me, for the task my God
   assigned me;
For the bright hopes yet to find me, and the good that I
   can do.

I live to learn their story who suffered for my sake;
To emulate their glory and follow in their wake:

Bards, patriots, martyrs, sages, the heroic of all ages,
Whose deeds crowd History's pages and Time's great
    volume make.

I live to hold communion with all that is divine,
To feel there is a union 'twixt Nature's heart and mine;
To profit by affliction, reap truth from fields of fiction,
Grow wiser from conviction, and fulfill God's grand
    design.

I live to hail the season, by gifted ones foretold,
When man shall live by reason, and not alone by gold;
When man to man united, and every wrong thing righted,
The whole world shall be lighted, as Eden was of old.

I live for those who love me, for those who know me
    true;
For the heaven that smiles above me, and awaits my
    spirit too;
For the cause that lacks assistance, for the wrong that
    needs resistance,
For the future in the distance, and the good that I can
    do.

—*G. Linnaeus Banks*

Winds of Fate[1]

ONE ship drives east and another drives west,
    While the self-same breezes blow;
It's the set of the sails and not the gales,
    That bids them where to go.

[1] Used by permission of the W. B. Conkey Co., Hammond, Ind.

Like the winds of the seas are the ways of the fates,
  As we voyage along through life;
It's the set of the soul that decides the goal,
  And not the storms or the strife.

—*Ella Wheeler Wilcox*

My Creed

IWOULD be true, for there are those who trust me;
  I would be pure, for there are those who care;
I would be strong, for there is much to suffer;
I would be brave, for there is much to dare.
I would be friend of all—the poor—the friendless;
I would be giving and forget the gift;
I would be humble, for I know my weakness;
I would look up—and laugh—and love—and lift.

—*Howard Arnold Walter*

My Kate

SHE was not as pretty as women I know,
  And yet all your best made of sunshine and snow
Drop to shade, melt to nought in the long-trodden ways,
While she's still remembered on warm and cold days—
                    My Kate.
Her air had a meaning, her movements a grace;
You turned from the fairest to gaze on her face;
And when you had once seen her forehead and mouth,
You saw as distinctly her soul and her truth—
                    My Kate.

Such a blue inner light from her eyelids outbroke,
You looked at her silence and fancied she spoke;
When she did, so peculiar yet soft was the tone,
Though the loudest spoke also, you heard her alone—
         My Kate.

I doubt if she said to you much that could act
As a thought or suggestion; she did not attract
In the sense of the brilliant or wise; I infer
'Twas her thinking of others made you think of her—
         My Kate.

She never found fault with you, never implied
Your wrong by her right; and yet men at her side
Grew nobler, girls purer, as through the whole town
The children were gladder that pulled at her gown—
         My Kate.

None knelt at her feet confessed lovers in thrall;
They knelt more to God than they used—that was all;
If you praised her as charming, some asked what you meant,
But the charm of her presence was felt when she went—
         My Kate.

The weak and the gentle, the ribald and rude,
She took as she found them, and did them all good;
It always was so with her—see what you have!
She has made the grass greener even here with her grave—
         My Kate.

        —*Elizabeth Barrett Browning*

Life's Mirror

THERE are loyal hearts, there are spirits brave,
 There are souls that are pure and true;
Then give to the world the best you have,
And the best will come back to you.

Give love, and love to your life will flow,
And strength in your inmost needs;
Have faith, and a score of hearts will show
Their faith in your work and deeds.

Give truth, and your gifts will be paid in kind,
And song a song will meet;
And the smile which is sweet will surely find
A smile that is just as sweet.

Give pity and sorrow to those who mourn;
You will gather in flowers again
The scattered seeds from your thought outborne,
Though the sowing seemed in vain.

For life is the mirror of king and slave,
'Tis just what we are and do;
Then give to the world the best you have
And the best will come back to you.

—Madeline S. Bridges

Tribute to Grass

LYING in the sunshine among the buttercups and dandelions of May, scarcely higher in intelligence than the minute tenants of that mimic wilderness, our earliest recollections are of grass; and when the fitful fever is ended and the foolish wrangle of the market and forum is closed, grass heals over the scar which our descent into the bosom of the earth has made, and the carpet of the infant becomes the blanket of the dead. Grass is the forgiveness of nature—her constant benediction. Fields trampled with battle, saturated with blood, torn with the ruts of cannon, grow green again with grass, and carnage is forgotten. Streets abandoned by traffic become grass-grown like rural lanes and are obliterated. Forests decay, harvests perish, flowers vanish, but grass is immortal. Beleaguered by the sullen hosts of Winter, it withdraws into the impregnable fortress of its subterranean vitality and emerges upon the first solicitation of Spring. Sown by the winds, by wandering birds, propagated by the subtle agriculture of the elements which are its ministers and servants, it softens the outline of the world. It bears no blazonry of bloom to charm the senses with fragrance or splendor, but its homely hue is more enchanting than the lily or the rose. It yields no fruit in earth or air, and yet, should its harvest fail for a single year, famine would depopulate the world.

—John J. Ingalls

How Do You Do?

"HOW can you, friend?" the Swedish say;
    The Dutch, "How do you fare?"
"How do you have yourself today?"
    Has quite a Polish air.
In Italy, "How do you stand?"
    Will greet you every hour;
In Turkey when one takes your hand,
    "Be under God's great power!"

"How do you carry you?" is heard
    When Frenchmen so inquire;
While Egypt's friendly greeting word
    Is "How do you perspire?"
"Thin may thy shadows never grow,"
    The Persian wish is true;
His Arab cousin, bowing low,
    Says, "Praise God! How are you?"
But oddest of them all is when
    Two Chinese meet, for thrice
They shake their own two hands, and then
    Ask, "Have you eaten rice?"

                  —H. Bedford Jones

The Grumble Family

THERE'S a family nobody likes to meet,
  They live, it is said, on Complaining Street,
In the city of Never-are-Satisfied,
The river of Discontent beside.
They growl at that and they growl at this,
Whatever comes there is something amiss;
And whether their station be high or humble,
They are known by the name of Grumble.

The weather is always too hot or cold,
Summer and winter alike they scold;
Nothing goes right with the folks you meet
Down on that gloomy Complaining Street.
They growl at the rain and they growl at the sun,
In fact, their growling is never done.
And if everything pleased them, there isn't a doubt
They'd growl that they'd nothing to grumble about!

But the queerest thing is that not one of the same
Can be brought to acknowledge his family name,
For never a Grumbler will own that he
Is connected with it at all, you see.
And the worst thing is that if any one stays
Among them too long he will learn their ways,
And before he dreams of the terrible jumble
He's adopted into the family of Grumble.

So it were wisest to keep our feet
From wandering into Complaining Street;

And never to growl, whatever we do,
Lest we be mistaken for Grumblers, too.
Let us learn to walk with a smile and song,
No matter if things do sometimes go wrong,
And then, be our station high or humble,
We'll never belong to the family of Grumble!

—Anon.

HEAVEN

The Holy City

LAST night I lay a-sleeping,
     There came a dream so fair;
I stood in old Jerusalem,
Beside the Temple there;
I heard the children singing,
And ever as they sang,
Methought the voice of angels
From heaven in answer rang,
     Jerusalem, Jerusalem,
     Lift up your gates and sing
     Hosanna in the highest,
     Hosanna to your King!

And then methought my dream was changed,
The streets no longer rang,
Hushed were the glad Hosannas
The little children sang;
The sun grew dark with mystery,
The morn was cold and chill,

As the shadow of a cross arose
Upon a lonely hill.
      Jerusalem, Jerusalem,
      Hark! how the angels sing,
      Hosanna in the highest,
      Hosanna to your King!

And once again the scene was changed,
New earth there seemed to be!
I saw the holy city
Beside the tideless sea;
The light of God was on its street,
The gates were open wide;
And all who would might enter,
And no one was denied.
No need of moon or stars by night,
Nor sun to shine by day;
It was the New Jerusalem,
That would not pass away.
      Jerusalem, Jerusalem,
      Sing, for the night is o'er,
      Hosanna in the highest,
      Hosanna for evermore!

                                        F. E. Weatherly

Nearer Home

ONE sweetly solemn thought
      Comes to me o'er and o'er:
I am nearer my home to-day
      Than I ever have been before;

Nearer my Father's house,
  Where the many mansions be;
Nearer the great white throne,
  Nearer the crystal sea;

Nearer the bound of life,
  Where we lay our burden down;
Nearer leaving the cross;
  Nearer gaining the crown:

But lying darkly between,
  Winding down through the night,
Is the silent, unknown stream,
  That leads at last to the light.

Closer and closer my steps
  Come to the dark abysm;
Closer Death to my lips
  Presses the awful chrism.

Oh, if my mortal feet
  Have almost gained the brink;
If it be I am nearer home
  Even to-day than I think!

Father, perfect my trust;
  Let my spirit feel in death,
That her feet are firmly set
  On the rock of a living faith!

—Phœbe Cary

The Land o' the Leal

I'M wearing awa', John,
  Like snaw when it's thaw, John,
I'm wearing awa'
    To the Land o' the Leal.
There's nae sorrow there, John,
There's neither cauld nor care, John,
The day is aye fair
    In the Land o' the Leal.

Ye wer aye leal and true, John,
Your task's ended noo, John,
And I'll welcome you
    To the Land o' the Leal.
Our bonnie bairn's there, John,
She was baith guid and fair, John;
Oh, we grudged her right sair
    To the Land o' the Leal!

Then dry that tearfu' e'e, John,
My soul langs to be free, John,
And angels wait on me
    To the Land o' the Leal.
Now fair ye weel, my ain John,
This warld's care is vain, John;
We'll meet and aye be fain
    In the Land o' the Leal.

—Lady Nairn

The Kingdom of God

I SAY to thee, do thou repeat
 To the first man thou mayest meet
In lane, highway, or open street—

That he and we and all men move
Under a canopy of love,
As broad as the blue sky above;

That doubt and trouble, fear and pain,
And anguish, all are shadows vain,
That death itself shall not remain;

That weary deserts we may tread,
A dreary labyrinth may thread,
Thro' dark ways underground be led;

Yet, if we will one Guide obey,
The dreariest path, the darkest way
Shall issue out in heavenly day;

And we, on divers shores now cast,
Shall meet, our perilous voyage past,
All in our Father's house at last,

And ere thou leave him, say thou this,
Yet one word more—they only miss
The winning of that final bliss,

Who will not count it true, that Love,
Blessing, not cursing, rules above,
And that in it we live and move.

And one thing further make him know,
That to believe these things are so,
This firm faith never to forego,

Despite of all which seems at strife
With blessing, all with curses rife,
That this *is* blessing, this *is* life.

—*Archbishop Trench*

HOME

Old Folks at Home

WAY down upon de Swanee ribber,
    Far, far away,
Dere's wha my heart is turning ebber,
    Dere's wha de old folks stay.
All up and down de whole creation,
    Sadly I roam,
Still longing for de old plantation,
    And for de old folks at home.

All round de little farm I wander'd
    When I was young,
Den many happy days I squander'd,
    Many de songs I sung.
When I was playing wid my brudder,
    Happy was I.
Oh! take me to my kind old mudder,
    Dere let me live and die.

162

One little hut among de bushes,
    One dat I love,
Still sadly to my mem'ry rushes,
    No matter where I rove.
When will I see the bees a-humming,
    All round de comb?
When will I hear de banjo tumming,
    Down in my good old home?

All de world am sad and dreary,
    Ebrywhere I roam,
Oh! darkies how my heart grows weary,
    Far from de old folks at home.

—*Stephen C. Foster*

Home, Sweet Home

MID pleasures and palaces though we may roam,
    Be it ever so humble, there's no place like home;
A charm from the sky seems to hallow us there,
Which, seek through the world, is ne'er met with else-
    where.
    Home, home, sweet, sweet home!
There's no place like home, oh, there's no place like home!

An exile from home, splendor dazzles in vain;
Oh, give me my lowly thatched cottage again!
The birds singing gayly, that came at my call—
Give me them—and the peace of mind, dearer than all!

163

Home, home, sweet, sweet home!
There's no place like home, oh, there's no place like home!

I gaze on the moon as I tread the drear wild,
And feel that my mother now thinks of her child,
As she looks on that moon from our own cottage door
Thro' the woodbine, whose fragrance shall cheer me no
    more.
    Home, home, sweet, sweet home!
There's no place like home, oh, there's no place like home!

How sweet 'tis to sit 'neath a fond father's smile,
And the caress of a mother to soothe and beguile!
Let others delight mid new pleasure to roam,
But give me, oh, give me, the pleasures of home,
    Home, home, sweet, sweet home!
There's no place like home, oh, there's no place like home!

To thee I'll return, overburdened with care;
The heart's dearest solace will smile on me there;
No more from that cottage again will I roam;
Be it ever so humble, there's no place like home.
    Home, home, sweet, sweet home!
There's no place like home, oh, there's no place like home!

—*John Howard Payne*

They Two

THEY are left alone in the dear old home,
    After so many years
When the house was full of frolic and fun

Of childish laughter and tears.
They are left alone, they two—once more,
  Beginning life over again,
Just as they did in the days of yore,
  Before they were nine or ten.

And the table is set for two these days;
  The children went one by one,
Away from home, on their separate ways,
  When the childhood days were done.
How healthily hungry they used to be,
  What romping they used to do;
And mother through weeping—can hardly see
  To set the table for two.

They used to gather around the fire
  While someone would read aloud,
But whether at study, or work, or play.
  'Twas a loving and merry crowd.
And now they are two that gather there
  At evening to read or sew,
And it seems almost too much to bear
  When they think of the long ago.

Ah, well—ah, well—'tis the way of the world
  Children stay but a little while,
And then into other scenes are whirled,
  Where other homes beguile.
But it matters not how far they roam,
  Their hearts are fond and true,
And there's never a home like the dear old home,
  Where the table is set for two.

                              —*Mrs. Frank A. Breck*

Hamlet's Soliloquy

TO be, or not to be; that is the question;
      Whether 'tis nobler in the mind to suffer
The slings and arrows of outrageous fortune,
Or to take arms against a sea of troubles,
And by opposing end them. To die: to sleep:
No more; and by a sleep to say we end
The heart-ache and the thousand natural shocks
That flesh is heir to; 'tis a consummation
Devoutly to be wished. To die; to sleep;
To sleep: perchance to dream; aye, there's the rub;
For in that sleep of death what dreams may come,
When we have shuffled off this mortal coil,
Must give us pause: there's the respect
That makes calamity of so long life;
For who would bear the whips and scorns of time,
The oppressor's wrong, the proud man's contumely,
The pangs of despis'd love, the law's delay,
The insolence of office, and the spurns
That patient merit of the unworthy takes,
When he himself might his quietus make
With a bare bodkin? Who would fardels bear,
To grunt and sweat under a weary life,
But that the dread of something after death—
The undiscover'd country from whose bourn
No traveler returns—puzzles the will
And makes us rather bear those ills we have
Than fly to others that we know not of?
Thus conscience does make cowards of us all,

And thus the native hue of resolution
Is sicklied o'er with the pale cast of thought,
And enterprises of great pith and moment
With this regard their currents turn awry,
And lose the name of action.

—William Shakespeare

The Mystic Borderland

THERE is a mystic borderland that lies
   Just past the limits of our work-day world,
And it is peopled with the friends we met
And loved a year, a month, a week or day,
And parted from with aching hearts, yet knew
That through the distance we must lose the hold
Of hand with hand, and only clasp the thread
Of memory. But still so close we feel this land,
So sure we are that these same hearts are true,
That when in waking dreams there comes a call
That sets the thread of memory aglow,
We know that just by stretching out the hand
In written word of love, or book, or flower,
The waiting hand will clasp our own once more
Across the distance, in the same old way.

—Helen Field Fischer

Cato's Soliloquy

IT must be so—Plato, thou reason'st well—
   Else whence this pleasing hope, this fond desire,

This longing after immortality?
Or whence this secret dread, and inward horror
Of falling into nought? Why shrinks the Soul
Back on herself, and startles at destruction?
'Tis the Divinity, that stirs within us;
'Tis Heav'n itself, that points out a hereafter,
And intimates eternity to man.
Eternity! thou pleasing, dreadful thought!
Through what variety of untried being,
Through what new scenes and changes must we pass!
The wide, th' unbounded prospect lies before me;
But shadows, clouds, and darkness rest upon it.
Here will I hold. If there's a power above us,
(And that there is, all Nature cries aloud
Through all her works,) He must delight in virtue;
And that which He delights in must be happy.
But when or where?—This world was made for Cæsar.
I'm weary of conjectures—this must end 'em.

Thus am I doubly arm'd—My death and life,
My bane and antidote are both before me.
This in a moment brings me to an end;
But this informs me I shall never die.
The Soul, secured in her existence, smiles
At the drawn dagger, and defies its point;
The stars shall fade away, the Sun himself
Grow dim with age, and Nature sink in years;
But thou shalt flourish in immortal youth,
Unhurt amidst the war of elements,
The wreck of matter and the crash of worlds.

—Joseph Addison

Hiawatha's Childhood

BY the shores of Gitche Gumee,
By the shining Big-Sea-Water,
Stood the wigwam of Nokomis,
Daughter of the Moon, Nokomis.
Dark behind it rose the forest,
Rose the black and gloomy pine-trees,
Rose the firs with cones upon them;
Bright before it beat the water,
Beat the clear and sunny water,
Beat the shining Big-Sea-Water.
      There the wrinkled old Nokomis
Nursed the little Hiawatha,
Rocked him in his linden cradle,
Bedded soft in moss and rushes,
Safely bound with reindeer sinews;
Stilled his fretful wail by saying,
"Hush! the Naked Bear will hear thee!"
Lulled him into slumber, singing,
"Ewa-yea! my little owlet!
Who is this, that lights the wigwam?
With his great eyes lights the wigwam?
Ewa-yea! my little owlet!"
      Many things Nokomis taught him
Of stars that shine in heaven;
Showed him Ishkoodah, the comet,
Ishkoodah, with fiery tresses;
Showed the Death-Dance of the spirits,
Warriors with their plumes and war-clubs,

Flaring far away to northward
In the frosty nights of winter;
Showed the broad white road in heaven,
Pathway of the ghosts, the shadows,
Running straight across the heavens,
Crowded with the ghosts, the shadows.

At the door on summer evenings,
Sat the little Hiawatha;
Heard the whispering of the pine-trees,
Heard the lapping of the waters,
Sounds of music, words of wonder;
"Minne-wawa!" said the pine-trees,
"Mudway-aushka!" said the water.

Saw the fire-fly Wah-wah-taysee,
Flitting through the dusk of evening,
With the twinkle of its candle
Lighting up the brakes and bushes,
And he sang the song of children,
Sang the song Nokomis taught him:
"Wah-wah-taysee, little firefly,
Little, flitting, white-fire insect,
Little, dancing, white-fire creature,
Light me with your little candle
Ere upon my bed I lay me,
Ere in sleep I close my eyelids!"

Saw the moon rise from the water,
Rippling, rounding from the water,
Saw the flecks and shadows on it,
Whispered, "What is that, Nokomis?"
And the good Nokomis answered:
"Once a warrior, very angry,
Seized his grandmother, and threw her

Up into the sky at midnight;
Right against the moon he threw her;
'Tis her body that you see there."
　　Saw the rainbow in the heaven,
In the eastern sky the rainbow,
Whispered, "What is that, Nokomis?"
And the good Nokomis answered:
" 'Tis the heaven of flowers you see there;
All the wild-flowers of the forest,
All the lilies of the prairie,
When on earth they fade and perish,
Blossom in that heaven above us."
　　When he heard the owls at midnight,
Hooting, laughing in the forest,
"What is that?" he cried in terror;
"What is that," he said, "Nokomis?"
And the good Nokomis answered:
"That is but the owl and owlet,
Talking in their native language,
Talking, scolding at each other."
　　Then the little Hiawatha
Learned of every bird its language,
Learned their names and all their secrets,
How they built their nests in summer,
Where they hid themselves in winter,
Talked with them whene'er he met them,
Called them "Hiawatha's Chickens."
Of all beasts be learned the language,
Learned their names and all their secrets,
How the beavers built their lodges,
Where the squirrels hid their acorns,
How the reindeer ran so swiftly,

Why the rabbit was so timid,
Talked with them whene'er he met them,
Called them "Hiawatha's Brothers."

—Henry Wadsworth Longfellow

KINDNESS

While the Days Are Going By

THERE are lonely hearts to cherish
  While the days are going by;
There are weary souls who perish,
  While the days are going by;
If a smile we can renew,
As our journey we pursue,
Oh, the good that we may do,
  While the days are going by.

There's no time for idle scorning,
  While the days are going by;
Let your face be like the morning,
  While the days are going by;
Oh, the world is full of sighs,
Full of sad and weeping eyes;
Help your fallen brothers rise,
  While the days are going by.

All the loving links that bind us
  While the days are going by;
One by one we leave behind us,
  While the days are going by;

But the seeds of good we sow,
Both in shade and shine will grow.
And will keep our hearts aglow,
While the days are going by.

—*George Cooper*

Scatter Seeds of Kindness

LET us gather up the sunbeams,
  Lying all around our path;
Let us keep the wheat and roses,
  Casting out the thorns and chaff;
Let us find our sweetest comfort
  In the blessings of today,
With a patient hand removing
  All the briers from the way.

Strange we never prize the music
  Till the sweet-voiced bird is flown!
Strange that we should slight the violets
  Till the lovely flowers are gone!
Strange that summer skies and sunshine
  Never seem one-half so fair,
As when winter's snowy pinions
  Shake the white down in the air.

If we knew the baby fingers,
  Pressed against the window pane,
Would be cold and stiff tomorrow—
  Never trouble us again—
Would the bright eyes of our darling

Catch the frown upon our brow?
Would the prints of rosy fingers
    Vex us then as they do now?

Ah! those little ice-cold fingers,
    How they point our memories back
To the hasty words and actions
    Strewn along our backward track!
How those little hands remind us,
    As in snowy grace they lie,
Not to scatter thorns, but roses,
    For our reaping by and by.

                    —*Mrs. Albert Smith*

Say It Now

IF you have a friend worth loving,
    Love him. Yes, and let him know
That you love him, ere life's evening
    Tinge his brow with sunset glow.
Why should good words ne'er be said.
Of a friend—till he is dead?

If you hear a song that thrills you,
    Sung by any child of song,
Praise it. Do not let the singer
    Wait deserved praises long.
Why should one who thrills your heart
Lack the joy you may impart?

If you hear a prayer that moves you
  By its humble, pleading tone,
Join it. Do not let the seeker
  Bow before its God alone.
Why should not your brother share
The strength of "two or three" in prayer?

If you see the hot tears falling
  From a brother's weeping eyes,
Share them. And by kindly sharing
  Own our kinship in the skies.
Why should anyone be glad
When a brother's heart is sad?

If a silvery laugh goes rippling
  Through the sunshine on his face,
Share it. 'Tis the wise man's saying—
  For both grief and joy a place.
There's health and goodness in the mirth
In which an honest laugh has birth.

If your work is made more easy
  By a friendly helping hand,
Say so. Speak out brave and truly
  Ere the darkness veil the land.
Should a brother workman dear
Falter for a word of cheer?

Scatter thus your seeds of kindness
  All enriching as you go—
Leave them. Trust the Harvest Giver;
  He will make each seed to grow.

So, until the happy end,
Your life shall never lack a friend.

—Anon.

Do It Now [1]

IF with pleasure you are viewing any work a man is
doing,
 If you like him or you love him, tell him now;
Don't withhold your approbation till the parson makes
oration
 As he lies with snowy lilies o'er his brow;
For, no matter how you shout it, he won't really care
about it;
 He won't know how many teardrops you have shed;
If you think some praise is due him, now's the time to
pass it to him,
 For he cannot read his tombstone when he's dead!

More than fame and more than money is the comment
kind and sunny,
 And the hearty, warm approval of a friend,
For it gives to life a savor and it makes you stronger,
braver,
 And it gives you heart and spirit to the end;
If he earns your praise—bestow it; if you like him, let
him know it;
 Let the words of true encouragement be said;
Do not wait till life is over and he's underneath the clover,
 For he cannot read his tombstone when he's dead!

—Berton Braley

[1] Used by permission of the author.

Give Them the Flowers Now

CLOSED eyes can't see the white roses;
　　Cold hands can't hold them, you know!
Breath that is stilled can not gather
　　The odors that sweet from them blow.
Death, with a peace beyond dreaming,
　　Its children of earth doth endow;
Life is the time we can help them;
　　So give them the flowers now!

Here are the struggles and striving;
　　Here are the cares and the tears;
Now is the time to be smoothing
　　The frowns and the furrows and fears.
What, to closed ears, are kind sayings?
　　What, to hushed heart, is deep vow?
Naught can avail after parting—
　　So give them the flowers now.

Just a kind word or a greeting;
　　Just a warm clasp or a smile—
These are the flowers that will lighten
　　The burdens for many a mile.
After the journey is over
　　What is the use of them? how
Can they carry them, who must be carried?
　　Oh, give them the flowers now!

Blooms from the happy heart's garden,
　　Plucked in the spirit of love;
Blooms that are earthly reflections

Of flowers that blossom above—
Words can not tell what a measure
Of blessing such gifts will allow
To dwell in the lives of many;
So give them the flowers now.

—*Anon.*

Give to the Living

IF we gave unto the living as we lavish on the dead,
Kindly thoughts and gentle phrases, tender words and
friendly praises,
Blotting out all imperfections, holding virtues up to
light;
If we left no daily token of our love and care unspoken—
Then would life be well worth living in a world all glad
and bright.

If we offered to the living, as we heap upon the dead,
Fragrant flowers of affection, blossoms of sweet recollec-
tion,
Waiting not till hands are folded on the quiet, pulseless
breast,
Then the passion of our pleading would not fall on ears
unheeding,
Nor our tears fall, unavailing, on the weary form at rest.

If we gave unto the living as we lavish on the dead
All our heart's long hidden treasure, all love's full, un-
stinted measure,

Adding, day by day, new jewels to the crown of human
  bliss,
Then life's burdens would weigh lightly, and the sun
  would shine more brightly,
And not Heaven itself were fairer than a world as glad
  as this.

—Ida Goldsmith Morris

Tell Him So

IF you hear a kind word spoken
  Of some worthy soul you know,
It may fill his heart with sunshine
  If you only tell him so.

If a deed, however humble,
  Helps you on your way to go,
Seek the one whose hand has helped **you,**
  Seek him out and tell him so!

If your heart is touched and tender
  Toward a sinner, lost and low,
It might help him to do better
  If you'd only tell him so!

Oh, my sisters, oh, my brothers,
  As o'er life's rough path you go.
If God's love has saved and kept you,
  Do not fail to tell men so!

—Anon.

Best of All

HE doeth well who doeth good
  To those of his own brotherhood;
He doeth better who doth bless
The stranger in his wretchedness;
Yet best, oh! best of all doth he
Who helps a fallen enemy.

—Anon.

What Is Good?

"WHAT is the real good?"
  I ask in musing mood.

"Order," said the law court;
  "Knowledge," said the school;
"Truth," said the wise man;
  "Pleasure," said the fool;
"Love," said the maiden;
  "Beauty," said the page;
"Freedom," said the dreamer;
  "Home," said the sage;
"Fame," said the soldier;
  "Equity," the seer.
Spake my heart full sadly:
  "The answer is not here."

Then within my bosom
  Softly this I heard:

180

"Each heart holds the secret:
   'Kindness is the word.' "

—John Boyle O'Reilly

LABOR

The Thinker [1]

BACK of the beating hammer
   By which the steel is wrought,
Back of the workshop's clamor,
   The seeker may find the *Thought;*
The Thought that is ever master
   Of iron and steam and steel,
That rises above disaster
   And tramples it under heel!

The drudge may fret and tinker,
   Or labor with dusty blows,
But back of him stands the Thinker,
   The clear-eyed man who *knows;*
For into each plow or saber,
   Each piece and part and whole,
Must go the Brains of Labor,
   Which gives the work a soul!

Might of the roaring boiler,
   Force of the engine's thrust,
Strength of the sweating toiler,
   Greatly in these we trust.
But back of them stands the Schemer,

[1] Used by permission of the author.

The Thinker who drives things through;
Back of the Job, the Dreamer,
Who's making the dream come true!
—*Berton Braley*

The True Aristocrat

WHO are the nobles of the earth,
  The true aristocrats,
Who need not bow their heads to lords,
  Nor doff to kings their hats?
Who are they but the men of toil,
  The mighty and the free,
Whose hearts and hands subdue the earth,
  And compass all the sea?

Who are they but the men of toil,
  Who cleave the forest down,
And plant, amid the wilderness,
  The hamlet and the town,
Who fight the battles, bear the scars,
  And give the world its crown
Of name, and fame, and history,
  And pomp of old renown?

These claim no guard of heraldry,
  And scorn the knightly rod;
Their coats of arms are noble deeds,
  Their peerage is from God!
They take not from ancestral graves
  The glory of their name,

But win, as once their fathers won,
    The laurel wreath of fame.

—W. Stewart

The Gospel of Labor

THIS is the Gospel of Labor—
    Ring it ye bells of the kirk,—
The Lord of love came down from above
    To live with the men who work.
This is the rose that he planted
    Here in the thorn-cursed soil—
Heaven is blessed with perfect rest;
    But the blessing of earth is toil.

—Henry Van Dyke

Song of the Shirt

WITH fingers weary and worn,
    With eyelids heavy and red,
A woman sat in unwomanly rags,
    Plying her needle and thread—
Stitch! stitch! stitch!
    In poverty, hunger and dirt,
And still with a voice of dolorous pitch
    She sang the "Song of the Shirt!"

"Work! work! work!
    While the cock is crowing aloof!

183

And work—work—work,
   Till the stars shine through the roof!
It's oh! to be a slave
   Along with the barbarous Turk,
Where a woman has never a soul to save,
   If this is Christian work!

"Work—work—work
   Till the brain begins to swim;
Work—work—work
   Till the eyes are heavy and dim!
Seam, and gusset, and band,
   Band, and gusset, and seam,
Till over the buttons I fall asleep,
   And sew them on in a dream!

"O men, with sisters dear!
   O men, with mothers and wives!
It is not linen you're wearing out,
   But human creatures lives!
Stitch—stitch—stitch!
   In poverty, hunger and dirt,—
Sewing at once, with a double thread,
   A shroud as well as a shirt!

"But why do I talk of Death,—
   That phantom of grisly bone?
I hardly fear his terrible shape,
   It seems so like my own,—
   It seems so like my own
Because of the fasts I keep;

O God! that bread should be so dear,
And flesh and blood so cheap!

"Work! work! work!
    My labor never flags;
And what are its wages?   A bed of straw,
    A crust of bread—and rags,
That shattered roof—and this naked floor—
    A table—a broken chair—
And a wall so blank, my shadow I thank
    For sometimes falling there!

"Work—work—work!
    From weary chime to chime!
Work—work—work!
    As prisoners work for crime!
Band, and gusset, and seam,
    Seam, and gusset, and band,—
Till the heart is sick and the brain benumbed,
    As well as the weary hand.

"Work—work—work!
    In the dull December light!
And work—work—work!
    When the weather is warm and bright!
While underneath the eaves
    The brooding swallows cling,
As if to show me their sunny backs,
    And twit me with the spring.

"Oh, but to breathe the breath
    Of the cowslip and primrose sweet,—

With the sky above my head,
   And the grass beneath my feet!
For only one short hour
   To feel as I used to feel,
Before I knew the woes of want
   And the walk that costs a meal!

"Oh, but for one short hour,—
   A respite, however brief!
No blessed leisure for love or hope,
   But only time for grief!
A little weeping would ease my heart;
   But in their briny bed
My tears must stop, for every drop
   Hinders needle and thread!"

With fingers weary and worn,
   With eyelids heavy and red,
A woman sat in unwomanly rags,
   Plying her needle and thread,—
Stitch! stitch! stitch!
   In poverty, hunger and dirt;
And still with a voice of dolorous pitch—
Would that its tone could reach the rich!—
   She sang the "Song of the Shirt."

                              —*Thomas Hood*

"Do It Right"

IF you have a thing to do—
  Do it Right;
Stick at it till you're through—
  Do it Right;
Give good and honest work—
It never pays to shirk—
  Do it Right;
Whether working fast or slow—
  Do it Right;
Don't do things just for show—
  Do them Right;
If things go wrong don't cry,
Just all the harder try—
  Do it Right;
If wealth you would acquire—
  Do it Right;
If to fame you would aspire—
  Do it Right;
Shun ill-gotten gain,
Strive for an honored name—
  Do it Right;

—*Samuel O. Buckner*

The Man With the Hoe [1]

(Written after seeing Millet's world-famous painting of a
brutalized toiler)
God made man in his own image in the
image of God made He him.—*Genesis*

BOWED by the weight of centuries he leans
   Upon his hoe and gazes on the ground,
The emptiness of ages in his face,
And on his back the burden of the world.
Who made him dead to rapture and despair,
A thing that grieves not and that never hopes,
Stolid and stunned, a brother to the ox?
Who loosened and let down this brutal jaw?
Whose was the hand that slanted back this brow?
Whose breath blew out the light within this brain?

Is this the Thing the Lord God made and gave
To have dominion over sea and land;
To trace the stars and search the heavens for power;
To feel the passion of Eternity?
Is this the dream He dreamed who shaped the suns
And markt their ways upon the ancient deep?
Down all the caverns of Hell to their last gulf
There is no shape more terrible than this—
More tongued with censure of the world's blind greed—
More filled with signs and portents for the soul—
More packt with danger to the universe.

1 From "The Man With the Hoe, and Other Poems," by Edwin Markham.
Published by Doubleday, Page & Co. Copyright 1899 and 1924 by the author,
and used by his permission.
  This poem has been called the "battle-cry of the next thousand years." It has
been translated into thirty languages.

What gulfs between him and the seraphim!
Slave of the wheel of labor, what to him
Are Plato and the swing of Pleiades?
What the long reaches of the peaks of song,
The rift of dawn, the reddening of the rose?
Thru this dread shape the suffering ages look;
Time's tragedy is in that aching stoop;
Thru this dread shape humanity betrayed,
Plundered, profaned and disinherited,
Cries protest to the Powers that made the world,
A protest that is also prophecy.

O masters, lords and rulers in all lands,
Is this the handiwork you give to God,
This monstrous thing distorted and soul-quencht?
How will you ever straighten up this shape;
Touch it again with immortality;
Give back the upward looking and the light;
Rebuild in it the music and the dream;
Make right the immemorial infamies,
Perfidious wrongs, immedicable woes?

O masters, lords and rulers in all lands,
How will the future reckon with this Man?
How answer his brute question in that hour
When whirlwinds of rebellion shake all shores?
How will it be with kingdoms and with kings—
With those who shaped him to the thing he is—
When this dumb Terror shall rise to judge the world,
After the silence of the centuries?

—*Edwin Markham*

189

Laugh It Off

ARE you worsted in a fight?
    Laugh it off.
Are you cheated of your right?—
    Laugh it off.
Don't make tragedy of trifles,
Don't shoot butterflies with rifles—
    Laugh it off.
Does your work get into kinks?—
    Laugh it off.
Are you near all sorts of brinks?
    Laugh it off.
If it's sanity you're after,
There's no recipe like laughter—
    Laugh it off.

—Henry Rutherford Elliot

Then Laugh [1]

BUILD for yourself a strong-box,
    Fashion each part with care;
When it's strong as your hand can make it,
    Put all your troubles there;
Hide there all thought of your failures
    And each bitter cup that you quaff;
Lock all your heartaches within it,
    Then sit on the lid and laugh.

Tell no one else its contents,
    Never its secrets share;
When you've dropped in your care and worry,
    Keep them forever there;
Hide them from sight so completely
    That the world will never dream half;
Fasten the strong-box securely—
    Then sit on the lid and laugh.

               —*Bertha Adams Backus*

The Way of the World [1]

LAUGH, and the world laughs with you,
    Weep, and you weep alone,
For the brave old earth must borrow its mirth—
    But has trouble enough of its own.
Sing and the hills will answer,
    Sigh, it is lost on the air;
The echoes rebound to a joyful sound
    And shrink from voicing care.

Rejoice, and men will seek you,
    Grieve, and they turn and go;
They want full measure of your pleasure,
    But they do not want your woe.
Be glad, and your friends are many
    Be sad, and you lose them all;
There are *none* to decline your nectared wine,
    But *alone* you must drink life's gall.

[1] Reprinted from "Poems of Passion" by Ella Wheeler Wilcox. By special permission W. B. Conkey Company, Hammond, Ind.

191

Feast, and your halls are crowded,
  Fast, and the world goes by.
Forget and forgive—it helps you to live,
  But no man can help you to die;
There's room in the halls of pleasure
  For a long and lordly train,
But, one by one, we must all march on
  Through the narrow aisle of pain.

—*Ella Wheeler Wilcox*

LEADERS

Leaders

SOME leaders lead too far ahead,
  High-visioned, unafraid;
Yet, ages after they are dead,
  We tread the paths they made.

Some leaders lead too far behind,
  Nor seem to keep the track,
Yet they bring on the deaf and blind,
  Who else would hold us back.

And some seem not to lead at all,
  Slow moving on the way,
Yet help the weary feet and small
  Of those who else would stray.

Lead on, O leaders of the race!
  Your work is long and wide;

192

We need your help in every place—
Before, behind, beside.

—Anon.

LIBERTY

Magna Charta

O N June 15, 1215, King John met the barons near Runnymeade on the Thames, England, and granted them the charter which they laid before him, now famous under the name "Magna Charta."

This charter contains sixty-three articles, some of which were merely temporary; the principles upon which the whole English judicial system is based are these:

"No freeman shall be taken or imprisoned, or disseised *, or outlawed, or banished . . . unless by the lawful judgment of his peers, or by the law of the land."

"We will sell to no man, we will not deny to any man, either justice or right."

Among the most important articles were the two which limited the power of the king in matters of taxation:

"No scutage or aid shall be imposed in our kingdom unless by the general council of our kingdom;" and

"For the holding of the general council of the kingdom . . . we shall cause to be summoned the archbishops, bishops, abbots, earls, and the greater barons of the realm, singly, by our letters. And furthermore, we shall cause to be summoned generally by our sheriffs and bailiffs, all others who hold of us in chief."

* Dispossessed of land.

193

A Psalm of Life

TELL me not, in mournful numbers,
    Life is but an empty dream!
For the soul is dead that slumbers,
    And things are not what they seem.

Life is real! life is earnest!
    And the grave is not its goal;
Dust thou art, to dust returnest,
    Was not spoken of the soul.

Not enjoyment, and not sorrow
    Is our destined end or way;
But to act, that each tomorrow
    Find us further than today.

Art is long, and time is fleeting,
    And our hearts, though stout and brave,
Still, like muffled drums, are beating
    Funeral marches to the grave.

In the world's broad field of battle,
    In the bivouac of life,
Be not like dumb, driven cattle!
    Be a hero in the strife!

Trust no future, howe'er pleasant!
    Let the dead past bury its dead!

Act—act in the living present!
    Heart within, and God o'erhead!

Lives of great men all remind us
    We can make our lives sublime,
And, departing, leave behind us
    Footprints on the sand of time—

Footprints, that perhaps another,
    Sailing o'er life's solemn main,
A forlorn and shipwrecked brother,
    Seeing, shall take heart again.

Let us, then, be up and doing,
    With a heart for any fate;
Still achieving, still pursuing,
    Learn to labor and to wait.

            —*Henry Wadsworth Longfellow*

Man's Mortality

LIKE as the damask rose you see,
    Or like the blossom on the tree,
Or like the dainty flower in May,
Or like the morning of the day,
Or like the sun, or like the shade,
Or like the gourd which Jonas had,
E'en such is man; whose thread is spun,
Drawn out, and cut, and so is done.
The rose withers; the blossom blasteth;
The flower fades; the morning hasteth;

The sun sets; the shadow flies;
The gourd consumes; and man he dies!

Like as the grass that's newly sprung,
Or like a tale that's new begun,
Or like the bird that's here to-day,
Or like the pearled dew of May,
Or like an hour, or like a span,
Or like the singing of a swan,
E'en such is man, who lives by breath,
Is here, now there, in life and death.
The grass withers; the tale is ended;
The bird is flown; the dew's ascended;
The hour is short; the span is long;
The swan's near death; man's life is done!

—*Simon Wastel*

LITTLE THINGS

One Step at a Time

ONE step at a time, and that well placed,
  We reach the grandest height;
One stroke at a time, earth's hidden stores
  Will slowly come to light;
One seed at a time, and the forest grows;
One drop at a time, and the river flows
  Into the boundless sea.

One word at a time, and the greatest book
  Is written and is read;

One stone at a time, and a palace rears
  Aloft its stately head;
One blow at a time, and the tree's cleft through,
And a city will stand where the forest grew
  A few short years before.

One foe at a time, and he subdued,
  And the conflict will be won;
One grain at a time, and the sands of life
  Will slowly all be run;
One minute, another, the hours thus fly;
One day at a time, and our lives speed by
  Into eternity!

One grain of knowledge, and that well stored,
  Another and more on them;
As time rolls on your mind will shine
  With many a garnered gem
Of thought and wisdom. And time will tell
"One thing at a time, and that done well,"
  Is wisdom's proven rule.

—Anonymous

LOVE

Woman's Love

MAN knows not love—such love as woman feels.
  In him it is a vast devouring flame—
Resistless fed—in its own strength consumed.

197

In woman's heart it enters step by step,
Concealed, disowned, until its gentler ray
Breathes forth a light, illuminating her world.
Man loves not for repose; he wooes the flower
To wear it as the victor's trophied crown;
Whilst woman, when she glories in her love,
More like the dove, in noiseless constancy,
Watches the nest of her affection till
'Tis shed upon the tomb of him she loves.

—Anon.

Comin' Thro' the Rye

GIN a body meet a body
    Comin' thro' the rye,
Gin a body kiss a body,
    Need a body cry?
Every lassie has her laddie—
    Ne'er a ane hae I;
Yet a' the lads they smile at me
    When comin' thro' the rye.
Amang the train there is a swain
    I dearly lo'e mysel';
But whaur his hame, or what his name,
    I dinna care to tell.

Gin a body meet a body
    Comin' frae the town,
Gin a body greet a body,
    Need a body frown?

Every lassie has her laddie—
　　Ne'er a ane hae I;
Yet a' the lads they smile at me
　　When comin' thro' the rye.
Amang the train there is a swain
　　I dearly lo'e mysel';
But whaur his hame, or what his name,
　　I dinna care to tell.

—Anonymous

"Believe Me, If All Those Endearing Young Charms"

BELIEVE me, if all those endearing young charms,
　　Which I gaze on so fondly to-day,
Were to change by to-morrow, and fleet in my arms,
　　Like fairy gifts, fading away,
Thou wouldst still be adored, as this moment thou art,
　　Let thy loveliness fade as it will,
And around the dear ruin each wish of my heart
　　Would entwine itself verdantly still.

It is not while beauty and youth are thine own,
　　And thy cheeks unprofaned by a tear,
That the fervor and faith of a soul can be known,
　　To which time will but make thee more dear.
No, the heart that has truly loved never forgets,
　　But as truly loves on to the close,
As the sun-flower turns on her god, when he sets,
　　The same look which she turned when he rose.

—Thomas Moore

The Rosary

THE hours I spent with thee, dear heart,
Are as a string of pearls to me;
I count them over—every one apart—
My rosary, my rosary.

Each hour a pearl, each pearl a prayer;
To still a heart in absence wrung;
I tell each bead unto the end,
And there, a cross is hung!

Oh, memories that bless and burn,
O barren gain, and bitter loss,
I kiss each bead, and strive at last to learn,
Sweetheart, to kiss the cross.

—*Robert Cameron Rogers*

Annie Laurie

MAXWELTON'S braes are bonnie
Where early fa's the dew,
And it's there that Annie Laurie
Gie'd me her promise true;
Gie'd me her promise true,
Which ne'er forgot will be;
And for bonnie Annie Laurie
I'd lay me doune and dee.

Her brow is like the snaw drift;
Her throat is like the swan;
Her face it is the fairest

That e'er the sun shone on—
That e'er the sun shone on—
And dark blue is her ee;
And for bonnie Annie Laurie
I'd lay me doune and dee.

Like dew on the gowan lying
Is the fa' o' her fairy feet;
And like the winds in summer sighing,
Her voice is low and sweet—
Her voice is low and sweet—
And she's a' the world to me;
And for bonnie Annie Laurie
I'd lay me doune and dee.

—Douglas of Fingland

Highland Mary

YE banks and braes and streams around
  The castle o' Montgomery,
Green be your woods, and fair your flowers,
  Your waters never drumlie!
There simmer first unfauld her robes,
  And there the langest tarry;
For there I took the last fareweel
  O' my sweet Highland Mary.

How sweetly bloomed the gay green birk,
  How rich the hawthorn's blossom,
As underneath their fragrant shade
  I clasped her to my bosom!

The golden hours on angel wings
  Flew o'er me and my dearie;
For dear to me as light and life
  Was my sweet Highland Mary.

Wi' mony a vow and locked embrace
  Our parting was fu' tender;
And pledging aft to meet again,
  We tore oursels asunder;
But, oh, fell death's untimely frost,
  That nipt my flower sae early!
Now green's the sod, and cauld the clay,
  That wraps my Highland Mary!

Oh, pale, pale now, those rosy lips,
  I aft hae kissed sae fondly!
And closed for aye the sparkling glance
  That dwelt on me sae kindly!
And moldering now in silent dust
  That heart that lo'ed me dearly!
But still within my bosom's core
  Shall live my Highland Mary.

—*Robert Burns*

Love's Young Dream

OH! the days are gone, when Beauty bright
    My heart's chain wove;
When my dream of life from morn till night
    Was love, still love.
    New hope may bloom,

And days may come
Of milder, calmer beam,
But there's nothing half so sweet in life
As love's young dream:
No, there's nothing half so sweet in life
As love's young dream.

Though the bard to purer fame may soar
When wild youth's past;
Though he wins the wise, who frowned before,
To smile at last;
He'll never meet
A joy so sweet,
In all his noon of fame,
As when first he sung to woman's ear
His soul-felt flame,
And, at every close, she blushed to hear
The one loved name.

No—that hallowed form is ne'er forgot
Which first love traced;
Still it lingering haunts the greenest spot
On memory's waste.
'Twas odour fled
As soon as shed;
'Twas morning's wingéd dream;
'Twas a light that ne'er can shine again
On life's dull stream:
Oh! 'twas light that ne'er can shine again
On life's dull stream.

—Thomas Moore

The Banks o' Doon

YE banks and braes o' bonnie Doon
   How can ye bloom sae fresh and fair?
How can ye chant, ye little birds,
   And I sae weary, fu' o' care?
Thou'lt break my heart, thou warbling bird,
   That wantons through the flowering thorn;
Thou minds me o' departed joys,
   Departed—never to return!

Aft hae I roved by bonnie Doon,
   To see the rose and woodbine twine;
And ilka bird sang o' its luve,
   And fondly sae did I o' mine.
Wi' lightsome heart I pu'd a rose,
   Fu' sweet upon its thorny tree;
And my fause luver stole my rose,
   But, ah! he left the thorn wi' me.

—*Robert Burns*

The Night Has a Thousand Eyes

THE night has a thousand eyes,
   And the day but one;
Yet the light of the bright world dies
   With the dying sun.

The mind has a thousand eyes,
   And the heart but one;

Yet the light of a whole life dies
When love is done.

—*Francis William Bourdillon*

A Song of the Camp

"GIVE us a song!" the soldiers cried,
  The outer trenches guarding,
When the heated guns of the camp allied
  Grew weary of bombarding.

The dark Redan, in silent scoff,
  Lay grim and threatening under;
And the tawny mound of the Malakoff
  No longer belched its thunder.

There was a pause. A guardsman said,
  "We storm the forts to-morrow;
Sing while we may, another day
  Will bring enough of sorrow."

They lay along the battery's side,
  Below the smoking cannon,—
Brave hearts from Severn and from Clyde,
  And from the banks of Shannon.

They sang of love, and not of fame;
  Forgot was Britain's glory;
Each heart recalled a different name,
  But all sang "Annie Laurie."

Voice after voice caught up the song,
  Until its tender passion
Rose like an anthem rich and strong,
  Their battle-eve confession.

Dear girl! her name he dared not speak;
  But as the song grew louder,
Something upon the soldier's cheek
  Washed off the stains of powder.

Beyond the darkening ocean burned
  The bloody sunset's embers,
While the Crimean valleys learned
  How English love remembers.

And once again a fire of hell
  Rained on the Russian quarters,
With scream of shot and burst of shell,
  And bellowing of the mortars!

And Irish Nora's eyes are dim
  For a singer dumb and gory;
And English Mary mourns for him
  Who sang of "Annie Laurie."

Sleep, soldiers! still in honored rest
  Your truth and valor wearing;
The bravest are the tenderest,—
  The loving are the daring.

                                      —*Bayard Taylor*

Annabel Lee

IT was many and many a year ago,
  In a kingdom by the sea,
That a maiden there lived whom you may know
  By the name of Annabel Lee;
And this maiden she lived with no other thought
  Than to love and be loved by me.

I was a child and she was a child,
  In this kingdom by the sea;
But we loved with a love that was more than love,
  I and my Annabel Lee;
With a love that the winged seraphs of heaven
  Coveted her and me.

And this was the reason that, long ago,
  In this kingdom by the sea,
A wind blew out of a cloud, chilling
  My beautiful Annabel Lee;
So that her high-born kinsman came
  And bore her away from me,
To shut her up in a sepulcher
  In this kingdom by the sea.

The angels, not half so happy in heaven,
  Went envying her and me.
Yes, that was the reason—as all men know,
  In this kingdom by the sea—
That the wind came out of the cloud by night,
  Chilling and killing my Annabel Lee.

But our love it was stronger far than the love
  Of those that were older than we,
  Of many far wiser than we.
And neither the angels in heaven above,
Nor the demons down under the sea,
Can ever dissever my soul from the soul
  Of the beautiful Annabel Lee:

For the moon never beams without bringing me dreams
  Of the beautiful Annabel Lee;
And the stars never rise but I feel the bright eyes
  Of the beautiful Annabel Lee;
And so, all the night-tide, I lie down by the side
Of my darling, my darling, my life, and my bride,
  In the sepulcher there by the sea,
  In her tomb by the sounding sea.

—Edgar Allan Poe

Lord Ullin's Daughter

A CHIEFTAIN to the Highlands bound,
  Cries, "Boatman, do not tarry!
And I'll give thee a silver pound
  To row us o'er the ferry."

"Now, who be ye would cross Lochgyle,
  This dark and stormy water?"
"Oh! I'm the chief of Ulva's isle,
  And this Lord Ullin's daughter.

"And fast before her father's men
    Three days we've fled together;
For, should he find us in the glen,
    My blood would stain the heather.

"His horsemen hard behind us ride;
    Should they our steps discover,
Then who will cheer my bonny bride
    When they have slain her lover?"

Out spoke the hardy island wight,
    "I'll go, my chief—I'm ready:—
It is not for your silver bright;
    But for your winsome lady:

"And by my word, the bonny bird
    In danger shall not tarry;
So, though the waves are raging white,
    I'll row you o'er the ferry."

By this the storm grew loud apace,
    The water-wraith was shrieking;
And in the scowl of heaven each face
    Grew dark as they were speaking.

But still as wilder blew the wind,
    And as the night grew drearer,
Adown the glen rode armed men,
    Their trampling sounded nearer.

"Oh! haste thee, haste!" the lady cries,
    "Though tempests round us gather;

209

I'll meet the raging of the skies,
  But not an angry father."

The boat has left a stormy land,
  A stormy sea before her,—
When, oh! too strong for human hand,
  The tempest gathered o'er her.

And still they rowed amidst the roar
  Of waters fast prevailing;
Lord Ullin reached that fatal shore,
  His wrath was changed to wailing.

For sore dismayed through storm and shade,
  His child he did discover:
One lovely hand she stretched for aid,
  And one was round her lover.

"Come back! come back!" he cried in grief,
  "Across this stormy water;
And I'll forgive your Highland chief,
  My daughter!—oh! my daughter!"

'Twas vain: the loud waves lashed the shore,
  Return or aid preventing;
The waters wild went o'er his child,
  And he was left lamenting.

—*Thomas Campbell*

Maud Muller

MAUD MULLER, on a summer's day,
Raked the meadow sweet with hay.
Beneath her torn hat glowed the wealth
Of simple beauty and rustic health.
Singing, she wrought, and her merry glee
The mock-bird echoed from his tree.

But when she glanced to the far-off town,
White from its hill-slope looking down,
The sweet song died, and a vague unrest
And a nameless longing filled her breast;
A wish, that she hardly dared to own,
For something better than she had known.

The Judge rode slowly down the lane,
Smoothing his horse's chestnut mane:
He drew his bridle in the shade
Of the apple-trees, to greet the maid,
And asked a draught from the spring that flowed
Through the meadow across the road.

She stooped where the cool spring bubbled up,
And filled for him her small tin cup,
And blushed as she gave it, looking down
On her feet so bare, and her tattered gown.
"Thanks!" said the Judge, "a sweeter draught
From a fairer hand was never quaffed."

He spoke of the grass, and flowers, and trees,
Of the singing birds and the humming bees;

Then talked of the haying, and wondered whether
The cloud in the west would bring foul weather.
And Maud forgot her brier-torn gown,
And her graceful ankles bare and brown,
And listened, while a pleased surprise
Looked from her long-lashed hazel eyes.

At last, like one who for delay
Seeks a vain excuse, he rode away.
Maud Muller looked and sighed: "Ah, me!
That I the Judge's bride might be!
He would dress me up in silks so fine,
And praise and toast me at his wine.

"My father should wear a broadcloth coat;
My brother should sail a painted boat;
I'd dress my mother so grand and gay,
And the baby should have a new toy each day;
And I'd feed the hungry and clothe the poor,
And all should bless me who left our door."

The Judge looked back as he climbed the hill,
And saw Maud Muller standing still.
"A form more fair, a face more sweet,
Ne'er has it been my lot to meet;
And her modest answer and graceful air
Show her wise and good as she is fair.

"Would she were mine, and I to-day,
Like her, a harvester of hay:
No doubtful balance of rights and wrongs,
Nor weary lawyers with endless tongues;

But low of cattle and song of birds,
And health, and quiet, and loving words."

But he thought of his sisters, proud and cold,
And his mother, vain of her rank and gold;
So, closing his heart, the Judge rode on,
And Maud was left in the field alone.
But the lawyers smiled that afternoon,
When he hummed in court an old love-tune;
And the young girl mused beside the well,
Till the rain on the unraked clover fell.

He wedded a wife of richest dower,
Who lived for fashion, as he for power;
Yet oft, in his marble hearth's bright glow,
He watched a picture come and go;
And sweet Maud Muller's hazel eyes,
Looked out in their innocent surprise.

Oft when the wine in his glass was red,
He longed for the wayside well instead;
And closed his eyes on his garnished rooms,
To dream of meadows and clover-blooms.
And the proud man sighed, with a secret pain,
"Ah, that I were free again!
Free as when I rode that day,
Where the barefoot maiden raked her hay."

She wedded a man unlearned and poor,
And many children played round her door;
But care and sorrow and wasting pain
Left their traces on heart and brain.

And oft when the summer sun shone hot
On the new-mown hay in the meadow lot,
And she heard the little spring brook fall
Over the roadside, through the wall,
In the shade of the apple-tree again
She saw a rider draw his rein,
And, gazing down with timid grace,
She felt his pleased eyes read her face.

Sometimes her narrow kitchen walls
Stretched away into stately halls;
The weary wheel to a spinet turned;
The tallow candle an astral burned;
And for him who sat by the chimney lug,
Dozing and grumbling o'er pipe and mug,
A manly form at her side she saw,
And joy was duty, and love was law.
Then she took up her burden of life again,
Saying only, "It might have been!"

Alas for maiden, alas for Judge,
For rich repiner and household drudge!
God pity them both! and pity us all,
Who vainly the dreams of youth recall;
For of all sad words of tongue or pen
The saddest are these: "It might have been!"
Ah, well! for us all some sweet hope lies
Deeply buried from human eyes;
And in the hereafter angels may
Roll the stone from its grave away!

—*John Greenleaf Whittier*

The Raven

ONCE upon a midnight dreary, while I pondered, weak
and weary,
  Over many a quaint and curious volume of forgotten
  lore,
While I nodded, nearly napping, suddenly there came a
  tapping,
  As of some one gently rapping, rapping at my chamber
  door.
  " 'Tis some visitor," I muttered, "tapping at my chamber door;
      Only this, and nothing more."

Ah, distinctly I remember, it was in the bleak December,
  And each separate dying ember wrought its ghost upon
  the floor.
Eagerly I wished the morrow; vainly I had sought to
  borrow
  From my books surcease of sorrow, sorrow for the lost
  Lenore,
  For the rare and radiant maiden whom the angels name
  Lenore,
      Nameless here forevermore.

And the silken sad uncertain rustling of each purple cur-
  tain
  Thrilled me—filled me with fantastic terrors never felt
  before;
So that now, to still the beating of my heart, I stood re-
  peating,

" 'Tis some visitor entreating entrance at my chamber
   door,
Some late visitor entreating entrance at my chamber
   door;
      This it is, and nothing more."

Presently my soul grew stronger; hesitating then no
   longer,
   "Sir," said I, "or madam, truly your forgiveness I
   implore;
But the fact is, I was napping, and so gently you came
   rapping,
   And so faintly you came tapping, tapping at my chamber door,
   That I scarce was sure I heard you." Here I opened
   wide the door;—
      Darkness there, and nothing more.

Deep into the darkness peering, long I stood there, wondering, fearing,
   Doubting, dreaming dreams no mortals ever dared to
   dream before;
But the silence was unbroken, and the stillness gave no
   token,
   And the only word there spoken was the whispered
   word "Lenore?"
   This I whispered, and an echo murmured back the
   word, "Lenore!"
      Merely this, and nothing more.

Back into the chamber turning, all my soul within me
   burning,

Soon again I heard a tapping, something louder than
before,
"Surely," said I, "surely, that is something at my window
lattice;
Let me see, then, what thereat is, and this mystery
explore;
Let my heart be still a moment, and this mystery explore;
'Tis the wind, and nothing more."

Open here I flung the shutter, when, with many a flirt
and flutter,
In there stepped a stately raven, of the saintly days of
yore.
Not the least obeisance made he; not a minute stopped or
stayed he;
But with mien of lord or lady, perched above my chamber door;
Perched upon a bust of Pallas, just above my chamber
door,
Perched, and sat, and nothing more.

Then this ebony bird beguiling my sad fancy into smiling,
By the grave and stern decorum of the countenance it
wore,
"Though thy crest be shorn and shaven, thou," I said,
"art sure no craven,
Ghastly, grim, and ancient raven, wandering from the
nightly shore.
Tell me what thy lordly name is on the Night's Plu-
tonian shore."
Quoth the raven, "Nevermore."

Much I marvelled this ungainly fowl to hear discourse so
    plainly,
  Though its answer little meaning, little relevancy bore;
For we cannot help agreeing that no living human being
  Ever yet was blessed with seeing bird above his cham-
    ber door,
  Bird or beast upon the sculptured bust above his cham-
    ber door,
        With such name as "Nevermore."

But the raven, sitting lonely on that placid bust, spoke
    only
  That one word, as if his soul in that one word he did
    outpour.
Nothing further then he uttered; not a feather then he
    fluttered;
  Till I scarcely more than muttered, "Other friends have
    flown before;
  On the morrow *he* will leave me, as my hopes have
    flown before."
        Then the bird said, "Nevermore."

Startled at the stillness broken by reply so aptly spoken,
  "Doubtless," said I, "what it utters is its only stock
    and store,
Caught from some unhappy master, whom unmerciful
    disaster
  Followed fast and followed faster, till his songs one
    burden bore,—
  Till the dirges of his hope that melancholy burden bore
        Of 'Never—nevermore.'"

But the raven still beguiling all my fancy into smiling,
  Straight I wheeled a cushioned seat in front of bird and
  bust and door;˙
Then, upon the velvet sinking, I betook myself to linking
  Fancy unto fancy, thinking what this ominous bird of
  yore,
  What this grim, ungainly, ghastly, gaunt, and ominous
  bird of yore
      Meant in croaking, "Nevermore."

Thus I sat engaged in guessing, but no syllable expressing
  To the fowl, whose fiery eyes now burned into my
  bosom's core;
This and more I sat divining, with my head at ease re-
  clining
  On the cushion's velvet lining that the lamplight gloated
  o'er,
  But whose velvet violet lining with the lamplight gloat-
  ing o'er
      She shall press, ah, nevermore!

Then, methought, the air grew denser, perfumed from an
  unseen censer
  Swung by seraphim whose footfalls tinkled on the
  tufted floor.
"Wretch," I cried, "thy God hath lent thee—by these
  angels he hath sent thee
  Respite—respite and nepenthe from thy memories of
  Lenore!
  Quaff, O quaff this kind nepenthe, and forget this lost
  Lenore!"
      Quoth the raven, "Nevermore!"

"Prophet!" said I, "thing of evil!—prophet still, if bird
  or devil!
  Whether tempter sent, or whether tempest tossed thee
    here ashore,
Desolate, yet all undaunted, on this desert land en-
  chanted—
  On this home by horror haunted—tell me truly, I
    implore:
  Is there—*is* there balm in Gilead?—tell me—tell me I
    implore!"
          Quoth the raven, "Nevermore!"

"Prophet!" said I, "thing of evil—prophet still, if bird or
  devil!
  By that heaven that bends above us—by that God we
    both adore—
Tell this soul with sorrow laden, if, within the distant
  Aidenn,
  It shall clasp a sainted maiden, whom the angels name
    Lenore—
  Clasp a rare and radiant maiden, whom the angels
    name Lenore?"
          Quoth the raven, "Nevermore!"

"Be that word our sign of parting, bird or fiend!" I
  shrieked, upstarting—
  "Get thee back into the tempest and the Night's Plu-
    tonian shore!
Leave no black plume as a token of that lie thy soul hath
  spoken!
  Leave my loneliness unbroken!—quit the bust above
    my door!

Take thy beak from out my heart, and take thy form
    from off my door!"
        Quoth the raven, "Nevermore!"

And the raven, never flitting, still is sitting, still is sitting
    On the pallid bust of Pallas just above my chamber
        door;
And his eyes have all the seeming of a demon's that is
        dreaming;
    And the lamplight o'er him streaming throws the shadow
        on the floor;
    And my soul from out that shadow that lies floating on
        the floor
        Shall be lifted—nevermore!

                                    —*Edgar Allan Poe*

Curfew Must Not Ring Tonight

ENGLAND'S sun was slowly setting
    O'er the hills so far away,
Filling all the land with beauty
    At the close of one sad day;
And the last rays kissed the forehead
    Of a man and maiden fair—
He with step so slow and weakened,
    She with sunny, floating hair;
He with sad bowed head, and thoughtful,
    She with lips so cold and white,
Struggling to keep back the murmur,
    "Curfew must not ring tonight."

"Sexton," Bessie's white lips faltered,
  Pointing to the prison old,
With its walls so dark and gloomy—
  Walls so dark, and damp, and cold—
"I've a lover in that prison,
  Doomed this very night to die,
At the ringing of the curfew,
  And no earthly help is nigh.
Cromwell will not come till sunset";
  And her face grew strangely white,
As she spoke in husky whispers,
  "Curfew must not ring tonight."

"Bessie," calmly spoke the sexton—
  Every word pierced her young heart
Like a thousand gleaming arrows,
  Like a deadly poisoned dart—
"Long, long years I've rung the curfew
  From that gloomy shadowed tow'r;
Every evening, just at sunset,
  It has told the twilight hour.
I have done my duty ever,
  Tried to do it just and right;
Now I'm old, I will not miss it;
  Girl, the curfew rings tonight!"

Wild her eyes and pale her features,
  Stern and white her thoughtful brow,
And within her heart's deep center,
  Bessie made a solemn vow.
She had listened while the judges
  Read, without a tear or sigh,

"At the ringing of the curfew
  Basil Underwood must die."
And her breath came fast and faster,
  And her eyes grew large and bright;
One low murmur, scarcely spoken—
  "Curfew must not ring tonight."

She with light step bounded forward,
  Sprang within the old church door,
Left the old man coming slowly,
  Paths he'd often trod before;
Not one moment paused the maiden,
  But with cheek and brow aglow,
Staggered up the gloomy tower,
  Where the bell swung to and fro;
Then she climbed the slimy ladder,
  Dark, without one ray of light,
Upward still, her pale lips saying,
  "Curfew shall not ring tonight."

She has reached the topmost ladder,
  O'er her hangs the great dark bell,
And the awful gloom beneath her,
  Like the pathway down to hell.
See, the ponderous tongue is swinging,
  'Tis the hour of curfew now;
And the sight has chilled her bosom,
  Stopped her breath, and paled her brow.
Shall she let it ring? No, never!
  Her eyes flash with sudden light,
As she springs and grasps it firmly—
  "Curfew shall not ring tonight."

Out she swung, far out, the city
  Seemed a tiny speck below;
There, 'twixt heaven and earth suspended,
  As the bell swung to and fro;
And the half-deaf sexton ringing
  (Years he had not heard the bell),
And he thought the twilight curfew
  Rang young Basil's funeral knell;
Still the maiden clinging firmly,
  Cheek and brow so pale and white,
Stilled her frightened heart's wild beating—
  "Curfew shall not ring tonight."

It was o'er—the bell ceased swaying,
  And the maiden stepped once more
Firmly on the damp old ladder,
  Where for hundred years before
Human foot had not been planted;
  And what she this night had done
Should be told in long years after:
  As the rays of setting sun
Light the sky with mellow beauty,
  Aged sires with heads of white,
Tell the children why the curfew
  Did not ring that one sad night.

O'er the distant hills came Cromwell;
  Bessie saw him, and her brow,
Lately white with sickening terror,
  Glows with sudden beauty now.
At his feet she told her story,
  Showed her hands all bruised and torn;

And her sweet young face so haggard,
    With a look so sad and worn,
Touched his heart with sudden pity,
    Lit his eyes with misty light;
"Go, your lover lives!" cried Cromwell;
    "Curfew shall not ring tonight."

—Rose Hartwick Thorpe

LOVE FOR OTHERS

The House by the Side of the Road [1]

THERE are hermit souls that live withdrawn
    In the place of their self-content;
There are souls like stars, that dwell apart,
    In a fellowless firmament;
There are pioneer souls that blaze their paths
    Where highways never ran—
But let me live by the side of the road
    And be a friend to man.

Let me live in a house by the side of the road,
    Where the race of men go by—
The men who are good and the men who are bad,
    As good and as bad as I.
I would not sit in the scorner's seat,
    Or hurl the cynic's ban—
Let me live in a house by the side of the road
    And be a friend to man.

[1] From "Dreams in Homespun," by Sam Walter Foss.

Used by special arrangement with the publishers, Lothrop, Lee & Shepard Co., Boston.

225

I see from my house by the side of the road,
  By the side of the highway of life,
The men who press with the ardor of hope,
  The men who are faint with the strife.
But I turn not away from their smiles nor their tears,
  Both parts of an infinite plan—
Let me live in a house by the side of the road
  And be a friend to man.

I know there are brook-gladdened meadows ahead
  And mountains of wearisome height;
That the road passes on through the long afternoon
  And stretches away to the night.
But still I rejoice when the travelers rejoice,
  And weep with the strangers that moan,
Nor live in my house by the side of the road
  Like a man who dwells alone.

Let me live in my house by the side of the road—
  It's here the race of men go by.
They are good, they are bad, they are weak, they are
    strong
  Wise, foolish—so am I;
Then why should I sit in the scorner's seat,
  Or hurl the cynic's ban?
Let me live in my house by the side of the road
  And be a friend to man.

                         —*Sam Walter Fost*

True Brotherhood [1]

GOD, what a world, if men in street and mart,
 Felt that same kinship of the human heart,
Which makes them, in the face of fire and flood,
Rise to the meaning of True Brotherhood.

—*Ella Wheeler Wilcox*

The Great Guest Comes In [2]

WHILE the cobbler mused, there passed his pane
 A beggar drenched by the driving rain;
He called him in from the stony street
And gave him shoes for his bruised feet.

The beggar went, and there came a crone
Her face with wrinkles of sorrow sown;
A bundle of fagots bowed her back,
And she was spent with the wrench and rack.

He gave her his loaf and steadied her load,
As she took her way on the weary road.
Then to his door came a little child,
Lost and afraid in the world so wild,

In the big, dark world. Catching it up,
He gave it the milk in the waiting cup,
And led it home to its mother's arms,
Out of the reach of the world's alarms.

[1] Used by permission of the W. B. Conkey Co., Hammond, Ind.
[2] Copyright by Edwin Markham. Used by his permission.

227

The day went down in the crimson West,
And with it the hope of the blessed guest;
And Conrad sighed as the world turned gray;
"Why is it, Lord, that Your feet delay?

"Did You forget that this was the day?"
Then, soft in the silence a voice was heard:
"Lift up your heart, for I kept My word.
Three times I came to your friendly door,

"Three times my shadow was on your floor;
I was a beggar with bruised feet;
I was a woman you gave to eat;
I was the child of the homeless street."

—Edwin Markham

Need of Loving

FOLKS need a lot of loving in the morning;
 The day is all before, with cares beset—
The cares we know, and they that give no warning;
 For love is God's own antidote for fret.

Folks need a heap of loving at the noontime—
 In the battle full, the moment snatched from strife,
Half way between the waking and the croontime,
 While bickering and worriment are rife.

Folks hunger so for loving at the night time,
 When wearily they take them home to rest—

228

At slumber song and turning-out-the-light time—
Of all the time for loving that's the best.

Folks want a lot of loving every minute—
The sympathy of others and their smile!
Till life's end, from the moment they begin it,
Folks need a lot of loving all the while.

—Strickland Gillilan

Abou Ben Adhem

ABOU BEN ADHEM (may his tribe increase!)
   Awoke one night from a deep dream of peace,
And saw, within the moonlight in his room,
Making it rich, and like a lily in bloom,
An Angel writing in a book of gold:
Exceeding peace had made Ben Adhem bold,
And to the Presence in the room he said,
"What writest thou?" The Vision raised its head,
And with a look made of all sweet accord
Answered, "The names of those who love the Lord."
"And is mine one?" said Abou. "Nay, not so,"
Replied the Angel. Abou spoke more low,
But cheerily still; and said, "I pray thee, then,
Write me as one that loves his fellow-men."

The Angel wrote, and vanished. The next night
It came again with a great wakening light,
And showed the names whom love of God had blessed,
And, lo! Ben Adhem's name led all the rest!

—James Henry Leigh Hunt

The Bigger Day

WE ARE done with little thinking,
  And we're done with little deeds;
We are done with petty conduct
  And we're done with narrow creeds;
We have grown to men and women,
  And we've noble work to do,
And today we are a people
  With a larger point of view.
In a big way we must labor,
  If our flag shall always fly,
In a big way we must suffer,
  In a big way some must die.

There must be no little dreaming
  In the visions that we see,
There must be no selfish planning
  In the joys that are to be.
We have set our faces eastward
  To the rising of the sun
That shall light a better nation,
  And there's big work to be done.
And the petty souls and narrow,
  Seeking only selfish gain
Shall be vanquished by the toilers
  Big enough to suffer pain.

It's a big task we have taken,
  'Tis for others we must fight.
We must see our duty clearly
  In a white and shining light.

We must quit our little circles
    Where we move in little ways,
And work as men and women
    For the bigger, better days.
We must quit our selfish thinking
    And our narrow views and creeds,
And as people, big and splendid
    We must do the bigger deeds.

—*G. E. Bishop*

Others [1]

LORD, help me live from day to day
    In such a self-forgetful way,
That even when I kneel to pray,
My prayer shall be for—*others*.

Help me in all the work I do,
To ever be sincere and true,
And know that all I'd do for you
Must needs be done for—*others*.

Let "Self" be crucified and slain,
And buried deep; and all in vain
May efforts be to rise again,
Unless to live for—*others*.

And when my work on earth is done,
And my new work in Heaven's begun,
May I forget the crown I've won,
While thinking still of—*others*.

Others, Lord, yes, others,
Let this my motto be,
Help me to live for others,
That I may live like Thee.

—*Charles D. Meigs*

Lifting and Leaning[1]

THERE are two kinds of people on earth today,
Just two kinds of people, no more, I say.

Not the good and the bad, for 'tis well understood
The good are half bad and the bad are half good.

Not the happy and sad, for the swift-flying years
Bring each man his laughter and each man his tears.

Not the rich and the poor, for to count a man's wealth,
You must first know the state of his conscience and
     health.

Not the humble and proud, for in life's busy span
Who puts on vain airs is not counted a man.

No! the two kinds of people on earth I mean
Are the people who lift and the people who lean.

Wherever you go you will find the world's masses
Are ever divided in just these two classes.

[1] Used by permission of the W. B. Conkey Co., Hammond, Ind.

And strangely enough you will find, too, I ween,
There is only one lifter to twenty who lean.

In which class are you? Are you easing the load
Of overtaxed lifters who toil down the road?

Or are you a leaner who lets other bear
Your portion of worry and labor and care?

—Ella Wheeler Wilcox

Keep Love in Your Life

KEEP love in your life, my friend,
　　If you would have perfect joy;
Keep love, never let her depart—
　　For who would his life destroy?
For life's no longer than love, my friend;
When love is no more, 'tis the journey's end.
And Regret and Fear shall your way attend.
Keep love in your life, my friend.

Keep love in your life alway,
　　Though tempted to bid her go;
Keep love the bride of your heart,
　　If you would a true life know.
For life's no longer than love, I say;
With the end of love comes the close of day,
And the chill of death 'mid the shadows gray.
Keep love in your life alway.

—Thomas Curtis Clark

Casabianca

Young Casabianca, a boy about thirteen years old, son to the admiral of the Orient, remained at his post (in the battle of the Nile) after the ship had taken fire, and all the guns had been abandoned; and perished in the explosion of the vessel, when the flames had reached the powder.

THE boy stood on the burning deck,
　Whence all but him had fled;
The flame that lit the battle's wreck,
　Shone round him o'er the dead.

Yet beautiful and bright he stood,
　As born to rule the storm;
A creature of heroic blood,
　A proud, though child-like form.

The flames roll'd on—he would not go,
　Without his father's word;
That father, faint in death below,
　His voice no longer heard.

He call'd aloud—"Say, father, say
　If yet my task is done?"
He knew not that the chieftain lay
　Unconscious of his son.

"Speak, father!" once again he cried,
　"If I may yet be gone!"

234

—And but the booming shots replied,
  And fast the flames roll'd on.

Upon his brow he felt their breath,
  And in his waving hair;
And look'd from that lone post of death,
  In still, yet brave despair:

And shouted but once more aloud,
  "My father! must I stay?"
While o'er him fast, through sail and shroud
  The wreathing fires made way.

They wrapt the ship in splendor wild,
  They caught the flag on high,
And stream'd above the gallant child,
  Like banners in the sky.

There came a burst of thunder sound—
  The boy—oh! where was he?
—Ask of the winds that far around
  With fragments strew'd the sea!

With mast, and helm, and pennon fair,
  That well had borne their part—
But the noblest thing that perish'd there,
  Was that young faithful heart.

                    —*Mrs. Felicia Dorothea Hemans*

A Woman's Question

DO YOU know you have asked for the costliest thing
Ever made by the hand above—
A woman's heart, and a woman's life,
And a woman's wonderful love?

Do you know you have asked for this priceless thing
As a child might ask for a toy—
Demanding what others have died to win,
With the reckless dash of a boy?

You have written my lesson of duty out,
Man-like you have questioned me;
Now stand at the bar of my woman's soul
Until I shall question thee.

You require your mutton shall always be hot,
Your socks and your shirts shall be whole;
I require your heart to be true as God's stars,
And pure as heaven your soul.

You require a cook for your mutton and beef;
I require a far better thing.
A seamstress you're wanting for stockings and shirts;
I look for a man and a king—

A king for a beautiful realm called home,
And a man that the Maker, God,

Shall look upon as he did the first,
  And say, "It is very good."

I am fair and young, but the rose will fade
  From my soft, young cheek one day;
Will you love then, mid the falling leaves,
  As you did mid the bloom of May?

Is your heart an ocean so strong and deep
  I may launch my all on its tide?
A loving woman finds heaven or hell
  On the day she is made a bride.

I require all things that are grand and true,
  All things that a man should be;
If you give this all, I would stake my life
  To be all you demand of me.

If you can not do this—a laundress and cook
  You can hire with little to pay;
But a woman's heart and a woman's life
  Are not to be won that way.

                              —*Elizabeth Barrett Browning*

A Maxim Revised

LADIES, to this advice give heed—
  In controlling men:
If at first you don't succeed,
  Why, cry, cry again.

                              —*Anon.*

God, Give Us Men!

GOD, give us men! A time like this demands
   Strong minds, great hearts, true faith and ready
      hands;
   Men whom the lust of office does not kill;
Men whom the spoils of office can not buy;
   Men who possess opinions and a will;
Men who have honor; men who will not lie;
Men who can stand before a demagogue
   And damn his treacherous flatteries without winking!
Tall men, sun-crowned, who live above the fog
   In public duty, and in private thinking;
For while the rabble, with their thumb-worn creeds,
Their large professions and their little deeds,
Mingle in selfish strife, lo! Freedom weeps,
Wrong rules the land and waiting Justice sleeps.

—Josiah Gilbert Holland

The Manly Man

THE world has room for the manly man, with the
   spirit of manly cheer;
The world delights in the man who smiles when his eyes
   keep back the tear;
It loves the man who, when things are wrong, can take
   his place and stand
With his face to the fight and his eyes to the light, and
   toil with a willing hand;

238

The manly man is the country's need, the moment's need,
    forsooth,
With a heart that beats to the pulsing troop of the lilied
    leagues of truth;
The world is his and it waits for him, and it leaps to
    hear the ring
Of the blow he strikes and the wheels he turns and ham-
    mers he dares to swing;
It likes the forward look on his face, the poise of his noble
    head,
And the onward lunge of his tireless will and the sweep
    of his dauntless tread!
Hurrah for the manly man who comes with sunlight on
    his face,
And the strength to do and the will to dare and the cour-
    age to find his place!
The world delights in the manly man, and the weak and
    evil flee
When the manly man goes forth to hold his own on land
    or sea!

—Anon.

MERCY

Mercy

THE quality of mercy is not strained;
    It droppeth as the gentle rain from heaven
Upon the place beneath: it is twice blest,—
It blesseth him that gives and him that takes:
'Tis mightiest in the mightiest; it becomes

The thronèd monarch better than his crown:
His sceptre shows the force of temporal power,
The attribute to awe and majesty,
Wherein doth sit the dread and fear of kings;
But mercy is above this sceptred sway,—
It is enthronèd in the hearts of kings,
It is an attribute to God himself;
And earthly power doth then show likest God's,
When mercy seasons justice.

—*William Shakespeare*

MONEY

Gold

GOLD! Gold! Gold! Gold!
  Bright and yellow, hard and cold,
Molten, graven, hammered, and rolled;
Heavy to get, and light to hold;
Hoarded, bartered, bought and sold,
Stolen, borrowed, squandered, doled;
Spurned by the young, but hugged by the old
To the very verge of the churchyard mould;
Price of many a crime untold;
Gold! Gold! Gold! Gold!
Good or bad, a thousand-fold!
  How widely its agencies vary!
To save, to ruin, to curse, to bless,
As even its minted coins express!
Now stamped with the image of Good Queen Bess,
  And now of a Bloody Mary!

—*Thomas Hood*

The Bravest Battle

THE bravest battle that ever was fought,
  Shall I tell you where and when?
On the maps of the world you will find it not;
  'Twas fought by the mothers of men.

Nay, not with cannon, or battle-shot,
  With sword, or nobler pen;
Nay, not with eloquent word or thought,
  From mouths of wonderful men.

But deep in a welled-up woman's heart—
  Of woman that would not yield,
But bravely, silently bore her part—
  Lo! there is that battlefield!

No marshaling troop, no bivouac song;
  No banners to gleam and wave!
But oh, these battles they last so long—
  From babyhood to the grave!

Yet faithful still as a bridge of stars,
  She fights in her walled-up town—
Fights on, and on, in the endless wars,
  Then silent, unseen, goes down!

O ye with banners and battle-shot,
  And soldier to shout and praise,

I tell you the kingliest victories fought
Are fought in these silent ways!

—Joaquin Miller

The Hand That Rocks the Cradle Is the Hand That Rules the World

BLESSINGS on the hand of women!
  Angels guard its strength and grace,
In the palace, cottage, hovel,
  Oh, no matter where the place;
Would that never storms assailed it,
  Rainbows ever gently curled;
For the hand that rocks the cradle
  Is the hand that rules the world.

Infancy's the tender fountain,
  Power may with beauty flow,
Mother's first to guide the streamlets,
  From them souls unresting grow—
Grow on for the good or evil,
  Sunshine streamed or evil hurled;
For the hand that rocks the cradle
  Is the hand that rules the world.

Woman, how divine your mission
  Here upon our natal sod!
Keep, oh, keep the young heart open
  Always to the breath of God!
All true trophies of the ages
  Are from mother-love impearled;

For the hand that rocks the cradle
 Is the hand that rules the world.

Blessings on the hand of women!
 Fathers, sons, and daughters cry,
And the sacred song is mingled
 With the worship in the sky—
Mingles where no tempest darkens,
 Rainbows evermore are hurled;
For the hand that rocks the cradle
 Is the hand that rules the world.

—*William Ross Wallace*

Which Loved Best?

"I LOVE you, Mother," said little Ben;
 Then, forgetting his work, his cap went on,
And he was off to the garden swing,
And left her the water and wood to bring.
"I love you, Mother," said rosy Nell—
"I love you better than tongue can tell";
Then she teased and pouted full half the day,
Till her mother rejoiced when she went to play.
"I love you, Mother," said little Fan;
"Today I'll help you all I can;
How glad I am that school doesn't keep!"
So she rocked the babe till it fell asleep.

Then, stepping softly, she fetched the broom,
And swept the floor and tidied the room;
Busy and happy all day was she,

Helpful and happy as child could be.
"I love you, Mother," again they said,
Three little children going to bed;
How do you think that mother guessed
Which of them really loved her best?

—*Joy Allison (Mary A. Cragin)*

Mother o' Mine

IF I were hanged on the highest hill,
Mother o' Mine, O mother o' mine!
I know whose love would follow me still,
Mother o' mine, O mother o' mine!

If I were drowned in the deepest sea,
Mother o' mine, O mother o' mine!
I know whose tears would come down to me,
Mother o' mine, O mother o' mine!

If I were damned of body and soul
Mother o' mine, O mother o' mine!
I know whose prayers would make me whole,
Mother o' mine, O mother o' mine!

—*Rudyard Kipling*

The Old Arm Chair

I LOVE it—I love it, and who shall dare
To chide me for loving that old arm chair!
I've treasured it long as a sainted prize—

I've bedewed it with tears, and embalmed it with sighs;
'Tis bound by a thousand bands to my heart,
Not a tie will break, not a link will start.
Would you learn the spell? a mother sat there;
And a sacred thing is that old arm chair.

In childhood's hour I lingered near
The hallowed seat with listening ear;
And gentle words that mother would give,
To fit me to die, and teach me to live.
She told me shame would never betide,
With truth for my creed, and God for my guide;
She taught me to lisp my earliest prayer,
As I knelt beside that old arm chair.

I sat and watched her many a day,
When her eyes grew dim and her locks were grey,
And I almost worshipped her when she smiled
And turned from her Bible to bless her child,
Years rolled on, but the last one sped—
My idol was shattered—my earth star fled:
I learnt how much the heart can bear,
When I saw her die in that old arm chair.

'Tis past! 'tis past! but I gaze on it now
With quivering breath and throbbing brow:
'Twas there she nursed me—'twas there she died,
And memory flows with lava tide—
Say it is folly, and deem me weak,
While the scalding tears run down my cheek.
But I love it—I love it, and cannot tear
My soul from my mother's old arm chair.

—*Eliza Cook*

Mothers—and Others

OTHERS weary of the noise,
Mothers play with girls and boys.

Others scold because we fell,
Mothers "kiss and make it well."

Others work with patient will,
Mothers labor later still.

Others' love is more or less,
Mothers love with steadiness.

Others pardon, hating yet;
Mothers pardon and forget.

Others keep the ancient score,
Mothers never shut the door.

Others grow incredulous,
Mothers still believe in us.

Others throw their faith away,
Mothers pray, and pray, and pray.

—*Amos R. Wells*

Mother's Love

DID you ever come to the place
When life seemed naught to you,

When your heart is filled with sorrow,
  And friends are mighty few;
When your faith in man is shaken,
  And everything seems a fraud,
Till at last you grow indifferent
  And doubt the love of God?
At one time you were happy,
  Had faith in all mankind;
But one by one your friends proved false—
  Faith now is left behind;
'Tis now you start to wandering
  Like a dog without a home,
And a kick here and a kick there
  As on and on you roam.

The friends whom once you thought were true
  Now seem to know you not.
The kindly things you did for them,
  Each one has been forgot.
While you were prosperous—you were fit
  To live and walk with them,
But when misfortune frowned on you,
  They were ready to condemn.
But there is one who still remains
  As true as the stars above;
No matter how debased you are,
  You still have mother's love.
Though you may sink deep into sin,
  Beside God, there is one other
Who is so willing to forgive—
  That one is your dear mother.

—Ross B. Clapp

Somebody's Mother

THE woman was old, and ragged and gray,
  And bent with the chill of a winter's day;
The streets were white with a recent snow,
And the woman's feet with age were slow.

At the crowded crossing she waited long,
Jostled aside by the careless throng
Of human beings who passed her by,
Unheeding the glance of her anxious eye.

Down the street with laughter and shout,
Glad in the freedom of "school is out,"
Came happy boys, like a flock of sheep,
Hailing the snow piled white and deep;
Past the woman, so old and gray,
Hasten the children on their way.

None offered a helping hand to her,
So weak and timid, afraid to stir,
Lest the carriage wheels or the horses' feet
Should trample her down in the slippery street.

At last came out of the merry troop
The gayest boy of all the group;
He paused beside her, and whispered low,
"I'll help you across, if you wish to go."

Her aged hand on his strong young arm
She placed, and so without hurt or harm,

He guided the trembling feet along,
Proud that his own were young and strong;
Then back again to his friends he went,
His young heart happy and well content.

"She's somebody's mother, boys, you know,
For all she's aged, and poor and slow;
And some one, some time, may lend a hand
To help my mother—you understand?
If ever she's poor, and old and gray,
And her own dear boy so far away."

Somebody's mother bowed low her head,
In her home that night, and the prayer she said
Was: "God be kind to that noble boy,
Who is somebody's son and pride and joy."

Faint was the voice, and worn and weak,
But heaven lists when its chosen speak;
Angels caught the faltering word,
And "Somebody's Mother's" prayer was heard.

—*Mary D. Brine*

MUSIC

A Lost Chord

SEATED one day at the organ,
   I was weary and ill at ease,
And my fingers wandered idly
   Over the noisy keys.

I do not know what I was playing,
  Or what I was dreaming then;
But I struck one chord of music
  Like the sound of a great Amen.

It flooded the crimson twilight
  Like the close of an angel's psalm,
And it lay on my fevered spirit
  With a touch of infinite calm.

It quieted pain and sorrow,
  Like love overcoming strife.
It seemed the harmonious echo
  From our discordant life.

It linked all perplexed meanings
  Into one perfect peace,
And trembled away into silence,
  As if it were loath to cease.

I have sought, but I seek it vainly,
  That one lost chord divine,
That came from the soul of the organ
  And entered into mine.

It may be that Death's bright angel
  Will speak in that chord again,
It may be that only in heaven
  I shall hear that grand Amen.

                    —*Adelaide Anne Procter*

Music

MUSIC is well said to be the speech of angels; in fact, nothing among the utterances allowed to man is felt to be so divine. It brings us near to the Infinite; we look for moments, across the cloudy elements, into the eternal sea of light, when song leads and inspires us. Serious nations, all nations that can still listen to the mandate of nature, have prized song and music as the highest; as a vehicle for worship, for prophecy, and for whatsoever in them was divine.

—Thomas Carlyle

NATURE

Out in the Fields With God

THE little cares that fretted me,
  I lost them yesterday,
Among the fields, above the sea,
  Among the winds at play;
Among the lowing of the herds,
  The rustling of the trees;
Among the singing of the birds,
  The humming of the bees.

The foolish fears of what may happen,
  I cast them all away
Among the clover-scented grass,
  Among the new-mown hay;
Among the rustling of the corn,

251

Where drowsy poppies nod,
Where ill thoughts die and good are born—
Out in the fields with God.

—*Elizabeth Barrett Browning*

Each a Part of All

THERE'S a part o' the sun in an apple;
  There's part o' the moon in a rose;
There's a part o' the flaming Pleiades
  In every leaf that grows.
Out of the vast comes nearness;
  For the God whose love we sing
Sends a little of His heaven
  To every living thing.

—*Augustus Wright Bamberger*

Mountains

FOR the lifting up of mountains,
  In brightness and in dread;

For the peaks where snow and sunshine
  Alone have dared to tread;

For the dark of silent gorges,
  Where mighty cedars nod;

For the majesty of the mountains,
I thank Thee, oh, my God!

—Lucy Larcom

(<i>From the poem "A Thanksgiving," in "The Poetical Works of
Lucy Larcom." This stanza is one of the most impressive descrip-
tions of mountains to be found in literature. It is comparable to
Joyce Kilmer's poem on "Trees."</i>)

Man's Littleness in Presence of the Stars

THOU, proud man, look upon yon starry vault,
Survey the countless gems which richly stud
The night's imperial chariot;—Telescopes
Will show the myriads more, innumerous
As the sea-sand;—each of those little lamps
Is the great source of light, the central sun
Round which some other mighty sisterhood
Of planets travel,—every planet stocked
With living beings impotent as thee.
Now, proud man—now, where is thy greatness fled?
What art thou in the scale of universe?
Less, less than nothing!

—Henry Kirke White

The Cataract of Lodore

Described in Rhymes for the Nursery

"HOW does the water
Come down at Lodore?"

My little boy asked me
Thus, once on a time;
And moreover he tasked me
To tell him in rhyme.
Anon at the word,
There first came one daughter,
And then came another,
To second and third
The request of their brother,
And to hear how the water
Comes down at Lodore,
With its rush and its roar,
As many a time
They had seen it before.

So I told them in rhyme,
For of rhymes I had store;
And 'twas in my vocation
For their recreation
That so I should sing;
Because I was Laureate
To them and the King.

From its sources which well
In the tarn on the fell;
From its fountains
In the mountains,
Its rills and its gills;
Through moss and through brake,
It runs and it creeps
For a while till it sleeps
In its own little lake.

And thence at departing,
Awakening and starting,
It runs through the reeds,
And away it proceeds,
Through meadow and glade,
In sun and in shade,
And through the wood-shelter,
Among crags in its flurry,
Helter-skelter,
Hurry-skurry.
Here it comes sparkling,
And there it lies darkling;
Now smoking and frothing
Its tumult and wrath in,
Till, in this rapid race
On which it is bent,
It reaches the place
Of its steep descent.

The cataract strong
Then plunges along,
Striking and raging
As if a war waging
Its caverns and rocks among;
Rising and leaping,
Sinking and creeping,
Swelling and sweeping,
Showering and springing,
Flying and flinging,
Writhing and wringing,
Eddying and whisking,
Spouting and frisking,

Turning and twisting
Around and around
With endless rebound:
Smiting and fighting,
A sight to delight in;
Confounding, astounding,
Dizzying and deafening the ear with its sound.

Collecting, projecting,
Receding and speeding,
And shocking and rocking,
And darting and parting,
And threading and spreading,
And whizzing and hissing,
And dripping and skipping,
And hitting and splitting,
And shining and twining,
And rattling and battling,
And shaking and quaking,
And pouring and roaring,
And waving and raving,
And tossing and crossing,
And flowing and going,
And running and stunning,
And foaming and roaming,
And dinning and spinning,
And dropping and hopping,
And working and jerking,
And guggling and struggling,
And heaving and cleaving,
And moaning and groaning;
And glittering and frittering,

And gathering and feathering,
And whitening and brightening,
And quivering and shivering,
And hurrying and skurrying,
And thundering and floundering;

Dividing and gliding and sliding,
And falling and brawling and sprawling,
And driving and riving and striving,
And sprinkling and twinkling and wrinkling,
And sounding and bounding and rounding,
And bubbling and troubling and doubling,
And grumbling and rumbling and tumbling,
And clattering and battering and shattering;

Retreating and beating and meeting and sheeting,
Delaying and straying and playing and spraying,
Advancing and prancing and glancing and dancing,
Recoiling, turmoiling and toiling and boiling,
And gleaming and streaming and steaming and beaming,
And rushing and flushing and brushing and gushing,
And flapping and rapping and clapping and slapping,
And curling and whirling and purling and twirling,
And thumping and plumping and bumping and jumping,
And dashing and flashing and splashing and clashing;
And so never ending, but always descending,
Sounds and motions for ever and ever are blending
All at once and all o'er, with a mighty uproar,—
And this way the water comes down at Lodore.

—*Robert Southey*

The Year Ahead

A FLOWER unblown: a Book unread:
   A Tree with fruit unharvested:
A Path untrod: a House whose rooms
Lack yet the heart's divine perfumes:
A Landscape whose wide border lies
In silent shade 'neath silent skies:
A wondrous Fountain yet unsealed:
A Casket with its gifts concealed—
This is the Year that for you waits
Beyond To-morrow's mystic gates.

                —Horatio Nelson Powers

Ring Out the Old, Ring In the New

R ING out, wild bells, to the wild sky,
   The flying clouds, the frosty light:
  The year is dying in the night—
Ring out, wild bells, and let him die.

Ring out the old, ring in the new—
  Ring, happy bells, across the snow:
  The year is going, let him go;
Ring out the false, ring in the true.

Ring out the grief that saps the mind,
  For those that here we see no more,

Ring out the feud of rich and poor,
Ring in redress to all mankind.

Ring out a slowly dying cause,
    And ancient forms of party strife;
    Ring in the nobler modes of life,
With sweeter manners, purer laws.

Ring out the want, the care, the sin,
    The faithless coldness of the times:
    Ring out, ring out my mournful rhymes,
But ring the fuller minstrel in.

Ring out false pride in place and blood,
    The civic slander and the spite;
    Ring in the love of truth and right,
Ring in the common love of good.

Ring out old shapes of foul disease,
    Ring out the narrowing lust of gold;
    Ring out the thousand wars of old,
Ring in the thousand years of peace.

Ring in the valiant man and free,
    The larger heart, the kindlier hand;
    Ring out the darkness of the land—
Ring in the Christ that is to be.

—Alfred Tennyson

A New Leaf

HE CAME to my desk with a quivering lip—
The lesson was done—
"Dear teacher, I want a new leaf," he said;
  "I have spoiled this one."
In place of the leaf so stained and blotted,
I gave him a new one all unspotted,
    And into his sad eyes smiled—
    "Do better now, my child."

I went to the throne with a quivering soul—
    The old year was done—
"Dear Father, hast Thou a new leaf for me?
  I have spoiled this one."
He took the old leaf, stained and blotted,
And gave me a new one all unspotted,
    And into my sad heart smiled—
    "Do better now, my child."

—Kathleen R. Wheeler

Another Year Is Dawning

ANOTHER YEAR is dawning!
  Dear Master, let it be,
In working or in waiting,
Another year with Thee.
Another year in leaning,
Upon Thy loving breast,
Of ever-deepening trustfulness,
Of quiet, happy rest.

260

Another year of mercies,
Of faithfulness and grace;
Another year of gladness,
In the shining of Thy face.
Another year of progress,
Another year of praise;
Another year of proving
Thy presence "all the days."

Another year of service,
Of witness for Thy love;
Another year of training
For holier works above.
Another year is dawning!
Dear Master, let it be
On earth, or else in heaven,
Another year for Thee!

—*Frances Ridley Havergal*

NOBILITY

Nobility

TRUE worth is in *being*, not *seeming*,—
  In doing, each day that goes by,
Some little good—not in dreaming
  Of great things to do by and by.
For whatever men say in their blindness,
  And spite of the fancies of youth,

There's nothing so kingly as kindness,
    And nothing so royal as truth.

We get back our mete as we measure—
    We cannot do wrong and feel right,
Nor can we give pain and gain pleasure,
    For justice avenges each slight.
The air for the wing of the sparrow,
    The bush for the robin and wren,
But always the path that is narrow
    And straight, for the children of men.

'Tis not in the pages of story
    The heart of its ills to beguile,
Though he who makes courtship to glory
    Gives all that he hath for her smile.
For when from her heights he has won her,
    Alas! it is only to prove
That nothing's so sacred as honor,
    And nothing so loyal as love!

We cannot make bargains for blisses,
    Nor catch them like fishes in nets;
And sometimes the thing our life misses
    Helps more than the thing which it gets.
For good lieth not in pursuing,
    Nor gaining of great nor of small,
But just in the doing, and doing
    As we would be done by, is all.

Through envy, through malice, through hating,
    Against the world, early and late,

No jot of our courage abating—
   Our part is to work and to wait.
And slight is the sting of his trouble
   Whose winnings are less than his worth;
For he who is honest is noble,
   Whatever his fortunes or birth.

—*Alice Cary*

OCEANS

Apostrophe to the Ocean

THERE is a pleasure in the pathless woods,
   There is a rapture on the lonely shore,
There is society where none intrudes,
   By the deep sea, and music in its roar.
   I love not man the less, but Nature more,
From these our interviews, in which I steal
   From all I may be, or have been before,
To mingle with the universe, and feel
What I can ne'er express, yet can not all conceal.

Roll on, thou deep and dark blue ocean, roll!
   Ten thousand fleets sweep over thee in vain;
Man marks the earth with ruin, his control
   Stops with the shore; upon the watery plain
   The wrecks are all thy deed, nor doth remain
A shadow of man's ravage, save his own,
   When for a moment, like a drop of rain,
He sinks into thy depths with bubbling groan,
Without a grave, unknelled, uncoffined, and unknown.,

263

His steps are not upon thy paths, thy fields
  Are not a spoil for him,—thou dost arise
And shake him from thee; the vile strength he wields
  For earth's destruction thou dost all despise,
  Spurning him from thy bosom to the skies,
And send'st him, shivering in thy playful spray
  And howling, to his gods, where haply lies
His pretty hope in some near port or bay,
And dashest him again to earth:—there let him lay.

The armaments which thunder-strike the walls
  Of rock-built cities, bidding nations quake,
And monarchs tremble in their capitals;
  The oak leviathans, whose huge ribs make
  Their clay creator the vain title take
Of lord of thee, and arbiter of war;—
  These are thy toys, and, as the snowy flake,
They melt into the nest of waves, which mar
Alike the Armada's pride or spoils of Trafalgar.

Thy shores are empires, changed in all save thee;
  Assyria, Greece, Rome, Carthage—what are they?
Thy waters wasted them while they were free,
  And many a tyrant since; their shores obey
  The stranger, slave, or savage; their decay
Has dried up realms to deserts: not so thou,
  Unchangeable save to thy wild waves' play;
Time writes no wrinkle on thy azure brow;
Such as creation's dawn beheld, thou rollest now.

Thou glorious mirror, where the Almighty's form
  Glasses itself in tempests; in all time,

Calm or convulsed; in breeze, or gale, or storm,
  Icing the pole, or in the torrid clime,
  Dark-heaving; boundless, endless, and sublime;—
The image of Eternity, the throne
  Of the Invisible; even from out thy slime
The monsters of the deep are made; each zone
Obeys thee; thou goest forth, dread, fathomless, alone.

And I have loved thee, Ocean! and my joy
  Of youthful sports was on thy breast to be
Borne, like thy bubbles, onward: from a boy
  I wanton'd with thy breakers—they to me
  Were a delight; and if the freshening sea
Made them a terror—'twas a pleasing fear,
  For I was as it were a child of thee,
And trusted to thy billows far and near,
And laid my hand upon thy mane—as I do here.

—*George Gordon Byron*

OLD AGE

Growing Old

A LITTLE more tired at the close of day,
    A little less anxious to have our way;
A little less anxious to scold and blame,
A little more care for a brother's name;
And so we are nearing the journey's end,
Where time and eternity meet and blend.

A little less care for bonds of gold,
A little more zest for the days of old,

A broader view and a saner mind,
And a little more love for all mankind;
And so we are faring down the way
That leads to the gates of a better day.

A little more love for the friends of youth,
A little more zeal for established truth;
A little more charity in our views,
A little less thirst for the daily news;
And so we are folding our tents away
And passing in silence at close of day.

A little more leisure to sit and dream,
A little more real the things unseen;
A little nearer to those ahead,
With visions of those long loved and dead;
And so we are going where all must go,
To the place the living may never know.

A little more laughter, a few more tears,
And we shall have told our increasing years.
The book is closed, and the prayers are said,
And we are part of the countless dead.
Thrice happy, then, if some soul can say,
"I live because he has passed my way."

—Rollin J. Wells

John Anderson

JOHN ANDERSON, my jo John,
 When we were first acquent,
Your locks were like the raven,
 Your bonny brow was brent;
But now your brow is bald, John,
 Your locks are like the snow;
But blessings on your frosty pow,
 John Anderson, my jo.

John Anderson, my jo John,
 We clamb the hill thegither,
And mony a canty day, John,
 We've had wi' ane anither;
Now we maun totter down, John,
 But hand in hand we'll go,
And sleep thegither at the foot,
 John Anderson, my jo.

       —*Robert Burns*

The Last Leaf

I SAW him once before
 As he passed by the door,
  And again
The pavement stones resound,
As he totters o'er the ground
  With his cane.

They say that in his prime,
Ere the pruning knife of time
   Cut him down,
Not a better man was found
By the crier on his round
   Through the town.

But now he walks the streets,
And he looks at all he meets
   So forlorn,
And he shakes his feeble head,
That it seems as if he said;
   "They are gone."

The mossy marbles rest
On the lips that he has press'd
   In their bloom;
And the names he loved to hear
Have been carved for many a year
   On the tomb.

My Grandmamma has said—
Poor old lady, she is dead
   Long ago—
That he had a Roman nose,
And his cheek was like a rose
   In the snow.

But now his nose is thin,
And it rests upon his chin
   Like a staff,
And a crook is in his back,

And a melancholy crack
   In his laugh

I know it is a sin
For me to sit and grin
   At him here;
But the old three-cornered hat,
And the breeches,—and all that,
   Are so queer!

And if I should live to be
The last leaf upon the tree
   In the spring,
Let them smile, as I do now,
At the old forsaken bough
   Where I cling.

                              —*Oliver Wendell Holmes*

The Boys

HAS there any old fellow got mixed with the boys?
   If there has, take him out, without making a noise.
Hang the Almanac's cheat and the Catalogue's spite!
Old Time is a liar! We're twenty to-night!

We're twenty! We're twenty! Who says we are more?
He's tipsy—young jackanapes!—show him the door!
"Gray temples at twenty?"—Yes! *white* if we please;
Where the snowflakes fall thickest there's nothing can
   freeze!

Was it snowing I spoke of? Excuse the mistake!
Look close—you will see not a sign of a flake!
We want some new garlands for those we have shed,
And these are white roses in place of the red.

We've a trick, we young fellows, you may have been told,
Of talking (in public) as if we were old;
That boy we call "Doctor," and this we call "Judge";
It's a neat little fiction—of course it's all fudge.

That fellow's the "Speaker"—the one on the right;
"Mr. Mayor," my young one, how are you to-night?
That's our "Member of Congress," we say when we
        chaff;
There's the "Reverend" What's-his-name?—don't make
    me laugh.

That boy with the grave mathematical look
Made believe he had written a wonderful book,
And the ROYAL SOCIETY thought it was *true!*
So they chose him right in; a good joke it was, too!

There's a boy, we pretend, with a three-decker brain,
That could harness a team with a logical chain;
When he spoke for our manhood in syllabled fire,
We called him "The Justice," but now he's "The Squire."

And there's a nice youngster of excellent pith:
Fate tried to conceal him by naming him Smith;
But he shouted a song for the brave and the free—
Just read on his medal, "My country," "of thee!"

You hear that boy laughing? You think he's all fun;
But the angels laugh, too, at the good he has done.
The children laugh loud as they troop to his call,
And the poor man that knows him laughs loudest of all!

Yes, we're boys—always playing with tongue or with
     pen;
And I sometimes have asked, Shall we ever be men?
Shall we always be youthful and laughing and gay,
Till the last dear companion drops smiling away?

Then here's to our boyhood, its gold and its gray!
The starts of its winter, the dews of its May!
And when we have done with our life-lasting toys,
Dear Father, take care of Thy children, THE BOYS!

                                        —*Oliver Wendell Holmes*

Too Late?

"IT IS too late!" Ah, nothing is too late—
     Cato learned Greek at eighty; Sophocles
Wrote his grand "Ædipus," and Simonides
Bore off the prize of verse from his compeers
When each had numbered more than fourscore years;
And Theophratus at fourscore and ten
Had begun his "Characters of Men."
Chaucer at Woodstock, with the nightingales,
At sixty wrote the "Canterbury Tales."
Goethe at Weimar, toiling to the last,
Completed "Faust" when eighty years were past.
What then, shall we sit idly down and say,

The night hath come; it is no longer day?
For age is opportunity no less
Than youth itself, though in another dress.
And as the evening twilight fades away,
The sky is filled with stars invisible by day.

—*Henry W. Longfellow*

OPPORTUNITY

Opportunity

MASTER of human destinies am I.
Fame, love, and fortune on my footsteps wait,
Cities and fields I walk; I penetrate
Deserts and seas remote, and, passing by
Hovel, and mart, and palace, soon or late
I knock unbidden, once at every gate!
If sleeping, wake—if feasting, rise before
I turn away. It is the hour of fate,
And they who follow me reach every state
Mortals desire, and conquer every foe
Save death; but those who doubt or hesitate,
Condemned to failure, penury and woe,
Seek me in vain and uselessly implore—
I answer not, and I return no more.

—*John James Ingalls*

Opportunity

THEY do me wrong who say I come no more
    When once I knock and fail to find you in;
For every day I stand outside your door,
    And bid you wake and rise to fight and win.

Wail not for precious chances passed away,
    Weep not for golden ages on the wane;
Each night I burn the records of the day,
    At sunrise every soul is born again.

Laugh like a boy at splendors that have sped,
    To vanished joys be blind and deaf and dumb:
My judgments seal the dead past with its dead,
    But never bind a moment yet to come.

Though deep in mire, wring not your hands and weep,
    I lend my arm to all who say, "I can."
No shamefaced outcast ever sank so deep
    But yet might rise and be again a man.

Dost thou behold thy lost youth all aghast?
    Dost reel from righteous retribution's blow?
Then turn from blotted archives of the past
    And find the future's pages white as snow.

Art thou a mourner? Rouse thee from thy spell!
    Art thou a sinner? Sins may be forgiven;
Each morning gives thee wings to flee from hell.
    Each night a star to guide thy feet to heaven.

                                    —*Hon. Walter Malone*

Opportunity [1]

WITH doubt and dismay you are smitten,
  You think there's no chance for you, son?
Why, the best books haven't been written,
  The best race hasn't been run,
The best score hasn't been made yet,
  The best song hasn't been sung,
The best tune hasn't been played yet;
  Cheer up, for the world is young!

No chance? Why the world is just eager
  For things that you ought to create;
Its store of true wealth is still meagre,
  Its needs are incessant and great;
It yearns for more power and beauty,
  More laughter and love and romance,
More loyalty, labor and duty,
  No chance—why there's nothing but chance!

For the best verse hasn't been rhymed yet,
  The best house hasn't been planned,
The highest peak hasn't been climbed yet,
  The mightiest rivers aren't spanned;
Don't worry and fret, faint-hearted,
  The chances have just begun,
For the best jobs haven't been started,
  The best work hasn't been done.

—*Berton Braley*

[1] Used by permission of the author.

274

The Task That Is Given to You [1]

TO EACH one is given a marble to carve for the wall;
A stone that is needed to heighten the beauty of all;
And only his soul has the magic to give it grace;
And only his hands have the cunning to put it in place.

Yes, the task that is given to each one, no other can do;
So the errand is waiting; it has waited through ages for
you.
And now you appear; and the hushed ones are turning
their gaze,
To see what you do with your chance in the chamber of
days.

—Edwin Markham

PALESTINE

Palestine

BLESSED land of Judea! thrice hallowed of song,
Where the holiest of memories pilgrim-like throng;
In the shade of thy palms, by the shores of thy sea,
On the hills of thy beauty, my heart is with thee.

With the eye of a spirit I look on that shore,
Where pilgrim and prophet have lingered before;
With the glide of a spirit I traverse the sod
Made bright by the steps of the angels of God.

[1] Copyright by Edwin Markham. Used by his permission.

Blue sea of the hills!—in my spirit I hear
The waters, Gennesaret, chime on my ear;
Where the Lowly and Just with the people sat down,
And thy spray on the dust of his sandals was thrown.

Beyond are Bethulia's mountains of green,
And the desolate hills of the wild Gadarene;
And I pause on the goat-crags of Tabor to see
The gleam of thy waters, O dark Galilee!

Hark, a sound in the valley! where swollen and strong,
Thy river, O Kishon, is sweeping along;
Where the Canaanite strove with Jehovah in vain,
And thy torrent grew dark with the blood of the slain.

There down from his mountains stern Zebulon came,
And Naphtali's stag, with his eyeballs of flame,
And the chariots of Jabin rolled harmlessly on,
For the arm of the Lord was Abinoam's son!

There sleep the still rocks and the caverns which rang
To the song which the beautiful prophetess sang,
When the princes of Issachar stood by her side,
And the shout of a host in its triumph replied.

Lo, Bethlehem's hill-site before me is seen,
With the mountains around, and the valleys between;
There rested the shepherds of Judah, and there
The song of the angels rose sweet on the air.

And Bethany's palm-trees in beauty still throw
Their shadows at noon on the ruins below;

But where are the sisters who hastened to greet
The lowly Redeemer, and sit at his feet?

I tread where the Twelve in their wayfaring trod;
I stand where they stood with the Chosen of God,
Where His blessing was heard and His lessons were taught,
Where the blind were restored and the healing was
    wrought.

Oh, here with his flock the sad Wanderer came;
These hills he toiled over in grief are the same;
The founts where he drank by the wayside still flow;
And the same airs are blowing which breathed on his
    brow!

And throned on her hills sits Jerusalem yet,
But with dust on her forehead, and chains on her feet;
For the crown of her pride to the mocker hath gone,
And the holy Shechinah is dark where it shone.

But wherefore this dream of the earthly abode
Of Humanity clothed in the brightness of God?
Were my spirit but turned from the outward and dim,
It could gaze, even now, on the presence of Him!

Not in clouds and in terrors, but gentle as when,
In love and in meekness, He moved among men;
And the voice which breathed peace to the waves of the
    sea
In the hush of my spirit would whisper to me.

And what if my feet may not tread where He stood,
Nor my ears hear the dashing of Galilee's flood,
Nor my eyes see the cross which He bowed Him to bear,
Nor my knees press Gethsemane's garden of prayer!

Yet, Loved of the Father, Thy Spirit is near,
To the meek and the lowly and peninent here,
And the voice of Thy love is the same even now
As at Bethany's tomb or on Olivet's brow.

Oh, the outward hath gone! but in glory and power
The Spirit surviveth the things of an hour;
Unchanged, undecaying, Its Pentecost flame
On the heart's secret altar is burning the same!

—*John Greenleaf Whittier*

PATIENCE

Let Be

WHEN the sky starts in a-rainin',
    Let it be.
There is no use of complainin',
    Don't you see?
It will keep on perseverin'
Till at last it's time for clearin'
An' the days are bright and cheerin';
    Let it be.

When a friend gits sour an' surly,
    Let 'im be.

Don't start up a hurly burly,
        Fightin' free.
He'll come 'round perhaps, with waitin';
Though plain facts you might be statin',
What's the good of irritatin'?
        Let 'im be.

—Anon.

PATRIOTISM

America

MY COUNTRY, 'tis of thee,
    Sweet land of liberty,
        Of thee I sing;
Land where my fathers died,
Land of the pilgrims' pride,
From every mountain-side
        Let freedom ring!

My native country, thee—
Land of the noble free—
        Thy name I love;
I love thy rocks and rills,
Thy woods and templed hills;
My heart with rapture thrills
        Like that above.

Let music swell the breeze,
And ring from all the trees
        Sweet freedom's song!

Let mortal tongues awake;
Let all that breathe partake;
Let rocks their silence break—
    The sound prolong!

Our fathers' God! to Thee,
Author of liberty,
    To Thee we sing;
Long may our land be bright
With freedom's holy light;
Protect us by thy might,
    Great God, our King!

—*Samuel Francis Smith*

The Star-Spangled Banner

OH, SAY, can you see, by the dawn's early light,
    What so proudly we hailed at the twilight's last
    gleaming,
Whose broad stripes and bright stars through the peril-
    ous fight,
    O'er the ramparts we watched were so gallantly stream-
    ing?
And the rockets' red glare, the bombs bursting in air,
Gave proof thro' the night that our flag was still there.
Oh, say, does that star-spangled banner yet wave
O'er the land of the free, and the home of the brave!

On the shore, dimly seen thro' the mists of the deep,
    Where the foe's haughty host in dread silence reposes

What is that which the breeze o'er the towering steep,
  As it fitfully blows, half conceals, half discloses?
Now it catches the gleam of the morning's first beam,
In full glory reflected, now shines on the stream.
'Tis the star-spangled banner; oh, long may it wave
O'er the land of the free, and the home of the brave!

Oh, thus be it ever when freemen shall stand
  Between their loved homes and the war's desolation;
Blest with victory and peace, may the heaven rescued
    land
    Praise the power that hath made and preserved us a
      nation!
Then conquer we must, when our cause it is just,
And this be our motto: "In God is our trust!"
And the star-spangled banner in triumph doth wave,
O'er the land of the free, and the home of the brave!

—*Francis Scott Key*

The Battle Hymn of the Republic

MINE eyes have seen the Glory of the Coming of the
    Lord;
He is treading out the vintage where the grapes of wrath
    are stored;
He hath loosed the fateful lightning of His terrible swift
    sword;
            His Truth is marching on.

I have seen Him in the watch-fires of a hundred circling
    camps;

They have builded Him an altar in the evening dews and
damps;
I have read His righteous sentence by the dim and flaring lamps;
His Day is marching on.

I have read a fiery Gospel, writ in burnished rows of
steel;
"As ye deal with My contemners, so with you My grace
shall deal;"
Let the Hero, born of woman, crush the serpent with His
heel;
Since God is marching on.

He has sounded forth His trumpet that shall never call
retreat;
He is sifting out the hearts of men before His Judgment
seat;
Oh, be swift, my soul, to answer Him; be jubilant, my
feet;
Our God is marching on.

In the beauty of the lilies, Christ was born across the sea,
With a glory in His bosom that transfigures you and me;
As He died to make men holy, let us die to make men
free;
While God is marching on.

He is coming like the glory of the morning on the wave;
He is wisdom to the mighty, He is succor to the brave;

So the world shall be His footstool and the soul of time
    His slave;
        Our God is marching on.

—Julia Ward Howe

Gettysburg Address

(Speech at the Dedication of the National Cemetery at Gettysburg
November 19, 1863)

FOURSCORE and seven years ago our fathers brought forth upon this continent a new nation, conceived in liberty, and dedicated to the proposition that all men are created equal. Now we are engaged in a great civil war, testing whether that nation, or any nation so conceived and so dedicated, can long endure. We are met on a great battlefield of that war. We have come to dedicate a portion of that field as a final resting-place for those who here gave their lives that that nation might live. It is altogether fitting and proper that we should do this. But in a larger sense we cannot dedicate, we cannot consecrate, we cannot hallow this ground. The brave men, living and dead, who struggled here, have consecrated it far above our poor power to add or detract. The world will little note, nor long remember, what we say here; but it can never forget what they did here. It is for us, the living, rather to be dedicated here to the unfinished work which they who fought here have thus far so nobly advanced. It is rather for us to be here dedicated to the great task remaining before us, that from these honored dead we take increased devotion to that cause for which they gave the last full measure of devotion; that we here highly resolve that these dead shall not have died in vain; that this nation, under God, shall have a new birth of freedom, and that government of the people, by the people, and for the people, shall not perish from the earth.

—Abraham Lincoln

America the Beautiful

O BEAUTIFUL for spacious skies,
For amber waves of grain,
For purple mountain majesties
Above the fruited plain;
America! America!
God shed His grace on thee,
And crown thy good with brotherhood,
From sea to shining sea.

O beautiful for pilgrim feet
Whose stern, impassioned stress
A thoroughfare for freedom beat
Across the wilderness;
America! America!
God mend thine every flaw,
Confirm thy soul in self-control,
Thy liberty in law.

O beautiful for glory tale
Of liberating strife,
When valiantly, for man's avail,
Men lavished precious life;
America! America!

May God thy gold refine,
Till all success be nobleness,
And every gain divine.

O beautiful for patriot dream
That sees beyond the years
Thine alabaster cities gleam,
Undimmed by human tears;
America! America!
God shed his grace on thee,
And crown thy good with brotherhood,
From sea to shining sea.

—Katharine Lee Bates

Your Flag and My Flag

YOUR flag and my flag,
    And how it flies today
In your land and my land
    And half a world away!
Rose-red and blood-red
    The stripes forever gleam;
Snow-white and soul-white—
    The good forefathers' dream;
Sky-blue and true blue, with stars to gleam aright—
The gloried guidon of the day, a shelter through the
    night.

Your flag and my flag!
    To every star and stripe
The drums beat as hearts beat

And fifers shrilly pipe!
Your flag and my flag—
    A blessing in the sky;
Your hope and my hope—
    It never hid a lie!
Home land and far land and half the world around,
Old Glory hears our glad salute and ripples to the sound!

Your flag and my flag!
    And, oh, how much it holds—
Your land and my land—
    Secure within its folds!
Your heart and my heart
    Beat quicker at the sight;
Sun-kissed and wind-tossed—
    Red and Blue and White.
The one flag—the great flag—the flag for me and you—
Glorified all else beside—the Red and White and Blue!

—*Wilbur D. Nesbit*

Love of Country

BREATHES there the man with soul so dead,
    Who never to himself hath said,
    "This is my own, my native land?"
Whose heart hath ne'er within him burned,
As home his footsteps he hath turned,
    From wandering on a foreign strand?
If such there breathes, go, mark him well:
For him no minstrel raptures swell;
High though his titles, proud his name,

Boundless his wealth as wish can claim,
Despite those titles, power, and pelf,
The wretch, concentered all in self,
Living, shall forfeit fair renown,
And, doubly dying, shall go down
To the vile dust from whence he sprung,
Unwept, unhonored, and unsung.

—*Sir Walter Scott*

The American Flag

WHEN Freedom, from her mountain height,
    Unfurled her standard to the air,
She tore the azure robe of night,
    And set the stars of glory there;
She mingled with its gorgeous dyes
The milky baldric of the skies,
And striped its pure, celestial white
With streakings of the morning light;
Then, from his mansion in the sun,
She called her eagle-bearer down,
And gave into his mighty hand
The symbol of her chosen land.

Majestic monarch of the cloud!
    Who rearest aloft thy regal form,
To hear the tempest-trumpings loud,
And see the lightning lances driven,
    When strive the warriors of the storm,
And rolls the thunder-drum of heaven—
Child of the Sun! to thee 'tis given

To guard the banner of the free,
To hover in the sulphur smoke,
To ward away the battle-stroke,
And bid its blendings shine afar,
Like rainbows on the cloud of war,
    The harbingers of victory!

Flag of the brave! thy folds shall fly,
The sign of hope and triumph high!
When speaks the signal-trumpet tone,
And the long line comes gleaming on,
Ere yet the life-blood, warm and wet,
Has dimmed the glistening bayonet,
Each soldier's eye shall brightly turn
To where thy sky-born glories burn,
And, as his springing steps advance,
Catch war and vengeance from the glance;
And when the cannon-mouthings loud
Heave in wild wreaths the battle-shroud,
And gory sabers rise and fall
Like shoots of flame on midnight's pall,
Then shall thy meteor glances glow,
    And cowering foes shall shrink beneath
Each gallant arm that strikes below
    That lovely messenger of death.

Flag of the seas! on ocean-wave
Thy stars shall glitter o'er the brave;
When death, careering on the gale,
Sweeps darkly round the bellied sail,
And frighted waves rush wildly back
Before the broadside's reeling rack,

Each dying wanderer of the sea
Shall look at once to heaven and thee,
And smile to see thy splendors fly
In triumph o'er his closing eye.

Flag of the free heart's hope and home,
  By angel-hands to valor given,
Thy stars have lit the welkin dome,
  And all thy hues were born in heaven.
Forever float that standard sheet!
  Where breathes the foe but falls before us,
With Freedom's soil beneath our feet,
  And Freedom's banner streaming o'er us!
                              —*Joseph Rodman Drake*

Our Country's Emblem

GOD bless our country's emblem
    That floats o'er land and sea;
God bless each waving star and stripe,
  And the men who kept it free—
Men who, 'mid smoke of battle,
  And murderous shot and shell,
Held high the gleaming colors
  Of the flag they loved so well.
                              —*Anonymous*

The Red, White and Blue

O COLUMBIA! the gem of the ocean,
  The home of the brave and the free;

289

The shrine of each patriot's devotion,
　A world offers homage to thee.
Thy mandates make heroes assemble,
　When Liberty's form stands in view;
Thy banners make tyranny tremble,
　When borne by the red, white and blue.
When borne by the red, white and blue,
　When borne by the red, white and blue.

When war winged its wide desolation,
　And threatened the land to deform,
The ark then of freedom's foundation,
　Columbia rode safe thro' the storm;
With her garlands of vict'ry around her,
　When so proudly she bore her brave crew,
With her flag proudly waving before her,
　The boast of the red, white and blue.
The boast of the red, white and blue,
　The boast of the red, white and blue.

Then, sons of Columbia, come hither,
　And join in our nation's sweet hymn;
May the wreaths they have won never wither,
　Nor the stars of their glory grow dim!
May the service, united, ne'er sever,
　But they to their colors prove true!
The Army and Navy forever,
　Three cheers for the red, white and blue.
Three cheers for the red, white and blue,
　Three cheers for the red, white and blue.

—D. T. Shaw

What Makes a Nation Great?

NOT serried ranks with flags unfurled,
Not armoured ships that gird the world,
Not hoarded wealth nor busy mills,
Not cattle on a thousand hills,
Not sages wise, nor schools nor laws,
Not boasted deeds in freedom's cause—
All these may be, and yet the state
In the eye of God be far from great.

That land is great which knows the Lord,
Whose songs are guided by His word;
Where justice rules 'twixt man and man,
Where love controls in art and plan;
Where, breathing in his native air,
Each soul finds joy in praise and prayer—
Thus may our country, good and great,
Be God's delight—man's best estate.

—Alexander Blackburn

America for Me

'TIS fine to see the Old World, and travel up and
down
Among the famous palaces and cities of renown,
To admire the crumbly castles and the statues of the
kings,—
But now I think I've had enough of antiquated things.

So it's home again, and home again, America for me!
My heart is turning home again, and there I long to be,
In the land of youth and freedom beyond the ocean bars,
Where the air is full of sunlight and the flag is full of stars.

Oh, London is a man's town, there's power in the air;
And Paris is a woman's town, with flowers in the hair;
And it's sweet to dream in Venice, and it's great to study Rome;
But when it comes to living there is no place like home.

I like the German fir-woods, in green battalions drilled;
I like the gardens of Versailles with flashing fountains filled;
But, oh, to take your hand, my dear, and ramble for a day
In the friendly western woodland where Nature has her way!

I know that Europe's wonderful, yet something seems to lack:
The Past is too much with her, and the people looking back.
But the glory of the Present is to make the Future free,—
We love our land for what she is and what she is to be.

Oh, it's home again, and home again, America for me!
I want a ship that's westward bound to plough the rolling sea,

To the blessed Land of Room Enough beyond the ocean
     bars,
Where the air is full of sunlight and the flag is full of
     stars.

                                              —*Henry Van Dyke*

The Flag Goes By

HATS off!
     Along the street there comes
A blare of bugles, a ruffle of drums,
A flash of color beneath the sky:
Hats off!
The flag is passing by!

    Blue and crimson and white it shines,
Over the steel-tipped, ordered lines.
Hats off!
The colors before us fly;
But more than the flag is passing by.

    Sea-fights and land-fights, grim and great,
Fought to make and to save the State:
Weary marches and sinking ships;
Cheers of victory on dying lips;

    Days of plenty and years of peace;
March of a strong land's swift increase;
Equal justice, right and law,
Stately honor and reverend awe;

Sign of a nation, great and strong
To ward her people from foreign wrong:
Pride and glory and honor,—all
Live in the colors to stand or fall.

Hats off!
Along the street there comes
A blare of bugles, a ruffle of drums;
And loyal hearts are beating high:
Hats off!
The flag is passing by!

—*Henry Holcomb Bennett*

God Save the People

WHEN wilt Thou save the people?
  O God of mercy, when?
Not kings and lords, but nations,
  Not thrones and crowns but men!
Flowers of Thy heart, O God, are they,
  Let them not pass like weeds away,
Their heritage a sunless day:
  God save the people!

Shall crime bring crime for ever,
  Strength aiding still the strong?
  Is it Thy will, O Father,
  That man shall toil for wrong?
"No," say Thy mountains; "No," Thy skies;
  Man's clouded sun shall brightly rise,

And songs ascend instead of sighs:
  God save the people!

  When wilt Thou save the people?
    O God of mercy, when?
  The people, Lord, the people,
    Not thrones and crowns, but men;
  God save the people! Thine they are,
    Thy children, as Thine angels fair,—
  From vice, oppression, and despair,
    God save the people!

—*Ebenezer Elliott*

Paul Revere's Ride

L ISTEN, my children, and you shall hear
    Of the midnight ride of Paul Revere,
On the eighteenth of April, in Seventy-five;
Hardly a man is now alive
Who remembers that famous day and year.

He said to his friend, "If the British march
By land or sea from the town to-night,
Hang a lantern aloft in the belfry arch
Of the North Church tower as a signal light,—
One if by land, and two if by sea;
And I on the opposite shore will be,
Ready to ride and spread the alarm
Through every Middlesex village and farm,
For the country folk to be up and to arm."

Then he said "Good-night!" and with muffled oar
Silently rowed to the Charlestown shore,
Just as the moon rose over the bay,
Where swinging wide at her moorings lay
The *Somerset*, British man-of-war;
A phantom ship, with each mast and spar
Across the moon like a prison bar,
And a huge black hulk, that was magnified
By its own reflection in the tide.

Meanwhile, his friend through alley and street
Wanders and watches, with eager ears,
Till in the silence around him he hears
The muster of men at the barrack door,
The sound of arms, and the tramp of feet,
And the measured tread of the grenadiers,
Marching down to their boats on the shore.

Then he climbed the tower of the Old North Church,
By the wooden stairs, with stealthy tread,
To the belfry chamber overhead,
And startled the pigeons from their perch
On the sombre rafters, that round him made
Masses and moving shapes of shade,—
By the trembling ladder, steep and tall,
To the highest window in the wall,
Where he paused to listen and look down
A moment on the roofs of the town
And the moonlight flowing over all.

Beneath, in the churchyard, lay the dead,
In their night encampment on the hill,

Wrapped in silence so deep and still
That he could hear, like a sentinel's tread,
The watchful night-wind, as it went
Creeping along from tent to tent,
And seeming to whisper, "All is well!"
A moment only he feels the spell
Of the place and the hour, and the secret dread
Of the lonely belfry and the dead;
For suddenly all his thoughts are bent
On a shadowy something far away,
Where the river widens to meet the bay,—
A line of black that bends and floats
On the rising tide like a bridge of boats.

Meanwhile, impatient to mount and ride,
Booted and spurred, with a heavy stride
On the opposite shore walked Paul Revere.
Now he patted his horse's side,
Now he gazed at the landscape far and near,
Then, impetuous, stamped the earth,
And turned and tightened his saddle girth;
But mostly he watched with eager search
The belfry tower of the Old North Church,
As it rose above the graves on the hill,
Lonely and spectral and sombre and still.
And lo! as he looks, on the belfry's height
A glimmer, and then a gleam of light!
He springs to the saddle, the bridle he turns,
But lingers and gazes, till full on his sight
A second lamp in the belfry burns.

A hurry of hoofs in a village street,
A shape in the moonlight, a bulk in the dark,
And beneath, from the pebbles, in passing, a spark
Struck out by a steed flying fearless and fleet;
That was all! And yet, through the gloom and the light,
The fate of a nation was riding that night;
And the spark struck out by that steed, in his flight,
Kindled the land into flame with its heat.
He has left the village and mounted the steep,
And beneath him, tranquil and broad and deep,
Is the Mystic, meeting the ocean tides;
And under the alders that skirt its edge,
Now soft on the sand, now loud on the ledge,
Is heard the tramp of his steed as he rides.

It was twelve by the village clock,
When he crossed the bridge into Medford town.
He heard the crowing of the cock,
And the barking of the farmer's dog,
And felt the damp of the river fog,
That rises after the sun goes down.

It was one by the village clock,
When he galloped into Lexington.
He saw the gilded weathercock
Swim in the moonlight as he passed,
And the meeting-house windows, black and bare,
Gaze at him with a spectral glare,
As if they already stood aghast
At the bloody work they would look upon.

It was two by the village clock,
When he came to the bridge in Concord town.
He heard the bleating of the flock,
And the twitter of birds among the trees,
And felt the breath of the morning breeze
Blowing over the meadow brown.
And one was safe and asleep in his bed
Who at the bridge would be first to fall,
Who that day would be lying dead,
Pierced by a British musket ball.

You know the rest. In the books you have read
How the British Regulars fired and fled,—
How the farmers gave them ball for ball,
From behind each fence and farmyard wall,
Chasing the redcoats down the lane,
Then crossing the fields to emerge again
Under the trees at the turn of the road,
And only pausing to fire and load.

So through the night rode Paul Revere;
And so through the night went his cry of alarm
To every Middlesex village and farm,—
A cry of defiance, and not of fear,
A voice in the darkness, a knock at the door,
And a word that shall echo for evermore!
For, borne on the night-wind of the Past,
Through all our history, to the last,
In the hour of darkness and peril and need,
The people will waken and listen to hear

The hurrying hoof-beats of that steed,
And the midnight message of Paul Revere.

—Henry Wadsworth Longfellow

Barbara Frietchie

UP FROM the meadows rich with corn,
Clear in the cool September morn,

The clustered spires of Frederick stand
Green-walled by the hills of Maryland.

Round about them orchards sweep,
Apple and peach-tree fruited deep,

Fair as a garden of the Lord
To the eyes of the famished rebel horde;

On that pleasant morn of the early fall
When Lee marched over the mountain wall,

Over the mountains, winding down,
Horse and foot into Frederick town.

Forty flags with their silver stars,
Forty flags with their crimson bars,

Flapped in the morning wind; the sun
Of noon looked down, and saw not one.

Up rose old Barbara Frietchie then,
Bowed with her fourscore years and ten;

Bravest of all in Frederick town,
She took up the flag the men hauled down;

In her attic-window the staff she set,
To show that one heart was loyal yet.

Up the street came the rebel tread,
Stonewall Jackson riding ahead.

Under his slouched hat left and right
He glanced: the old flag met his sight.

"Halt!"—the dust-brown ranks stood fast;
"Fire!"—out blazed the rifle-blast.

It shivered the window, pane and sash,
It rent the banner with seam and gash.

Quick, as it fell, from the broken staff
Dame Barbara snatched the silken scarf;

She leaned far out on the window-sill,
And shook it forth with a royal will.

"Shoot, if you must, this old grey head,
But spare your country's flag," she said.

A shade of sadness, a blush of shame,
Over the face of the leader came;

The nobler nature within him stirred
To life at that woman's deed and word:

"Who touches a hair on yon grey head
Dies like a dog! March on!" he said.

All day long through Frederick street
Sounded the tread of marching feet.

All day long that free flag tost
Over the heads of the rebel host.

Ever its torn folds rose and fell
On the loyal winds that loved it well;

And through the hill-gaps sunset light
Shone over it with a warm good-night.

Barbara Frietchie's work is o'er,
And the rebel rides on his raids no more.

Honor to her! and let a tear
Fall, for her sake, on Stonewall's bier.

Over Barbara Frietchie's grave,
Flag of freedom and union, wave!

Peace, and order, and beauty draw
Round thy symbol of light and law;

And ever the stars above look down
On thy stars below in Frederick town!

—John Greenleaf Whittier

302

Rule, Britannia

WHEN Britain first, at Heaven's command,
  Arose from out the azure main,
This was the charter of her land,
  And guardian angels sung the strain:
    Rule, Britannia! Britannia rules the waves!
    Britons never shall be slaves.

The nations, not so blest as thee,
  Must, in their turn, to tyrants fall,
Whilst thou shalt flourish, great and free,
  The dread and envy of them all:
            Rule, Britannia, &c.

Still more majestic shalt thou rise,
  More dreadful from each foreign stroke;
As the loud blast that tears the skies
  Serves but to root thy native oak:
            Rule, Britannia, &c.

Thee haughty tyrants ne'er shall tame;
  All their attempts to hurl thee down
Will but arouse thy gen'rous flame,
  And work their woe—but thy renown:
            Rule, Britannia, &c.

To thee belongs the rural reign;
  Thy cities shall with commerce shine:
All thine shall be the subject main,
  And every shore encircle thine:
            Rule, Britannia, &c.

The Muses, still with Freedom found,
Shall to thy happy coast repair;
Blest isle! with matchless beauty crown'd,
And manly hearts to guard the fair:
Rule, Britannia, &c.

—*James Thomson*

God Save the King

The National Song of Britain

GOD save our gracious King
Long live our noble King,
God save the King:
Send him victorious,
Happy and glorious,
Long to reign over us;
God save the King.

Through every changing scene,
O Lord, preserve our King;
Long may he reign:
His heart inspire and move
With wisdom from above,
And in a nation's love
His throne maintain,

Thy choicest gifts in store,
On him be pleased to pour;
Long may he reign:
May he defend our laws,

And ever give us cause
To sing with heart and voice,
    God save the King.

                                              —*Henry Carey*

The Marseillaise

The National Song of France

YE sons of toil awake to glory!
    Hark! hark!! what myriads bid you rise!
Your children, wives and grandsires hoary,
    Behold their tears and hear their cries!
Shall hateful tyrants, mischief breeding,
        With hireling hosts, a ruffian band,
        Affright and desolate the land,
    While peace and liberty lie bleeding?

CHORUS:
    To arms, to arms, ye brave!
    Th' avenging sword unsheathe!
    March on, march on,
    All hearts resolved
    On victory or death!

With luxury and pride surrounded
    The vile, insatiate despots dare,
Their thirst for gold and power unbounded,
    To mete and vend the light and air.
Like beasts of burden would they load us,
        Like gods would bid their slaves adore,

305

But man is man and who is more?
Then shall they longer lash and goad us?

Oh, Liberty, can man resign thee,
  Once having felt thy gen'rous flame?
Can dungeons, belts and bars confine thee?
  Or whips thy noble spirit tame?
Too long the world has wept bewailing
    That falsehood's dagger tyrants wield;
    But freedom is our sword and shield.
And all their arts are unavailing.

—Rouget de Lisle

The Garibaldi Hymn

The Italian National Hymn

COME, arm ye! Come, arm ye!
  From vineyards of olives, from grape-mantled
  bowers,
Where landscapes are laughing in mazes of flowers;
From mountains, all lighted by sapphire and amber,
From cities of marble, from temples and marts,
Arise, all ye valiants! your manhood proclaiming,
Whilst thunders are meeting, and sabers are flaming,
For honor, for glory, the bugles are sounding,
To quicken your pulses and gladden your hearts.
Then hurl our fierce foemen far from us forever,
The Day is dawning, the Day is dawning, which shall be
  our own.

—Luigi Mercantini

Prophecy

FOR I dipt into the future,
    Far as human eye could see,
Saw the vision of the world,
    And all the wonder that would be;

Saw the heavens fill with commerce,
    Argosies of magic sails,
Pilots of the purple twilight,
    Dropping down with costly bales;

Heard the heavens fill with shouting,
    And there rain'd a ghastly dew
From the nations' airy navies
    Grappling in the central blue;

Far along the world-wide whisper
    Of the south-wind rushing warm,
With the standards of the peoples
    Plunging thro' the thunder storm;

Till the war-drum throbb'd no longer,
    And the battle-flags were furl'd
In Parliament of man,
    The Federation of the world.

There the common sense of most
    Shall hold a fretful realm in awe,

And the kindly earth shall slumber,
Lapt in universal law.

—From "Locksley Hall,"
By Alfred Tennyson, 1842

A Message of Peace

WERE half the power that fills the world with terror,
   Were half the wealth bestowed on camps and
     courts,
Given to redeem the human mind from error
   There were no need of arsenals or forts!

The warrior's name would be a name abhorred!
   And every nation, that should lift again
Its hand against a brother, on its forehead
   Would wear forevermore the curse of Cain!

Down the dark future, through long generations,
   The echoing sounds grow fainter and then cease;
And like a bell, with solemn, sweet vibrations,
   I hear once more the voice of Christ say, "Peace!"

Peace! and no longer from its brazen portals
   The blast of war's great organ shakes the skies!
But beautiful as songs of the immortals,
   The holy melodies of love arise.

—Henry W. Longfellow

Peace [1]

WHAT was the first prophetic word that rang,
    When down the starry sky the angels sang?
That night they came as envoys of the birth—
What word but peace, "peace and good will on earth"?

And what was the last word the Master said,
That parting night when they broke brother bread?
That night He knew men would not let Him live—
Oh, what but "peace I leave" and "peace I give"?

And yet behold; near twice a thousand years
And still the battle wrath, the grief, the tears!
Let mercy speed the hour when swords shall cease
And men cry back to God, "There shall be peace!"
                   —*Edwin Markham*

"He Shall Speak Peace"

HATRED and greed and pride shall die,
    Cannon and sword shall prostrate lie;
Warring shall end, the world shall cry—
    For He shall speak peace.

Rivers shall nevermore run red,
Terror shall hide his bloody head,
Life shall no more for lust be shed—
    For He shall speak peace.

[1] Copyrighted by Edwin Markham. Used by his permission.

They shall not strive in earth again,
Honor will come to dwell with men;
Children will bide in safety then—
  For He shall speak peace.

Desolate plains, now bleak and cold,
Burst forth again in green and gold;
Birds of the trenches sing, as of old—
  For He shall speak peace.

—*Thomas Curtis Clark*

The World Hymn

AROUSE, arouse, ye friends of right,
  Be bold for freedom's cause!
See that our common liberty
  Pervades all nations' laws.
See that the banner of the free
  O'er all the earth shall wave;
And in the strength of God above
  Go forth the world to save.

Be brave, be brave, ye sons of men;
  Lift freedom's banner high!
As many bled and died of old
  To raise it to the sky.
Let every tyrant be o'erthrown,
  And right, not might, hold sway;
That for all nations of the earth
  May dawn a brighter day.

Ye people of all lands, arise,
    And banish war and crime;
Let man to man be fair and just
    In every land and clime.
Let people for the people rule,
    Democracy be king;
Maintain the rights of all mankind
    And every living thing.

Let martial drums now muffled be,
    And battle flags be furled;
The parliament of man now meet
    To federate the world;
One language to mankind be given,
    One hope, one aim, one cause,
With equal measures, weights and coins,
    And just and righteous laws.

                        —*J. Gilchrist Lawson*

The Reign of Peace

SOME day, some happy day,
    All forms of strife shall cease,
And may it be not far away—
    The time when all is peace;
On every sea, on every shore,
The sound of war shall be no more.

Some time, some happy time,
    And may that time be near—

Injustice, cruelty and crime
    From earth shall disappear;
For Christ shall come to be our King,
And every tongue with joy shall sing.

That time, that happy time,
    Which this whole world shall bless,
Will bring to view a sight sublime—
    The reign of righteousness;
For Christ alone shall be our King,
And every tongue His praise shall sing.

His love, His wondrous love,
    Shall soften every heart,
As it comes down from heaven above,
    While sin shall then depart,
And every tongue with joy shall sing,
When Christ has come to be our King.

—*Mary Starck*

The Church Triumphant

THESE things shall be! a loftier race
    Than e'er the world has known shall rise
With flame of freedom in their souls
    And light of knowledge in their eyes.

They shall be gentle, brave, and strong
    To spill no drop of blood, but dare
All that may plant man's lordship firm,
    On earth, and fire, and sea, and air.

312

Nation with nation, land with land,
    Unarmed shall live as comrades free;
In every heart and brain shall throb
    The pulse of one fraternity.

Man shall love man with heart so pure
    And fervent as the young-eyed throng
Who chant their heavenly psalms before
    God's face with undiscordant song.

New arts shall bloom of loftier mould,
    And mightier music thrill the skies,
And every life shall be a song,
    When all the earth is paradise.

There shall be no more sin, nor shame,
    Though pain and passion may not die;
For man shall be at one with God
    In bonds of firm necessity.

—John Addington Symonds

Bugle Song of Peace

BLOW, bugle, blow!
    The day has dawned at last.
Blow, blow, blow!
The fearful night is past.
The prophets realize their dreams:
Lo! in the east the glory gleams.
Blow, bugle, blow!
The day has dawned at last.

Blow, bugle, blow!
The soul of man is free.
The rod and sword of king and lord
Shall no more honored be;
For God alone shall govern men,
And Love shall come to earth again,
Blow, bugle, blow!
The soul of man is free.

Blow, bugle, blow!
The rivers run with blood,
But greed and strife, and lust for life
Are passing with the flood.
The world's great heart with grief is bowed,
The gory beast of war is cowed,
Blow, bugle, blow!
The day has dawned at last.

—Thomas Curtis Clark

"He Shall Speak Peace unto the Nations"

(Zechariah 9:10)

A STORMY sea! Waves dashing high!
    The frail boat rocks upon the deep.
(How can the Lord unconscious lie,
    Head pillowed, in the stern—asleep?)

The winds sweep down on Galilee,
    And fiercer grows the storm, until

314

Strong men cry out in fear! Then He,
   In conscious power, speaks: "Peace, be still."

A world war-wrecked! In fury tossed
   By storms of rage and jealous hate!
(The Lord unmindful of the cost;
   Unheeding—till it be too late!)

Yet say not so! He hears the cry—
   And still "He maketh wars to cease."
The crucible is 'neath His eye.
   In His own time "He shall speak peace."

—Lila V. Walters

Tubal Cain

OLD Tubal Cain was a man of might
   In the days when Earth was young;
By the fierce red light of his furnace bright
   The strokes of his hammer rung;
And he lifted high his brawny hand
   On the iron glowing clear,
Till the sparks rushed out in scarlet showers,
   As he fashioned the sword and spear.
And he sang—"Hurra for my handiwork!
   Hurra for the spear and sword!
Hurra for the hand that shall wield them well,
   For he shall be king and lord!"

To Tubal Cain came many a one,
   As he wrought by his roaring fire,

And each one prayed for a strong steel blade
  As the crown of his desire:
And he made them weapons sharp and strong,
  Till they shouted loud for glee,
And gave him gifts of pearl and gold,
  And spoils of the forest free.
And they sang—"Hurra for Tubal Cain,
  Who hath given us strength anew!
Hurra for the smith, hurra for the fire,
  And hurra for the metal true!"

But a sudden change came o'er his heart
  Ere the setting of the sun,
And Tubal Cain was filled with pain
  For the evil he had done;
He saw that men, with rage and hate,
  Made war upon their kind,
That the land was red with the blood they shed
  In their lust for carnage blind.
And he said "Alas! that ever I made,
  Or that skill of mine should plan,
The spear and the sword for men whose joy
  Is to slay their fellow man."

And for many a day old Tubal Cain
  Sat brooding o'er his woe;
And his hand forebore to smite the ore
  And his furnace smouldered low.
But he rose at last with a cheerful face,
  And a bright courageous eye,

And bared his strong right arm for work,
  While the quick flames mounted high.
And he sang—"Hurra for my handicraft!"
  And the red sparks lit the air;
"Not alone for the blade was the bright steel made;"
  And he fashioned the first ploughshare.

And men, taught wisdom from the past,
  In friendship joined their hands,
Hung the sword in the hall, the spear on the wall,
  And ploughed the willing lands;
And sang—"Hurra for Tubal Cain!
  Our staunch good friend is he;
And for the ploughshare and the plough
  To him our praise shall be.
But while oppression lifts its head,
  Or a tyrant would be lord,
Though we may thank him for the plough,
  We'll not forget the sword!"

                              —*Charles Mackay*

Christmas Bells

I HEARD the bells on Christmas Day
  Their old familiar carols play,
      And wild and sweet
      The words repeat
Of peace on earth, good will to men.

And thought how, as the day had come,
The belfries of all Christendom

Had rolled along
The unbroken song
Of peace on earth, good will to men.

Till ringing, singing on its way,
The world revolved from day to day,
A voice, a chime,
A chant sublime
Of peace on earth, good will to men.

Then pealed the bells more loud and deep;
"God is not dead; nor doth he sleep;
The Wrong shall fail,
The Right prevail,
With peace on earth, good will to men."

—H. W. Longfellow

P E P

"Pep"

VIGOR, vitality, vim and punch—
That's pep!
The courage to act on a sudden hunch—
That's pep!
The nerve to tackle the hardest thing,
With feet that climb, and hands that cling,
And a heart that never forgets to sing—
That's pep!

Sand and grit in a concrete base—
That's pep!

318

Friendly smile on an honest face—
      That's pep!
The spirit that helps when another's down,
That knows how to scatter the blackest frown,
That loves its neighbor and loves its town—
      That's pep!

To say "I will"—for you know you can—
      That's pep!
To look for the best in every man—
      That's pep!
To meet each thundering knockout blow,
And come back with a laugh, because you know
You'll get the best of the whole show—
      That's pep!

              —Grace G. Bostwick

PERSEVERANCE

It Couldn't Be Done [1]

By Edgar A. Guest

SOMEBODY said that it couldn't be done,
    But he with a chuckle replied
That "maybe it couldn't," but he would be one
    Who wouldn't say so till he'd tried.
So he buckled right in with a trace of a grin
    On his face. If he worried he hid it.
He started to sing as he tackled the thing
    That couldn't be done—and he did it!

[1] From Mr. Guest's book "The Path to Home." Copyright 1919, and reprinted
by permission of the publishers, Reilly & Lee Co., Chicago.

Somebody scoffed, "Oh, you'll never do that—
    At least no one ever has done it;"
But he took off his coat and he took off his hat,
    And the first thing we knew he'd begun it.
With the lift of his chin and a bit of a grin,
    Without doubting or quiddit,
He started to sing as he tackled the thing,
    That couldn't be done—and he did it!

There are thousands to tell you it cannot be done,
    There are thousands to prophesy failure;
There are thousands to point out to you, one by one,
    The dangers that wait will assail you.
But just buckle in with a bit of a grin,
    Then take off your coat and go to it;
Just start in to sing as you tackle the thing
    That "cannot be done"—and you'll do it!

Excelsior

THE shades of night were falling fast,
    As through an Alpine village passed
A youth, who bore, 'mid snow and ice,
A banner with the strange device—
        Excelsior!

His brow was sad; his eye beneath
Flashed like a faulchion from its sheath;
And like a silver clarion rung

The accents of that unknown tongue—
  Excelsior!

In happy homes he saw the light
Of household fires gleam warm and bright,
Above, the spectral glaciers shone,
And from his lips escaped a groan—
  Excelsior!

"Try not the pass," the old man said:
"Dark lowers the tempest overhead;
The roaring torrent is deep and wide!"
And loud that clarion voice replied,
  Excelsior!

"Oh stay," the maiden said, "and rest
Thy weary head upon this breast!"
A tear stood in his bright blue eye,
But still he answered, with a sigh,
  Excelsior!

"Beware the pine-tree's withered branch!
Beware the awful avalanche!"
This was the peasant's last good-night:
A voice replied, far up the height,
  Excelsior!

At break of day, as heavenward
The pious monks of Saint Bernard
Uttered the oft-repeated prayer,
A voice cried, through the startled air,
  Excelsior!

A traveller, by the faithful hound,
Half-buried in the snow was found,
Still grasping in his hand of ice
That banner with the strange device,
    Excelsior!

There in the twilight cold and gray,
Lifeless, but beautiful, he lay,
And from the sky, serene and far,
A voice fell, like a falling star—
    Excelsior!

—Henry Wadsworth Longfellow

Hang To Your Grit!

DON'T give up hoping when the ship goes down,
  Grab a spar or something—just refuse to drown.
Don't think you are dying just because you're hit,
Smile in face of danger and hang to your grit.
Folks die too easy—they sort of fade away;
Make a little error and give up in dismay.
Kind of man that's needed is the man of ready wit,
To laugh at pain and trouble and keep up his grit.

—Louis E. Thayer

The Only Way To Win

IT takes a little courage
  And a little self-control
And some grim determination,

If you want to reach the goal.
It takes a deal of striving,
   And a firm and stern-set chin,
No matter what the battle,
   If you really want to win.

There's no easy path to glory,
   There's no rosy road to fame.
Life, however we may view it,
   Is no simple parlor game;
But its prizes call for fighting,
   For endurance and for grit;
For a rugged disposition
   And a "don't-know-when-to-quit."

You must take a blow or give one,
   You must risk and you must lose,
And expect that in the struggle
   You will suffer from the bruise.
But you mustn't wince or falter,
   If a fight you once begin;
Be a man and face the battle—
   That's the only way to win.

—Anon.

Keep a-Goin'

IF you strike a thorn or rose,
   Keep a-goin!
If it hails or if it snows,
   Keep a-goin!
'Taint no use to sit an' whine

When the fish ain't on your line;
Bait your hook an' keep a-tryin'—
    Keep a-goin!

When the weather kills your crop,
    Keep a-goin!
Though 'tis work to reach the top,
    Keep a-goin!
S'pose you're out o' ev'ry dime,
Gittin' broke ain't any crime;
Tell the world you're feelin' *prime*—
    Keep a-goin!

When it looks like all is up,
    Keep a-goin!
Drain the sweetness from the cup,
    Keep a-goin!
See the wild birds on the wing,
Hear the bells that sweetly ring,
When you feel like singin', sing—
    Keep a-goin!

—Frank L. Stanton

The Quitter

IT ain't the failures he may meet
    That keeps a man from winnin',
It's the discouragement complete
    That blocks a new beginnin';
You want to quit your habits bad;
    And, when the shadows flittin'

324

Make life seem worthless an' sad,
    You want to quit your quittin'!

You want to quit a-layin' down
    An' sayin hope is over,
Because the fields are bare an' brown
    Where once we lived in clover.
When jolted from the water-cart,
    It's painful to be hittin'
The earth; but make another start.
    Cheer up, an' quit your quittin'!

Although the game seems rather stiff,
    Don't be a doleful doubter;
There's always one more innin' if
    You're not a down-and-outer.
But fortune's pretty sure to flee
    From folks content with sittin'
Around an' sayin' life's N. G.—
    You've got to quit your quittin'.

—Anon.

Always Finish

IF a task is once begun,
    Never leave it till it's done.
Be the labor great or small,
Do it well or not at all.

—Anon.

325

Sacred Poetry

HOW beautiful is genius when combined
   With holiness! Oh, how divinely sweet
The tones of earthly harp, whose chords are touch'd
By the soft hand of Piety, and hung
Upon Religion's shrine, there vibrating
With solemn music in the ear of God.
And must the Bard from sacred themes refrain?
Sweet were the hymns in patriarchal days,
That, kneeling in the silence of his tent,
Or on some moonlit hill, the shepherd pour'd
Unto his heavenly Father. Strains survive
Erst chanted to the lyre of Israel,
More touching far than ever poet breathed
Amid the Grecian isles, or later times
Have heard in Albion, land of every lay.
Why therefore are ye silent, ye who know
The trance of adoration, and behold
Upon your bended knees the throne of Heaven,
And Him Who sits thereon? Believe it not,
That Poetry, in purer days the nurse,
Yea, parent oft of blissful piety,
Should silent keep from service of her God,
Nor with her summons, loud but silver-toned,
Startle the guilty dreamer from his sleep,
Bidding him gaze with rapture or with dread
On regions where the sky for ever lies
Bright as the sun himself, and trembling all
With ravishing music, or where darkness broods
O'er ghastly shapes, and sounds not to be borne.

—John Wilson

For A' That and A' That

IS there, for honest poverty,
  That hangs his head, and a' that?
The coward-slave, we pass him by,
  And dare be poor for a' that;
    For a' that, and a' that,
      Our toils obscure, and a' that;
    The rank is but the guinea stamp;
      The man's the gowd for a' that.

What tho' on hamely fare we dine,
  Wear hodden-grey, and a' that;
Gie fools their silks, and knaves their wine,
  A man's a man, for a' that.
    For a' that, and a' that,
      Their tinsel show, and a' that:
    The honest man, tho' ne'er sae poor,
      Is King o' men for a' that.

Ye see yon birkie, ca'd a lord,
  Wha struts, and stares, and a' that;
Tho' hundreds worship at his word,
  He's but a coof for a' that:
    For a' that, and a' that,
      His riband, star, and a' that,
    The man of independent mind,
      He looks and laughs at a' that.

A king can mak' a belted knight,
  A marquis, duke, and a' that;
But an honest man's aboon his might,
  Guid faith, he maunna fa' that!
    For a' that, and a' that,
      Their dignities, and a' that,
    The pith o' sense, and pride o' worth,
      Are higher ranks than a' that.

Then let us pray that come it may,
  As come it will for a' that,
That sense and worth, o'er a' the earth,
  May bear the gree, and a' that;
    For a' that, and a' that,
      It's coming yet, for a' that;
    That man to man, the warld o'er,
      Shall brothers be for a' that.

—*Robert Burns*

PRAYER

I Thank Thee, Lord

I THANK Thee, Lord, for mine unanswered prayers,
  Unanswered save Thy quiet, kindly "Nay,"
Yet it seemed hard among my heavy cares
  That bitter day.

I wanted joy; but Thou didst know for me
  That sorrow was the gift I needed most,

328

And in its mystic depth I learned to see
    The Holy Ghost.

I wanted health; but Thou didst bid me sound
    The secret treasuries of pain,
And in the moans and groans my heart oft found
    Thy Christ again.

I wanted wealth: 'twas not the better part,
    There is a wealth with poverty oft given,
And thou didst teach me of the gold of heart,
    Best gift of heaven.

I thank Thee, Lord, for these unanswered prayers,
    And for Thy word, the quiet, kindly "Nay."
'Twas Thy withholding lightened all my cares
    That blessed day.

                    —Anon.

Prayer

LORD, what a change within us one short hour
    Spent in Thy presence will avail to make!
What heavy burdens from our bosoms take!
What parched grounds refresh as with a shower!
We kneel, and all around us seems to lower;
We rise, and all, the distant and the near,
Stands forth in sunny outline, brave and clear;
We kneel, how weak! we rise, how full of power!
Why, therefore, should we do ourselves this wrong,
Or others—that we are not always strong—

That we are sometimes overborne with care—
That we should ever weak or heartless be,
Anxious or troubled—when with us is prayer,
And joy and strength and courage are with Thee?
—*Richard C. Trench*

Sweet Hour of Prayer!

SWEET hour of prayer! sweet hour of prayer!
That calls me from a world of care,
And bids me at my Father's throne
Make all my wants and wishes known:
In seasons of distress and grief,
My soul has often found relief;
And oft escaped the tempter's snare,
By thy return, sweet hour of prayer!

Sweet hour of prayer! sweet hour of prayer!
Thy wings shall my petition bear
To Him whose truth and faithfulness
Engage the waiting soul to bless:
And since He bids me seek His face,
Believe His word, and trust His grace,
I'll cast on Him my every care,
And wait for thee, sweet hour of prayer!

Sweet hour of prayer! sweet hour of prayer!
May I thy consolation share,
Till, from Mount Pisgah's lofty height,
I view my home and take my flight;
This robe of flesh I'll drop, and rise

To seize the everlasting prize;
And shout, while passing through the air,
Farewell, farewell, sweet hour of prayer!

—William W. Walford

RAIN

Rain Song

IT isn't raining rain to me,
 It's raining daffodils;
In ev'ry dimpling drop I see
 Wildflowers on the hills.
A cloud of gray engulfs the day
 And overwhelms the town;
It isn't raining rain to me,
 It's raining roses down.

It isn't raining rain to me,
 But fields of clover bloom,
Where any buccaneering bee
 May find a bed and room.
A health, then, to the happy,
 A fig to him who frets;
It isn't raining rain to me,
 It's raining violets.

—Robert Loveman

True Rest

REST is not quitting
 The busy career;
Rest is the fitting
 Of self to one's sphere.

'Tis the brook's motion,
 Clear without strife,
Fleeting to ocean,
 After this life.

'Tis loving and serving,
 The highest and best;
'Tis onward, unswerving,
 And this is true rest.

—Johann Wolfgang Goethe

Right Is Right

FOR right is right, since God is God,
 And right the day must win;
To doubt would be disloyalty,
 To falter would be sin.

—F. W. Faber

SATISFACTION

A Perfect Day

WHEN you come to the end of a perfect day,
    And you sit alone with your thought,
While the chimes ring out with a carol gay,
For the joy that the day has brought,
Do you think what the end of a perfect day
Can mean to a tired heart,
When the sun goes down with a flaming ray
And the dear friends have to part.

Well this is the end of a perfect day,
Near the end of a journey too,
But it leaves a thought that is big and strong,
With a wish that is kind and true,
For mem'ry has painted this perfect day
With colors that never fade,
And we find at the end of a perfect day,
The soul of a friend we've made.

—Carrie Jacobs-Bond

SCIENCE

Domestic Science

GIVE me a spoon of oleo, Ma,
    And the sodium alkali,
For I'm going to make a pie, Mamma!
    I'm going to make a pie.

For Dad will be hungry and tired, Ma,
    And his tissues will decompose;
So give me a gram of phosphate,
    And the carbon and cellulose.
Now give me a chunk of casein, Ma,
    To shorten the thermic fat,
And give me the oxygen bottle, Ma,
    And look at the thermostat.
And if the electric oven is cold
    Just turn it on half an ohm,
For I want to have supper ready
    As soon as Dad comes home.

—Farm Journal

SHIPWRECK

The Wreck of the Hesperus

IT was the schooner Hesperus,
    That sailed the wintry sea;
And the skipper had taken his little daughter,
    To bear him company.

Blue were her eyes as the fairy-flax,
    Her cheeks like the dawn of day,
And her bosom white as the hawthorn buds
    That ope in the month of May.

The skipper he stood beside the helm,
    His pipe was in his mouth,

And he watched how the veering flaw did blow
    The smoke now west, now south.

Then up and spake an old sailòr,
    Had sailed the Spanish Main,
"I pray thee put into yonder port,
    For I fear a hurricane.

"Last night, the moon had a golden ring,
    And to-night no moon we see!"
The skipper, he blew a whiff from his pipe,
    And a scornful laugh laughed he.

Colder and louder blew the wind,
    A gale from the north-east;
The snow fell hissing in the brine,
    And the billows frothed like yeast.

Down came the storm, and smote amain
    The vessel in its strength;
She shuddered and paused, like a frightened steed,
    Then leaped her cable's length.

"Come hither! come hither! my little daughter,
    And do not tremble so;
For I can weather the roughest gale
    That ever wind did blow."

He wrapped her warm in his seaman's coat
    Against the stinging blast;
He cut a rope from a broken spar,
    And bound her to the mast.

"O father! I hear the church-bells ring,
  O say what may it be?"
"'Tis the fog-bell on a rock-bound coast!"
  And he steered for the open sea.

"O father! I hear the sound of guns,
  O say what may it be?"
"Some ship in distress, that cannot live
  In such an angry sea!"

"O father! I see a gleaming light,
  O say what may it be?"
But the father answered never a word,—
  A frozen corpse was he.

Lashed to the helm, all stiff and stark,
  With his face turned to the skies,
The lantern gleamed through the gleaming snow
  On his fixed and glassy eyes.

Then the maiden clasped her hands and prayed
  That savèd she might be;
And she thought of Christ, who stilled the wave
  On the Lake of Galilee.

And fast through the midnight dark and drear,
  Through the whistling sleet and snow,
Like a sheeted ghost, the vessel swept
  Towards the reef of Norman's Woe.

And ever the fitful gusts between
  A sound came from the land;

It was the sound of the trampling surf,
  On the rocks and the hard sea-sand.

The breakers were right beneath her bows,
  She drifted a dreary wreck,
And a whooping billow swept the crew
  Like icicles from her deck.

She struck where the white and fleecy waves
  Looked soft as carded wool,
But the cruel rocks, they gored her side
  Like the horns of an angry bull.

Her rattling shrouds, all sheathed in ice,
  With the masts went by the board;
Like a vessel of glass, she stove and sank,
  Ho! ho! the breakers roared!

At daybreak, on the bleak sea-beach,
  A fisherman stood aghast,
To see the form of a maiden fair,
  Lashed close to a drifting mast!

—Henry W. Longfellow

SKEPTICISM

There Is No Unbelief

THERE is no unbelief,
  Whoever plants a seed beneath the sod,
And waits to see it push away the clod,
  Trusts he in God.

There is no unbelief,
Whoever says, when clouds are in the sky,
Be patient, heart, light breaketh by and by,
    Trusts the Most High.

There is no unbelief,
Whoever sees, 'neath winter's fields of snow,
The silent harvests of the future grow,
    God's power must know.

There is no unbelief,
Whoever lies down on his couch to sleep,
Content to lock each sense in slumber deep,
    Knows God will keep.

There is no unbelief,
Whoever says tomorrow, the unknown,
The future, trusts that power alone,
    None dare disown.

There is no unbelief,
The heart that looks on where dear eyelids close,
And dares to live when life has only woes,
    God's comfort knows.

There is no unbelief,
For thus by day and night unconsciously
The heart lives by the faith the lips deny,
    God knoweth why.

                              —*Elizabeth York Case*

Hammers and Anvil

I PAUSED last eve beside the blacksmith's door,
  And heard the anvil ring, the vesper's chime,
And looking in I saw upon the floor
  Old hammers, worn with beating years of time.
"How many anvils have you had?" said I,
  "To wear and batter all these hammers so?"
"Just one," he answered. Then with twinkling eye:
  "The anvil wears the hammers out, you know."
And so, I thought, the anvil of God's Word
  For ages skeptics' blows have beat upon
But though the noise of falling blows was heard
  The anvil is unchanged; the hammers gone.

—John Clifford, D.D.

Have You Lost Faith?

WHEN faith in God goes, man, the thinker, loses his
  greatest thought.
When faith in God goes, man, the worker, loses his greatest motive.
When faith in God goes, man, the sinner, loses his strongest help.
When faith in God goes, man, the sufferer, loses his secur-
  est refuge.
When faith in God goes, man, the lover, loses his fairest vision.
When faith in God goes, man, the mortal, loses his only
  hope.

—Anon.

339

Hustle and Grin

SMILE, and the world smiles with you;
"Knock," and you go it alone;
For the cheerful grin will let you in
Where the "kicker" is never known.

Growl, and the way looks dreary;
Laugh, and the path is bright;
For a welcome smile brings sunshine, while
A frown shuts out the light.

Sigh, and you "rake in" nothing;
Work, and the prize is won;
For the nervy man with backbone can
By nothing be outdone.

Hustle! and fortune awaits you;
Shirk! and defeat is sure;
For there's no chance of deliverance
For the chap who can't endure!

Sing, and the world's harmonious;
Grumble, and things go wrong,
And all the time you are out of rhyme
With the busy, hustling throng.

—*Anon.*

A Smile

LET others cheer the winning man,
    There's one I hold worth while;
'Tis he who does the best he can,
Then loses with a smile.
Beaten he is, but not to stay
Down with the rank and file;
That man will win some other day,
Who loses with a smile.

—Anon.

Smile

LIKE a bread without the spreadin',
    Like a puddin' without sauce,
Like a mattress without beddin',
    Like a cart without a hoss,
Like a door without a latch-string,
    Like a fence without a stile,
Like a dry an' barren creek bed—
    Is the face without a smile.

Like a house without a dooryard,
    Like a yard without a flower,
Like a clock without a main spring,
    That will never tell the hour;
A thing that sort o' makes yo' feel
    A hunger all the while—

Oh, the saddest sight that ever was
   Is a face without a smile!

The face of man was built for smiles,
   An' thereby he is blest
Above the critters of the field,
   The birds an' all the rest;
He's just a little lower
   Than the angels in the skies,
An' the reason is that he can smile;
   Therein his glory lies!

So smile an' don't forgit to smile,
   An' smile, an' smile ag'in;
'Twill help loosen up the cords o' care
   An' ease the weights o' sin;
'Twill help you all along the way,
   An' cheer you mile by mile;
An' so, whatever is your lot,
   Jes' smile, an' smile, an' smile.

—Anon.

Try Smiling

WHEN the weather suits you not,
   Try smiling.
When your coffee isn't hot,
   Try smiling.
When your neighbors don't do right,
Or your relatives all fight,
Sure 'tis hard, but then you might
   Try smiling.

Doesn't change the things, of course,
    Just smiling.
But it cannot make them worse,
    Just smiling.
And it seems to help your case,
Brightens up a gloomy place,
Then, it sort o' rests your face—
    Just smiling.

—Anon.

Let Us Smile

THE thing that goes the farthest toward making life
    worth while,
That costs the least and does the most, is just a pleasant
    smile.
The smile that bubbles from the heart that loves its
    fellow men,
Will drive away the clouds of gloom and coax the sun
    again.
It's full of worth and goodness, too, with manly kindness
    blent;
It's worth a million dollars, and it doesn't cost a cent.

There is no room for sadness when we see a cheery
    smile;
It always has the same good look; it's never out of style;
It nerves us on to try again when failure makes us blue;
The dimples of encouragement are good for me and you.
It pays the highest interest—for it is merely lent;
It's worth a million dollars, and it doesn't cost a cent.

343

A smile comes very easy—you can wrinkle up with cheer
A hundred times before you can squeeze out a salty tear;
It ripples out, moreover, to the heartstrings that will tug,
And always leaves an echo that is very like a hug.
So, smile away! Folks understand what by a smile is
    meant;
It's worth a million dollars, and it doesn't cost a cent.
                                        —*Wilbur D. Nesbit*

Keep Smiling

MY father smiled this morning when
        He came downstairs, you see,
At mother; and, when he smiled, then
        She turned and smiled at me;
And when she smiled at me I went
        And smiled at Mary Ann
Out in the kitchen; and she lent
        It to the baker's man.

So then he smiled at someone whom
        He saw when going by,
Who also smiled, and, ere he knew,
        Had twinkles in his eye;
So he went to his office then,
        And smiled right at his clerk,
Who put some more ink on his pen,
        And smiled back from his work.

And when this clerk went home he smiled
        Right at his wife; and she
Smiled over at his little child,
        As happy as could be;

And then the little girlie took
  The smile to school; and, when
She smiled at teacher from her book,
  Teacher smiled back again.

And then the teacher passed on one
  To little Jim McBride,
Who couldn't get his lessons done
  No matter how he tried;
And Jimmy took it home, and told
  How teacher smiled at him
When he was tired, and didn't scold,
  But said, "Don't worry, Jim."

And when I happened to be there
  That very night to play,
Jim's mother had a smile to spare,
  Which came across my way;
And then I took it for awhile
  Back home, and mother said:
"Here is that very selfsame smile
  Come back with us to bed."

—*Anon.*

SNOW

The Beautiful Snow

[During the early part of the Civil War, one dark Saturday night in midwinter, there died in the Commercial Hospital of Cincinnati a young woman over whose head only two and twenty summers had passed. She had once

345

been possessed of enviable beauty, and, as she herself said, had been "flattered and sought for the charms of her face." But alas! upon her fair brow was written that terrible word—prostitute. A highly educated and accomplished woman, she might have shone in the best of society. The evil hour that marked her downfall was the door from childhood, and, having spent a young life of disgrace and shame, the poor friendless one died the melancholy death of a broken-hearted outcast.

Among her personal effects was found the manuscript, "Beautiful Snow," which was at once carried to Enos B. Reed, at that time editor of *"The National Union."* In the columns of that paper on the morning following the girl's death, the poem appeared in print for the first time. When the paper containing the poem came out on Sunday morning, the body of the victim had not received burial.

Mr. T. B. Reed, one of the first American poets, was so taken with its strange pathos that he immediately followed the corpse to its final resting-place.

Such, according to the *"Boston Standard,"* are the plain facts concerning her whose "Beautiful Snow" shall long be remembered as one of the brightest poems in American literature.]

OH! the snow, the beautiful snow,
　Filling the sky and the earth below!
Over the housetops, over the street,
Over the heads of the people you meet;
　　　Dancing,
　　　　Flirting,
　　　　　Skimming along.

Beautiful snow! it can do no wrong.
Flying to kiss a fair lady's cheek,
Clinging to lips in a frolicsome freak,
Beautiful snow from the heaven above,
Pure as an angel, gentle as love!

Oh! the snow, the beautiful snow!
How the flakes gather and laugh as they go
Whirling about in their maddening fun!
It plays in its glee with every one,
   Chasing,
    Laughing,
     Hurrying by;
It lights on the face and it sparkles the eye,
And even the dogs, with a bark and a bound,
Snap at the crystals that eddy around.
The town is alive and its heart in a glow,
To welcome the coming of beautiful snow!

How the wild crowd goes swaying along,
Hailing each other with humor and song!
How the gay sledges, like meteors, flash by,
Bright for a moment, then lost to the eye;
   Ringing,
    Singing,
     Dancing they go
Over the crust of the beautiful snow—
Snow so pure when it falls from the sky,
To be trampled in mud by the crowd rushing by,
To be trampled and tracked by the thousands of feet,
Till it blends with the horrible filth in the street.
Once I was pure as the snow—but I fell!

347

Fell, like the snowflakes, from heaven—to hell;
Fell to be scoffed, to be spit on and beat;
   Pleading,
    Cursing,
     Dreading to die,
Selling my soul to whoever would buy,
Dealing in shame for a morsel of bread,
Hating the living and fearing the dead.
Merciful God! have I fallen so low?
And yet I was once like the beautiful snow!

Once I was fair as the beautiful snow,
With an eye like its crystal, a heart like its glow;
Once I was loved for my innocent grace,
Flattered and sought for the charms of my face!
   Father,
    Mother,
     Sisters, all,
God and myself, I have lost by my fall.
The veriest wretch that goes shivering by
Will make a wide sweep lest I wander too nigh;
For of all that is on or about me, I know,
There is nothing that's pure but the beautiful snow.

How strange it should be that the beautiful snow
Should fall on a sinner with nowhere to go!
How strange it would be, when the night comes again,
If the snow and the ice struck my desperate brain!
   Fainting,
    Freezing,
     Dying alone;
Too wicked for prayer, too weak for my moan

To be heard in the streets of the crazy town,
Gone mad in the joy of the snow coming down;
To lie and to die in my terrible woe,
With a bed and a shroud of the beautiful snow.

—John W. Watson

The First Snowfall

THE snow had begun in the gloaming,
  And busily all the night
Had been heaping field and highway
  With a silence deep and white.

Every pine and fir and hemlock
  Wore ermine too dear for an earl,
And the poorest twig on the elm tree
  Was ridged inch-deep with pearl.

From sheds new-roofed with Carrara
  Came Chanticleer's muffled crow;
The stiff rails were softened to swan's-down,
  And still fluttered down the snow.

I stood and watched by the window
  The noiseless work of the sky,
And the sudden flurries of snowbirds,
  Like brown leaves whirling by.

I thought of a mound in sweet Auburn
  Where a little headstone stood;

How the flakes were folding it gently
    As did robins the babes in the wood.

Up spoke our own little Mabel,
    Saying, "Father, who makes it snow?"
And I told of the good All-father
    Who cares for us here below.

Again I looked at the snowfall,
    And thought of the leaden sky
That arched o'er our first great sorrow,
    When the mound was heaped so high.

I remembered the gradual patience
    That fell from that cloud like snow,
Flake by flake, healing and hiding
    The scar that renewed our woe.

And again to the child I whispered,
    "The snow that husheth all,
Darling, the merciful Father
    Alone can make it fall."

Then, with eyes that saw not, I kissed her
    And she, kissing back, could not know
That *my* kiss was given to her sister,
    Folded close under deepening snow.

                    —*James Russell Lowell*

Solitude

(From "The Search After Happiness")

SWEET Solitude, thou placid queen,
  Of modest air, and brow serene!
'Tis thou inspirest the sage's themes,
The poet's visionary dreams.

Parent of Virtue, nurse of Thought,
By thee were saints and patriarchs taught;
Wisdom from thee her treasures drew,
And in thy lap fair Science grew.

Whate'er exalts, refines and charms,
Invites to thought, to virtue warms,
Whate'er is perfect, fair, and good,
We owe to thee, sweet Solitude!

In these blest shades, oh, still maintain
Thy peaceful, unmolested reign!
Let no disordered thoughts intrude
On thy repose, sweet Solitude!

With thee the charms of life shall last,
Although its rosy bloom be past,
Shall still endure when time shall spread
His silver blossoms o'er my head.

No more with this vain world perplexed,
Thou shalt prepare me for the next;

The springs of life shall gently cease,
And angels point the way to peace.

—Hannah More

SUCCESS

If—

IF you can keep your head when all about you
  Are losing theirs and blaming it on you;
If you can trust yourself when all men doubt you,
  But make allowance for their doubting too;
If you can wait and not be tired by waiting,
  Or, being lied about, don't deal in lies,
Or, being hated, don't give way to hating,
  And yet don't look too good, nor talk too wise;

If you can dream—and not make dreams your master;
  If you can think—and not make thoughts your aim;
If you can meet with triumph and disaster
  And treat those two impostors just the same;
If you can bear to hear the truth you've spoken
  Twisted by knaves to make a trap for fools,
Or watch the things you gave your life to broken,
  And stoop and build 'em up with wornout tools;

If you can make one heap of all your winnings
  And risk it on one turn of pitch-and-toss,
And lose, and start again at your beginnings
  And never breathe a word about your loss;

If you can force your heart and nerve and sinew
    To serve your turn long after they are gone,
And so hold on when there is nothing in you
    Except the Will which says to them: "Hold on";

If you can talk with crowds and keep your virtue,
    Or walk with kings—nor lose the common touch;
If neither foes nor loving friends can hurt you;
    If all men count with you, but none too much;
If you can fill the unforgiving minute
    With sixty seconds' worth of distance run—
Yours is the Earth and everything that's in it,
    And—which is more—you'll be a Man, my son!

                        —*Rudyard Kipling*

Success! [1]

IT'S doing your job the best you can,
    And being just to your fellow man;
It's making money, but holding friends,
And staying true to your aims and ends;
It's figuring how and learning why,
And looking forward and thinking high;
And dreaming a little and doing much;
It's keeping always in closest touch
With what is finest in word and deed;
It's being thorough, yet making speed;
It's daring blithely the field of chance
While making labor a brave romance;
It's going onward despite defeat
And fighting staunchly, but keeping sweet;

[1] Used by permission of the author.

It's being clean and it's playing fair;
It's laughing lightly at Dame Despair;
It's looking up at the stars above,
And drinking deeply of life and love;
It's struggling on with the will to win,
But taking loss with a cheerful grin;
It's sharing sorrow, and work, and mirth,
And making better this good old earth;
It's serving, striving through strain and stress,
It's doing your noblest—that's Success!

—*Berton Braley*

Settin' on de Fence

HONEY, see dat jay-bird dah,
  Sittin' on de fence?
Firs' he look dis way, den dat,
  Lak he ain't got sense.
Flap his wings an' crane his neck—
  Ain' no use to try
Figu'in from the way he ac's
  Wha he's gwine to fly.

Lookit how dat squirrel am perched
  On dat topmos' rail.
See him? how he turn his haid,
  How he flip his tail?
Watch him close as you can watch;
  Den you ain't begun
Findin' out which way he's gwine
  When he sta'ts to run!

Sittin' on de fence, mah boy,
  Wond'rin what to do
Ain' gwine bring no bacon home—
  No suh! Not fo' you.
Know yo' min' an' go ahead;
  Do de bes' you can!
Dat's de way you proves yo'se'f
  An' shows yo'se'f a man.

—Anon.

To Whom Shall the World Henceforth Belong? [1]

TO whom shall the world henceforth belong.
  And who shall go up and possess it?

—To the Great-Hearts—the Strong
Who will suffer no wrong,
And who shall go up and possess it.

—To the Men of Bold Sight
Whose souls, seized of Light,
Found a work to be done and have done it.

—To the Valiant who fought
For a soul-lifting thought,
Saw the fight to be won and have won it.

—To the Men of Great Mind
Set on lifting their kind,
Who, regardless of danger, will do it.

[1] Used by permission of author.

—To the Men of Good Will,
Who would cure all Life's ill,
And whose passion for peace will ensue it.

—To the Men who will bear
Their full share of Life's care,
And will rest not till wrongs be all righted.

—To the Stalwarts who toil
'Mid the seas of turmoil,
Till the Haven of Safety be sighted.

—To the Men of Good Fame
Who everything claim—
This world and the next—in their Master's great name—

—To these shall the world henceforth belong,
And they shall go up and possess it;
Overmuch, overlong, has the world suffered wrong,
We are here by God's help to redress it.

—*John Oxenham*

One Thing

THE man who seeks one thing in life, and but one,
   May hope to achieve it before life is done;
But he who seeks all things wherever he goes,
Only reaps from the hopes which around him he sows
A harvest of barren regrets.

—*Owen Meredith*

356

TEMPTATION

The Spider and the Fly

(A Fable)

"WILL you walk into my parlor?" said the spider to
the fly;
" 'Tis the prettiest little parlor that ever you did spy.
The way into my parlor is up a winding stair,
And I have many pretty things to show when you are
there."
"O no, no," said the little fly, "to ask me is in vain,
For who goes up your winding stair can ne'er come down
again."

"I'm sure you must be weary, dear, with soaring up so
high;
Will you rest upon my little bed?" said the spider to the
fly.
"There are pretty curtains drawn around, the sheets are
fine and thin,
And if you like to rest awhile, I'll snugly tuck you in."
"O no, no," said the little fly, "for I've often heard it
said,
They *never, never wake* again, who sleep upon *your* bed."

Said the cunning spider to the fly, "Dear friend, what
shall I do,
To prove the warm affection I've always felt for you?
I have within my pantry good store of all that's nice;

357

I'm sure you're very welcome; will you please to take a
slice?"
"O no, no," said the little fly, "kind sir, that cannot be;
I've heard what's in your pantry, and I do not wish to
see."

"Sweet creature!" said the spider, "you're witty and
you're wise,
How handsome are your gauzy wings, how brilliant are
your eyes!
I have a little looking-glass upon my parlor shelf,
If you'll step in one moment, dear, you shall behold
yourself."
"I thank you, gentle sir," she said, "for what you're
pleased to say,
And bidding you good-morning *now,* I'll call *another*
day."

The spider turned him round about, and went into his
den,
For well he knew the silly fly would soon be back again:
So he wove a subtle web, in a little corner sly,
And set his table ready to dine upon the fly.
Then he came out to his door again, and merrily did sing
"Come hither, hither, pretty fly, with the pearl and silver
wing:
Your robes are green and purple; there's a crest upon
your head;
Your eyes are like the diamond bright, but mine are
dull as lead."

Alas, alas! how very soon this silly little fly,
Hearing his wily flattering words, came slowly flitting by.
With buzzing wings she hung aloft, then near and nearer
  drew
Thinking only of her brilliant eyes, and green and pur-
  ple hue;
Thinking only of her crested head—*poor foolish thing!*
  At last,
Up jumped the cunning spider, and fiercely held her fast.
He dragged her up his winding stair, into his dismal den,
Within his little parlor; but she ne'er came out again!

And now, dear little children, who may this story read,
To idle, silly, flattering words, I pray you ne'er give
  heed;
Unto an evil counselor close heart, and ear, and eye,
And take a lesson from this tale of the Spider and the Fly.

—*Mary Howitt*

THANKSGIVING

We Thank Thee, Lord [1]

FOR all thy ministries—
  For morning mist and gently falling dew;
For summer rains, for winter ice and snow;
For whispering wind and purifying storm;
For the reft clouds that show the tender blue;
For the forked flash and long, tumultuous roll;
For mighty rains that wash the dim earth clean;
For the sweet promise of the seven-fold bow;

[1] Used by permission of the author.

For the soft sunshine and the still, calm night;
For dimpled laughter of soft summer seas;
For latticed splendor of the sea-borne moon;
For gleaming sands and granite-fronted cliffs;
For Might so mighty and for Love so true, with equal
   mind,
We thank thee, Lord.

—John Oxenham

Thanksgiving [1]

FOR all things beautiful, and good, and true;
   For things that seemed not good yet turned to good;
For all the sweet compulsions of Thy will
That chastened, tried, and wrought us to Thy shape;
For things unnumbered that we take of right,
And value first when they are withheld;
For light and air; sweet sense of sound and smell;
For ears to hear the heavenly harmonies;
For eyes to see the unseen in the seen;
For vision of the Worker in the work;
For hearts to apprehend Thee everywhere;—
We thank Thee, Lord.

—John Oxenham

[1] Used by permission of the author.

Thanks for Everything

FOR all that God in mercy sends;
  For health and children, home and friends,
For comfort in the time of need,
For every kindly word and deed,
For happy thoughts and holy talk,
For guidance in our daily walk,
  For everything give thanks!

For beauty in this world of ours,
For verdant grass and lovely flowers,
For song of birds, for hum of bees,
For refreshing summer breeze,
For hill and plain, for streams and wood,
For the great ocean's mighty flood,
  For everything give thanks!

For sweet sleep which comes with night,
For the returning morning's light,
For the bright sun that shines on high,
For the stars glittering in the sky,
For these and everything we see,
O Lord, our hearts we lift to thee.
  For everything give thanks!

—Miss Helen Isabella Tupper

The Deacon's Masterpiece
or "The One-Hoss Shay"

HAVE you heard of the wonderful one-hoss shay,
That was built in such a logical way
It ran a hundred years to a day,
And then, of a sudden, it—ah, but stay,
I'll tell you what happened without delay,
Scaring the parson into fits,
Frightening people out of their wits,—
Have you heard of that, I say?

Seventeen hundred and fifty-five.
Georgius Secundus was then alive,—
Snuffy old drone from the German hive.
That was the year when Lisbon-town
Saw the earth open and gulp her down,
And Braddock's army was done so brown,
Left without a scalp to its crown.
It was on the terrible Earthquake-day
That the Deacon finished the one-hoss shay.

Now in building of chaises, I tell you what,
There is always *somewhere* a weakest spot,—
In hub, tire, felloe, in spring or thill,
In panel, or crossbar, or floor, or sill,
In screw, bolt, thoroughbrace,—lurking still,
Find it somewhere you must and will,—
Above or below, or within or without,—

And that's the reason, beyond a doubt,
A chaise *breaks down*, but doesn't *wear out*.

But the Deacon swore (as Deacons do),
With an "I dew vum," or an "I tell yeou,")
He would build one shay to beat the taown
'N the keounty 'n' all the kentry raoun';
It should be so built that it *couldn'* break daown:
—"Fur," said the Deacon, " 't's mighty plain
Thut the weakes' places mus' stan' the strain;
'N the way t' fix it, uz I maintain,
                    Is only jest
T' make that place uz strong uz the rest."

So the Deacon inquired of the village folk
Where he could find the strongest oak,
That couldn't be split nor bent nor broke,—
That was for spokes and floor and sills;
He sent for lancewood to make the thills;
The crossbars were ash, from the straightest trees;
The panels of white-wood, that cuts like cheese,
But lasts like iron for things like these;
The hubs of logs from the "Settler's ellum,"—
Last of its timber,—they couldn't sell 'em,
Never an axe had seen their chips,
And the wedges flew from between their lips,
Their blunt ends frizzled like celery-tips;
Step and prop-iron, bolt and screw,
Spring, tire, axle, and linchpin too,
Steel of the finest, bright and blue;
Thoroughbrace bison-skin, thick and wide;
Boot, top, dasher, from tough old hide

Found in the pit when the tanner died.
That was the way he "put her through."—
"There!" said the Deacon, "naow she'll dew!"

Do! I tell you, I rather guess
She was a wonder, and nothing less!
Colts grew horses, beards turned gray,
Deacon and deaconess dropped away,
Children and grandchildren—where were they?
But there stood the stout old one-hoss shay
As fresh as on Lisbon-earthquake-day!

EIGHTEEN HUNDRED;—it came and found
The Deacon's masterpiece strong and sound.
Eighteen hundred increased by ten;—
"Hahnsum kerridge" they called it then.
Eighteen hundred and twenty came;—
Running as usual; much the same.
Thirty and forty at last arrive,
And then come fifty, and FIFTY-FIVE.

Little of all we value here
Wakes on the morn of its hundredth year
Without both feeling and looking queer.
In fact, there's nothing that keeps its youth,
So far as I know, but a tree and truth.
(This is a moral that runs at large;
Take it. You're welcome. No extra charge.)
FIRST OF NOVEMBER,—the Earthquake-day,—
There are traces of age in the one-hoss shay,
A general flavor of mild decay,
But nothing local as one may say.

There couldn't be,—for the Deacon's art
Had made it so like in every part
That there wasn't a chance for one to start.
For the wheels were just as strong as the thills,
And the floor was just as strong as the sills,
And the panels just as strong as the floor,
And the whippletree neither less nor more,
And the back cross-bar as strong as the fore,
And spring and axle and hub *encore.*
And yet, *as a whole,* it is past a doubt
In another hour it will be *worn out!*

First of November, 'Fifty-five!
This morning the parson takes a drive.
Now, small boys, get out of the way!
Here comes the wonderful one-hoss shay,
Drawn by a rat-tailed, ewe-necked bay.
"Huddup!" said the parson. Off went they.
The parson was working his Sunday's text,—
Had got to *fifthly,* and stopped perplexed
At what the—Moses—was coming next.
All at once the horse stood still,
Close by the meet'n'-house on the hill.
—First a shiver, and then a thrill,
Then something decidedly like a spill,—
And the parson was sitting up on a rock,
At half-past nine by the meet'n'-house clock,—
Just the hour of the Earthquake shock!
—What do you think the parson found,
When he got up and stared around?
The poor old chaise in a heap or mound,

As if it had been to the mill and ground!
You see, of course, if you're not a dunce,
How it went to pieces all at once,—
All at once, and nothing first,—
Just as bubbles do when they burst.

End of the wonderful one-hoss shay,
Logic is logic. That's all I say.

—*Oliver Wendell Holmes*

TIME

The Old Clock on the Stairs

SOMEWHAT back from the village street,
Stands the old-fashioned country seat.
Across its antique portico
Tall poplar trees their shadows throw;
And from its station in the hall
An ancient time-piece says to all,
  "Forever—never!
  Never—forever!"

Half way up the stairs it stands,
And points and beckons with its hands,
From its case of massive oak,
Like a monk, who under his cloak
Crosses himself, and sighs, alas!
With sorrowful voice, to all who pass,
  "Forever—never!
  Never—forever!"

By day its voice is low and light,
But in the silent dead of night,
Distinct as a passing footstep's fall
It echoes along the vacant hall,
Along the ceiling, along the floor,
And seems to say at each chamber door,
  "Forever—never!
   Never—forever!"

In that mansion used to be
Free-hearted hospitality;
His great fires by the chimney roared,
The stranger feasted at his board;
But like the skeleton at the feast,
The warning time-piece never ceased,
  "Forever—never!
   Never—forever!"

There groups of merry children played,
There youth and maidens dreaming strayed;
O precious hours, O golden prime,
And affluence of love and time;
E'en as a miser counts his gold,
Those hours the ancient time-piece told,
  "Forever—never!
   Never—forever!"

From the chamber, clothed in white,
The bride came forth on her wedding-night;
There in that silent room below,
The dead lay in his shroud of snow;
And in the hush that followed the prayer,

We heard the old clock on the stair,—
  "Forever—never!
  Never—forever!"

All are scattered now and fled:
Some are married, some are dead;
And when I ask, with throbs of pain,
"Ah, when shall they all meet again,
As in the days long since gone by?"
The ancient time-piece makes reply,
  "Forever—never!
  Never—forever!"

Never here, forever there!
Where all parting, pain and care,
And death and time shall disappear,
Forever there, but never here!
The horologe of eternity
Sayeth this incessantly,
  "Forever—never!
  Never—forever!"

               —Henry W. Longfellow

Advertisement of a Lost Day

LOST! lost! lost!
  A gem of countless price,
Cut from the living rock,
  And graved in Paradise.
Set round with three times eight
  Large diamonds, clear and bright,

And each with sixty smaller ones,
    All changeful as the light.

Lost—where the thoughtless throng
    In fashion's mazes wind,
Where trilleth folly's song,
    Leaving a sting behind;
Yet to my hand 'twas given
    A golden harp to buy,
Such as the white-robed choir attune
    To deathless minstrelsy.

Lost! lost! lost!
    I feel all search is vain;
That gem of countless cost
    Can ne'er be mine again.
I offer no reward,
    For till these heart-strings sever,
I know that Heaven-intrusted gift
    Is reft away forever.

But when the sea and land
    Like burning scroll have fled,
I'll see it in His hand
    Who judgeth quick and dead;
And when of scath and loss
    That man can ne'er repair,
The dread inquiry meets my soul,
    What shall it answer there?

                    —*Mrs. Lydia Sigourney*

He Lives Long Who Lives Well

WOULDST thou live long? The only means are these—
'Bove Galen's diet, or Hippocrates':
Strive to live well; tread in the upright ways,
And rather count thy actions than thy days:
Then thou hast lived enough amongst us here,
For every day well spent I count a year.
Live well, and then, how soon soe'er thou die,
Thou art of age to claim eternity.
But he that outlives Nestor, and appears
To have passed the date of gray Methuselah's years,
If he his life to sloth and sin doth give,
I say he only WAS—he did not LIVE.

—*Thomas Randolph*

The Isle of the Long Ago

OH, a wonderful stream is the River Time,
As it runs through the realm of tears,
With a faultless rhythm and a musical rhyme,
And a boundless sweep and a surge sublime,
As it blends with the Ocean of Years.

How the winters are drifting like flakes of snow,
And the summers like buds between,
And the year in the sheaf, so they come and they go,
On the river's breast, with its ebb and flow,
As it glides in the shadow and sheen.

There's a magical isle up the river Time,
　　Where the softest of airs are playing;
There's a cloudless sky and a tropical clime,
And a song as sweet as a vesper chime,
　　And the Junes with the roses are straying.

And the name of that Isle is the Long Ago,
　　And we bury our treasures there;
There are brows of beauty and bosoms of snow;
There are heaps of dust—but we loved them so!
　　There are trinkets and tresses of hair.

There are fragments of song that nobody sings;
　　And a part of an infant's prayer;
There's a lute unswept, and a harp without strings;
There are broken vows and pieces of rings,
　　And the garments she used to wear.

There are hands that are waved when the fairy shore
　　By the mirage is lifted in air,
And we sometimes hear through the turbulent roar
Sweet voices we heard in the days gone before,
　　When the wind down the river is fair.

Oh, remembered for aye be the blessed Isle,
　　All the day of our life until night;
When the evening comes with its beautiful smile,
And our eyes are closing to slumber awhile,
　　May that "Green wood" of Soul be in sight!

　　　　　　　　　　—Benjamin Franklin Taylor

Woodman, Spare That Tree

WOODMAN, spare that tree!
　Touch not a single bough!
In youth it sheltered me,
　And I'll protect it now.
'Twas my forefather's hand
　That placed it near his cot:
There, woodman, let it stand;
　Thy ax shall harm it not!

That old familiar tree,
　Whose glory and renown
Are spread o'er land and sea—
　And wouldst thou hew it down?
Woodman, forbear thy stroke!
　Cut not its earth-bound ties!
Oh! spare that aged oak,
　Now towering to the skies.

When but an idle boy
　I sought its grateful shade;
In all their gushing joy,
　Here, too, my sisters played.
My mother kissed me here,
　My father pressed my hand:
Forgive this foolish tear,
　But let that old oak stand!

My heart-strings round thee cling,
   Close as thy bark, old friend!
Here shall the wild bird sing,
   And still thy branches bend.
Old tree, the storm still brave!
   And, woodman, leave the spot!
While I've a hand to save
   Thy ax shall harm it not.

                  —*George P. Morris*

What Do We Plant?

WHAT do we plant when we plant the tree?
   We plant the ship, which will cross the sea.
We plant the mast to carry the sails,
We plant the plank to withstand the gales,
The keel, the keelson, and beam and knee;
We plant the ship when we plant the tree.

What do we plant when we plant the tree?
We plant the houses for you and me.
We plant the rafters, the shingles, the floors,
We plant the studding, the lath, the doors,
The beams and siding, all parts that be;
We plant the house when we plant the tree.

What do we plant when we plant the tree?
A thousand things that we daily see,
We plant the spire that out-towers the crag,
We plant the staff for our country's flag—

We plant the shade, from the hot sun free;
We plant all these when we plant the tree.

—Henry Abbey

Plant a Tree

HE who plants a tree
   Plants a hope.
  Rootlets up through fibres blindly grope;
Leaves unfold into horizons free.
   So man's life must climb
   From the clods of time
   Unto heavens sublime.
Canst thou prophesy, thou little tree,
What the glory of thy boughs shall be?

He who plants a tree
   Plants a joy:
   Plants a comfort that will never cloy;
Every day a fresh reality,
   Beautiful and strong,
   To whose shelter throng
   Creatures blithe with song.
If thou couldst but know, thou happy tree,
Of the bliss that shall inhabit thee!

He who plants a tree,—
   He plants peace.
  Under its green curtains jargons cease.
Leaf and zephyr murmur soothingly;
   Shadows soft with sleep

Down tired eyelids creep,
Balm of slumber deep.
Never hast thou dreamed thou blessèd tree,
Of the benediction thou shalt be.

He who plants a tree,—
He plants youth;
Vigor won for centuries in sooth;
Life of time, that hints eternity!
Boughs their strength uprear;
New shoots, every year,
On old growths appear;
Thou shalt teach the ages, sturdy tree,
Youth of soul is immortality.

He who plants a tree,—
He plants love,
Tents of coolness spreading out above
Wayfarers he may not live to see.
Gifts that grow are best;
Hands that bless are blest;
Plant! life does the rest!
Heaven and earth help him who plants a tree,
And his work its own reward shall be.

—*Lucy Larcom*

The Primeval Forest

(*From the Introduction of "Evangeline"*)

THIS is the forest primeval. The murmuring pines
and the hemlocks,

Bearded with moss, and in garments green, indistinct in
the twilight,
Stand like Druids of old, with voices sad and prophetic;
Stand like harpers hoar, with beards that rest on their
bosoms.
Loud from its rocky caverns, the deep-voiced neighboring
ocean
Speaks, and in accents disconsolate answers the wail of
the forest.
This is the forest primeval; but where are the hearts that
beneath it
Leaped like the roe when he hears in the woodland the
voice of the huntsman?

—Henry Wadsworth Longfellow

Trees[1]

I THINK that I shall never see
A poem lovely as a tree.

A tree whose hungry mouth is prest
Against the earth's sweet flowing breast;

A tree that looks at God all day,
And lifts her leafy arms to pray;

A tree that may in summer wear
A nest of robins in her hair;

Upon whose bosom snow has lain;
Who intimately lives with rain.

Poems are made by fools like me,
But only God can make a tree.

—Joyce Kilmer

What God Has Promised

GOD hath not promised
Skies always blue,
Flower-strewn pathways
All our lives through;
God hath not promised
Sun without rain,
Joy without sorrow,
Peace without pain.

But God hath promised
Strength for the day,
Rest for the labour
Light for the way,
Grace for the trials,
Help from above,
Unfailing sympathy,
Undying Love.

—*Miss Annie Johnson Flint*

If All the Skies Were Sunshine

IF all the skies were sunshine
Our faces would be fain
To feel once more upon them
The cooling splash of rain.

377

If all the world were music,
  Our hearts would often long
For one sweet strain of silence
  To break the endless song.

If life were always merry
  Our souls would seek relief
And rest from weary laughter
  In the quiet arms of grief.

—Henry Van Dyke

Trouble

BETTER never trouble Trouble
  Until Trouble troubles you;
For you only make your trouble
  Double-trouble when you do;
And the trouble—like a bubble—
  That you're troubling about,
May be nothing but a cipher
  With its rim rubbed out.

—David Keppel

Calvary and Easter

A SONG of sunshine through the rain,
  Of Spring across the snow;
A balm to heal the hurts of pain,
A peace surpassing woe.

Lift up your heads, ye sorrowing ones,
And be ye glad of heart,
For Calvary and Easter Day,
Earth's saddest day and gladdest day,
Were just three days apart!

With shudder of despair and loss
The world's deep heart was wrung,
As, lifted high upon His cross,
The Lord of Glory hung—
When rocks were rent, and ghostly forms
Stole forth in street and mart;
But Calvary and Easter Day,
Earth's blackest day and whitest day,
Were just three days apart.

—*Susan Coolidge*

TRUSTING GOD

Psalm 23 (Poetical Version)

THE Lord's my shepherd; I'll not want;
    He makes me down to lie
In pastures green: He leadeth me
    The quiet waters by.

My soul He doth restore again;
    And me to walk doth make
Within the paths of righteousness,
    E'en for His own name's sake.

Yea, though I walk through death's dark vale,
　　Yet will I fear none ill;
For Thou art with me: and Thy rod
　　And staff me comfort still.

My table Thou hast furnished
　　In presence of my foes;
My head Thou dost with oil anoint,
　　And my cup overflows.

Goodness and mercy all my life
　　Shall surely follow me;
And in God's house forever more
　　My dwelling-place shall be.

—The Bible

Rocked in the Cradle of the Deep

ROCKED in the cradle of the deep,
　　I lay me down in peace to sleep;
Secure I rest upon the wave,
For Thou, O Lord, hast power to save.

I know Thou wilt not slight my call,
For Thou dost mark the sparrow's fall;
And calm and peaceful is my sleep,
Rocked in the cradle of the deep.

And such the trust that still were mine,
Though stormy winds swept o'er the brine,

380

Or though the tempest's fiery breath
Roused me from sleep to wreck and death.

In ocean's caves still safe with Thee,
The germ of immortality;
And calm and peaceful is my sleep,
Rocked in the cradle of the deep.

—*Emma Willard*

Disappointment

"DISAPPOINTMENT—His appointment,"
   Change one letter, then I see
That the thwarting of my purpose
   Is God's better choice for me.
His appointment must be blessing,
   Though it may come in disguise,
For the end from the beginning
   Open to His wisdom lies.

"Disappointment—His appointment,"
   Whose? The Lord's, Who loves me best
Understands and knows me fully,
   Who my faith and love would test;
For, like loving earthly parent,
   He rejoices when He knows
That His child accepts, unquestioned,
   All that from His wisdom flows.

"Disappointment—His appointment,"
   "No good thing will He withhold,"

From denials oft we gather
   Treasures of His love untold.
Well He knows each broken purpose
   Leads to fuller, deeper trust,
And the end of all His dealings
   Proves our God is wise and just.

"Disappointment—His appointment,"
   Lord, I take it, then, as such,
Like the clay in hands of potter,
   Yielding wholly to Thy touch,
All my life's plan is Thy moulding,
   Not one single .choice be mine;
Let me answer, unrepining—
   Father, "Not my will, but Thine."

                        —Anon.

God Knoweth Best

PRECIOUS thought, my Father knoweth,
   In His love I rest;
For whate'er my Father doeth
   Must be always best.
Well I know the heart that planneth,
   Nought but good for me;
Joy and sorrow interwoven;
   Love in all I see.

Precious thought, my Father knoweth,
   Careth for His child;

Bids me nestle closer to Him
  When the storm beats wild.
Tho' my earthly hopes are shattered,
  And the tear drops fall,
Yet He is Himself my solace,
  Yea, my Friend, my all.

Oh, to trust Him then more fully,
  Just to simply move
In the conscious, calm enjoyment
  Of the Father's love;
Knowing that life's chequered pathway
  Leadeth to His rest,
Satisfied the way He taketh
  Must be always best.

—Anon.

Life and the Weaver

LIFE is a woven fabric;
  The pattern and web are wrought
By the dark threads and the golden
  That into the loom are shot.

You cannot judge God's purpose
  By the thrust of a single thread,
What to you may be dark, mysterious,
  May be gloriously bright instead.

For He holds in mind a pattern
  As fair as His love is strong,

Which grows each day in the weaving;
  Not a single thread goes wrong.

No warp in His hands shall tangle,
  No slumber His eyelids close;
We only can thwart His purpose
  When our stubborn wills impose.

Our tangled and broken efforts
  To walk in His kind commands
Will give life an added luster,
  Restored by His loving hands.

So trust in the Weaver's wisdom,
  In His love and unfailing care,
And the fabric of life, completed,
  Some day will be wondrous fair.

—A. W. Dewar

The Tapestry Weavers

LET us take to our hearts a lesson—no lesson can
  braver be—
From the ways of the tapestry weavers on the other side
  of the sea.
Above their heads the pattern hangs, they study it with
  care,
And while their fingers deftly work, their eyes are fas-
  tened there.
They tell this curious thing, besides, of the patient, plod-
  ding weaver;

He works on the wrong side evermore, but works for the
right side ever.
It is only when the weaving stops, and the web is tossed
and turned,
And he sees his real handiwork, that his marvelous skill
is learned.
Ah, the sight of its delicate beauty, how it pays him for
all it cost,
No rarer, daintier work than his was ever done by the
frost.
Thus the master bringeth him golden hire and giveth
him praises as well,
And how happy the heart of the weaver is, no tongue
but his own can tell.

The years of man are the looms of God let down from
the place of the sun,
Wherein we are weaving always, till the mystic web is
done.
Weaving kindly; but weaving surely, each for himself,
his fate,
We may not see how the right side looks, we can only
weave and wait.
But looking above for the pattern, no weaver hath need
to fear,
Only let him look clear into heaven—the perfect pattern
is there.
If he keeps the face of the Savior forever and always
in sight,
His toil shall be sweeter than honey, his weaving is sure
to be right.

And when his task is ended, and the web is turned and
    shown,
He shall hear the voice of the Master, it shall say to
    him, "Well done!"
And the white-winged angels of heaven to bear him
    thence shall come down,
And God shall give him gold for his hire, not coin, but
    a fadeless crown.

—Rev. Anson J. Chester, D.D.

Thy Will Be Done

NOT in dumb resignation
    We lift our heads on high;
Not like the nerveless fatalist
    Content to do and die;
Our faith springs like the eagle,
    Who soars to meet the sun,
And cries exultingly unto Thee,
    "O Lord, Thy will be done."

Thy will it bids the weak be strong,
    It bids the strong be just.
No lips to fawn, no hands to beg,
    No brow to seek the dust.
Wherever a man oppresses man
    Beneath the liberal sun,
O Lord, be there! Thine arm to bare;
    Thy righteous will be done.

—John Hay

He Careth

WHAT can it mean? Is it aught to Him,
 That the nights are long and the days are dim?
Can He be touched by the grief I bear,
Which saddens the heart and whitens the hair?
About His throne are eternal calms
And strong glad music of happy psalms,
And bliss unruffled by any strife—
How can He care for my little life?

And yet, I want Him to care for me,
While I live in this world where sorrows be!
When the lights die down from the path I take,
When strength is feeble and friends forsake,
When love, and music that once did bless,
Have left me in silence and loneliness,
And my life song changes to sobbing prayers,
Then my heart cries out for a God who cares.

When shadows hang over the whole day long,
And my spirit is bowed with shame and wrong,
When I am not good, and the deeper shade
Of conscious sin makes me afraid,
And this busy world has too much to do
To stay in its course to help me through,
And I long for a Saviour—can it be
That the God of the universe cares for me?

O wonderful story of deathless love!
Each child is dear to that heart above;
He fights for me when I cannot fight;

He comforts me in the gloom of night;
He lifts the burden, for He is strong;
He stills the sigh and awakes the song;
The sorrow that bears me down, He bears,
And loves and pardons, because He cares.

Let all who are sad take heart again;
We are not alone in our hours of pain;
Our Father stoops from His throne above;
To soothe and quiet us with His love;
He leaves us not when the storm is high;
And we have safety, for He is nigh;
Can there be trouble, which He doth not share?
Oh, rest in peace, for the Lord will care!

—*Marianne Farningham*

Trust the Great Artist

TRUST the Great Artist. He
Who paints the sky and sea
With shadowed blue, who clothes the land
In garb of green, and in the spring
Sets all earth blossoming—
He guides your destiny.

The magic hand
That colors dawn with flaming rose,
That ere the falling night,
For every soul's delight,
Pours out the streaming gold—
That hand too holds your life.

His grasp, amid the strife,
Would shape you to His will:
Let Him his wish fulfill.
What though the testings irk,
Fret not: mar not His work.
Trust the Great Artist, He
Who made the earth and sea.

—*Thomas Curtis Clark*

He Leadeth Me

HE leadeth me! oh! blessed thought,
O words with heavenly comfort fraught;
Whate'er I do, where'er I be,
Still 'tis God's hand that leadeth me.

Chorus
He leadeth me! He leadeth me!
By His own hand He leadeth me;
His faithful follower I would be,
For by His hand He leadeth me.

Sometimes 'mid scenes of deepest gloom,
Sometimes where Eden's bowers bloom,
By waters still, o'er troubled sea—
Still 'tis God's hand that leadeth me.

Lord, I would clasp Thy hand in mine,
Nor ever murmur nor repine,
Content, whatever lot I see,
Since 'tis my God that leadeth me.

And when my task on earth is done,
When by Thy grace, the victory's won,
E'en death's cold wave I will not flee,
Since God through Jordan leadeth me.

—Rev. Joseph H. Gilmore

Our Master

WE may not climb the heavenly steeps
  To bring the Lord Christ down;
In vain we search the lowest deeps,
  For Him no depths can drown.

But warm, sweet, tender, even yet
  A present help is He;
And faith has still its Olivet,
  And love its Galilee.

Through Him the first fond prayers are said
  Our lips of childhood frame;
The last low whispers of our dead
  Are burdened with His name.

O Lord and Master of us all,
  Whate'er our name or sign,
We own Thy sway, we hear Thy call,
  We test our lives by Thine!

—John G. Whittier

God's Goodness [1]

BE not dismayed, whate'er betide,
   God will take care of you;
Beneath His wing of love abide,
   God will take care of you.

Through days of toil when heart doth fail,
   God will take care of you;
When dangers fierce your path assail,
   God will take care of you.

All you may need He will provide,
   God will take care of you;
Nothing you ask will be denied,
   God will take care of you.

No matter what may be the test,
   God will take care of you;
Lean, weary one, upon His breast,
   God will take care of you.

God will take care of you,
   Through every day, o'er all the way;
He will take care of you,
   God will take care of you.

—*C. D. Martin*

[1] Copyright 1905 by John A. Davis.   Used by permission.

De Good Lawd Know My Name

I JES' don' know ef de kohn'll grow,
   But I plans hit jes' de same;
I jes' don' know ef de wind'll blow,
But I watch an' pray, an' I reap an' sow,
An' de sun he rise, an' de ribber flow,
   An' de good Lawd know my name.

I jes' can't tell ef de cotton sell,
   But I toils on jes' de same;
De birds they build where de spring sap swell,
An' dey know enough for a rainy spell,
An' dat's lots more than dey gwine to tell.—
   And de good Lawd know my name.

So I watch an' pray as I goes my way,
   An' I toils on jes' de same;
De rose is sweet, but de rose can't stay,
But I'm mighty glad when it blooms my way;
De night fall dark, but de Lawd send day,
   An' de good Lawd know my name.

—Frank L. Stanton

God's Sunshine [1]

N EVER once—since the world began,
   Has the sun ever stopped shining;
His face very often we could not see,
And we grumbled at His inconstancy,

[1] Used by permission of author.

But the clouds were really to blame, not He,
    For behind them he was shining.

And so—behind life's darkest clouds
    God's love is always shining;
We veil it at times with our faithless fears,
And darken our sight with our foolish tears,
But in time the atmosphere always clears,
    For His love is always shining.

—John Oxenham

Abide With Me

ABIDE with me: fast falls the eventide;
    The darkness deepens; Lord, with me abide:
When other helpers fail, and comforts flee,
Help of the helpless, oh, abide with me!

Swift to its close ebbs out life's little day;
Earth's joys grow dim, its glories pass away;
Change and decay in all around I see:
O Thou Who changeth not, abide with me!

I need Thy presence every passing hour:
What but Thy grace can foil the tempter's pow'r?
Who like Thyself my guide and stay can be?
Through cloud and sunshine, oh, abide with me!

I fear no foe with Thee at hand to bless;
Ills have no weight, and tears no bitterness;

Where is death's sting? where, grave, thy victory?
I triumph still, if Thou abide with me.

Hold Thou Thy cross before my closing eyes;
Shine through the gloom, and point me to the skies.
Heaven's morning breaks, and earth's vain shadows flee—
In life, in death, O Lord, abide with me!

—*Henry F. Lyte*

Some Time We'll Understand

NOT now, but in the coming years,
It may be in the better land,
We'll read the meaning of our tears,
And there, some time, we'll understand.

CHORUS
Then trust in God through all thy days;
Fear not! for He doth hold thy hand;
Though dark thy way, still sing and praise:
Some time, some time, we'll understand.

We'll catch the broken threads again,
And finish what we here began;
Heaven will the mysteries explain,
And then, ah, then, we'll understand.

We'll know why clouds instead of sun
Were over many a cherished plan;
Why song has ceased when scarce begun;
'Tis there, some time, we'll understand.

Why what we long for most of all
 Eludes so oft our eager hand;
Why hopes are crushed and castles fall,
 Up there, some time, we'll understand.

God knows the way, He holds the key,
 He guides us with unerring hand;
Some time with tearless eyes we'll see;
 Yes, there, up there, we'll understand.

—*Maxwell N. Cornelius, D.D.*

TRUTH

Truth Never Dies

TRUTH never dies. The ages come and go.
 The mountains wear away, the stars retire.
Destruction lays earth's mighty cities low;
 And empires, states and dynasties expire;
But caught and handed onward by the wise,
 Truth never dies.

Though unreceived and scoffed at through the years;
 Though made the butt of ridicule and jest;
Though held aloft for mockery and jeers,
 Denied by those of transient power possessed,
Insulted by the insolence of lies,
 Truth never dies.

It answers not. It does not take offense,
 But with a mighty silence bides its time;

As some great cliff that braves the elements
　　And lifts through all the storms its head sublime,
It ever stands, uplifted by the wise;
　　And never dies.

As rests the Sphinx amid Egyptian sands;
　　As looms on high the snowy peak and crest;
As firm and patient as Gibraltar stands,
　　So truth, unwearied, waits the era blest
When men shall turn to it with great surprise.
　　Truth never dies.

—Anon.

USEFULNESS

The Life That Counts

THE life that counts must toil and fight;
　　Must hate the wrong and love the right;
Must stand for truth by day and night:
　　This is the life that counts.

The life that counts must aim to rise
Above the earth to sunlit skies;
Must fix its gaze on Paradise—
　　That is the life that counts.

The life that counts must helpful be;
In darkest night make melody;
Must wait the dawn on bended knee—
　　This is the life that counts.

396

The life that counts must helpful be;
The cares and needs of others see;
Must seek the slave of sin to free—
    That is the life that counts.

                                    —*A. W. S.*

VICE

The Price He Paid [1]

I SAID I would have my fling,
    And do what a young man may:
And I didn't believe a thing
    That the parsons had to say.
I didn't believe in a God
    That gives us blood like fire,
Then flings us into hell because
    We answer the call of desire.

And I said: "Religion is rot,
    And the laws of the world are nil;
For the bad man is he who is caught
    And cannot foot his bill.
And there is no place called hell;
    And heaven is only a truth,
When a man has his way with a maid,
    In the fresh keen hour of youth.

"And money can buy us grace,
    If it rings on the plate of the church;

[1] Used by permission of the W. B. Conkey Co., Hammond, Ind.

And money can neatly erase,
    Each sign of a sinful smirch."
For I saw men everywhere,
    Hotfooting the road of vice:
And women and preachers smiled on them
    As long as they paid the price.

So I had my joy of life:
    I went the pace of the town;
And then I took me a wife,
    And started to settle down.
I had gold enough and to spare
    For all of the simple joys
That belong with a house and a home
    And a brood of girls and boys.

I married a girl with health
    And virtue and spotless fame.
I gave in exchange my wealth
    And a proud old family name.
And I gave her the love of a heart
    Grown sated and sick of sin!
My deal with the devil was all cleaned up,
    And the last bill handed in.

She was going to bring me a child,
    And when in labor she cried,
With love and fear I was wild—
    But now I wish she had died.
For the son she bore me was blind
    And crippled and weak and sore!

398

And his mother was left a wreck.
　　It was so she settled my score.

I said I must have my fling,
　　And they knew the path I would go;
Yet no one told me a thing
　　Of what I needed to know.
Folks talk too much of a soul
　　From heavenly joys debarred—
And not enough of the babes unborn,
　　By the sins of their fathers scarred.

—Ella Wheeler Wilcox

WAR

Somebody's Darling

INTO a ward of the whitewashed halls,
　　Where the dead and dying lay,
Wounded by bayonets, shells and balls,
　　Somebody's Darling was borne one day.
Somebody's Darling, so young and so brave,
　　Wearing yet on his pale, sweet face,
Soon to be hid by the dust of the grave,
　　The lingering light of his boyhood's grace.

Matted and damp are the curls of gold,
　　Kissing the snow of the fair young brow;
Pale are the lips of delicate mould—
　　Somebody's Darling is dying now.
Back from his beautiful blue-veined brow,

Brush all the wandering waves of gold;
Cross his hands on his bosom now—
Somebody's Darling is still and cold.

Kiss him once for somebody's sake,
  Murmur a prayer both soft and low;
One bright curl from his fair mates take—
  They were somebody's pride, you know;
Somebody's hand hath rested there—
  Was it a mother's soft and white?
And have the lips of a sister fair
  Been baptized in the waves of light?

God knows best! He has somebody's love;
  Somebody's heart enshrined him there;
Somebody wafted his name above,
  Night and morn, on the wings of prayer.
Somebody wept when he marched away,
  Looking so handsome, brave and grand,
Somebody's kiss on his forehead lay,
  Somebody clung to his parting hand.

Somebody's waiting and watching for him—
  Yearning to hold him again to her heart;
And there he lies with his blue eyes dim,
  And the smiling child-like lips apart.
Tenderly bury the fair young dead,
  Pausing to drop on his grave a tear
Carve in the wooden slab at his head:
  "Somebody's Darling lies sleeping here."

—Marie R. LaCoste

The Charge of the Light Brigade
At Balaklava

HALF a league, half a league,
  Half a league onward,
All in the valley of death,
  Rode the six hundred.

Into the valley of death
  Rode the six hundred;
For up came an order which
  Some one had blundered.
"Forward, the light brigade!
Take the guns!" Nolan said:
Into the valley of death,
  Rode the six hundred.

"Forward the light brigade!"
No man was there dismayed—
Not though the soldier knew
  Some one had blundered:
Theirs not to make reply,
Theirs not to reason why,
Theirs but to do and die—
Into the valley of death,
  Rode the six hundred.

Cannon to right of them,
Cannon to left of them,
Cannon in front of them,
  Volleyed and thundered.
Stormed at with shot and shell,

Boldly they rode and well;
Into the jaws of death,
Into the mouth of hell,
    Rode the six hundred.

Flashed all their sabres bare,
Flashed all at once in air,
Sabring the gunners there,
Charging an army, while
    All the world wondered.
Plunged in the battery smoke,
With many a desperate stroke
The Russian line they broke;
Then they rode back, but not—
    Not the six hundred.

Cannon to right of them,
Cannon to left of them,
Cannon behind them,
    Volleyed and thundered:
Stormed at with shot and shell,
While horse and hero fell,
They that had fought so well,
Came through the jaws of death,
Back from the mouth of hell,
All that was left of them
    Left of six hundred.

When can their glory fade?
Oh, the wild charge they made!
    All the world wondered.
Honor the charge they made!

Honor the Light Brigade,
Noble six hundred!

—*Alfred Tennyson*

Bingen On The Rhine

A SOLDIER of the Legion lay dying in Algiers,
There was lack of woman's nursing, there was
dearth of woman's tears;
But a comrade stood beside him, while his life-blood ebbed
away,
And bent, with pitying glances, to hear what he might say.
The dying soldier faltered, and he took that comrade's
hand,
And he said, "I nevermore shall see my own, my native
land;
Take a message, and a token, to some distant friends of
mine,
For I was born at Bingen,—at Bingen on the Rhine.

"Tell my brothers and companions, when they meet and
crowd around,
To hear my mournful story, in the pleasant vineyard
ground,
That we fought the battle bravely, and when the day was
done,
Full many a corse lay ghastly pale beneath the setting sun;
And mid the dead and dying, were some grown old in
wars,—
The death-wound on their gallant breasts, the last of
many scars;

And some were young, and suddenly beheld life's morn decline,

And one had come from Bingen,—fair Bingen on the Rhine.

"Tell my mother that her other son shall comfort her old age;

For I was still a truant bird that thought his home a cage;

For my father was a soldier, and even as a child,

My heart leaped forth to hear him tell of struggles fierce and wild;

And when he died, and left us to divide his scanty hoard,

I let them take whate'er they would; but kept my father's sword;

And with boyish love I hung it where the bright light used to shine,

On the cottage wall at Bingen,—calm Bingen on the Rhine.

"Tell my sister not to weep for me, and sob with drooping head,

When the troops come marching home again with glad and gallant tread,

But to look upon them proudly with a calm and steadfast eye,

For her brother was a soldier too, and not afraid to die;

And if a comrade seek her love, I ask her in my name,

To listen to him kindly, without regret or shame,

And to hang the old sword in its place, (my father's sword and mine,)

For the honor of old Bingen—dear Bingen on the Rhine.

"There's another—not a sister; in the happy days gone by
You'd have known her by the merriment that sparkled
    in her eye;
Too innocent for coquetry—too fond for idle scorning,—
O friend, I fear the lightest heart makes sometimes heavi-
    est mourning!
Tell her the last night of my life (for, ere the moon be
    risen,
My body will be out of pain, my soul be out of prison),
I dreamed I stood with *her,* and saw the yellow sunlight
    shine
On the vine-clad hills of Bingen,—fair Bingen on the
    Rhine.

"I saw the blue Rhine sweep along,—I heard, or seemed
    to hear
The German songs we used to sing, in chorus sweet and
    clear;
And down the pleasant river, and up the slanting hill,
The echoing chorus sounded, through the evening calm and
    still;
And her glad blue eyes were on me, as we passed, with
    friendly talk,
Down many a path beloved of yore, and well-remembered
    walk!
And her little hand lay lightly, confidingly in mine,
But we'll meet no more at Bingen,—loved Bingen on the
    Rhine."

His trembling voice grew faint and hoarse his grasp was
    childish, weak,—

His eyes put on a dying look,—he sighed and ceased to
speak.

His comrade bent to lift him, but the spark of life had
fled,—

The soldier of the legion in a foreign land is dead!

And the soft moon rose up slowly, and calmly she looked
down

On the red sand of the battle-field, with bloody corses
strewn;

Yes, calmly on that dreadful scene her pale light seemed to
shine,

As it shone on distant Bingen,—fair Bingen on the Rhine.

—Caroline E. Norton

The Destruction of Sennacherib

THE Assyrian came down like the wolf on the fold,
And his cohorts were gleaming in purple and gold;
And the sheen of their spears was like stars on the sea,
When the blue wave rolls nightly on deep Galilee.

Like the leaves of the forest when summer is green,
That host with their banners at sunset were seen;
Like the leaves of the forest when autumn hath blown,
That host on the morrow lay withered and strown.

For the Angel of Death spread his wings on the blast,
And breathed in the face of the foe as he passed;
And the eyes of the sleepers wax'd deadly and chill,
And their hearts but once heaved, and for ever grew still!

And there lay the steed with his nostril all wide,
But through it there roll'd not the breath of his pride;
And the foam of his gasping lay white on the turf,
And cold as the spray of the rock-beating surf.

And there lay the rider distorted and pale,
With the dew on his brow and the rust on his mail;
And the tents were all silent, the banners alone,
The lances unlifted, the trumpet unblown.

And the widows of Ashur are loud in their wail;
And the idols are broke in the temple of Baal;
And the might of the Gentile, unsmote by the sword,
Hath melted like snow in the glance of the Lord.

—*Lord Byron*

General Joseph Warren's Address

(At the Battle of Bunker Hill)

STAND! the ground's your own, my braves!
  Will ye give it up to slaves?
Will ye look for greener graves?
  Hope ye mercy still?
What's the mercy despots feel?
Hear it in that battle peal!
Read it on yon bristling steel!
  Ask it, ye who will!

Fear ye foes who kill for hire?
Will ye to your homes retire?

407

Look behind you! they're afire!
And before you, see
Who have done it! From the vale
On they come!—and will ye quail?
Leaden rain and iron hail
Let their welcome be!

In the God of battles trust!
Die we may, and die we must;
But, oh, where can dust to dust
Be consigned so well
As where heaven its dews shall shed
On the martyred patriot's bed?
And the rocks shall raise their head,
Of his deeds to tell.

—*John Pierpont*

The Night Before the Battle of Waterloo

THERE was a sound of revelry by night,
And Belgium's capital had gathered then
Her beauty and her chivalry, and bright
The lamps shone over fair women and brave men:
A thousand hearts beat happily; and when
Music arose with its voluptuous swell,
Soft eyes looked love to those which spake again
And all went merry as a marriage bell;
But hush! hark! a deep sound strikes like a rising knell!

Did ye not hear it?—No, 'twas but the wind,
Or the car rattling o'er the stony street:

On with the dance! let joy be unconfined:
No sleep till morn when youth and pleasure meet,
To chase the glowing hours with flying feet.
But hark that heavy sound breaks in once more,
As if the clouds its echo would repeat
And nearer, clearer, deadlier than before!
Arm! arm! it is—it is the cannon's opening roar!

Within a windowed niche of that high hall
Sate Brunswick's fated chieftain: he did hear
That sound the first amidst the festival,
And caught its tone with death's prophetic ear;
And when they smiled because he deemed it near,
His heart more truly knew that peal too well
Which stretched his father on a bloody bier
And roused the vengeance blood alone could quell:
He rushed into the field, and foremost fighting, fell.

Ah! then and there was hurrying to and fro,
And gathering tears and trembling of distress,
And cheeks all pale, which, but an hour ago,
Blushed at the praise of their own loveliness;
And these were sudden partings, such as press
The life from out young hearts, and choking sighs
Which ne'er might be repeated; who could guess
If ever more should meet those mutual eyes
Since upon night so sweet such awful morn could rise?

And there was mounting in hot haste: the steed,
The mustering squadron and the clattering car,
Went pouring forward with impetuous speed
And swiftly forming in the ranks of war;

And the deep thunder peal on peal afar;
And near, the beat of the alarming drum
Roused up the soldier ere the morning star;
While thronged the citizens with terror dumb
Or whispered with white lips, "The foe! They come! They
    come!"

                        —*Lord Byron*

Face To Face With Reality [1]

WHAT did you see out there, my lad,
    That has set that look in your eyes?
You went out a boy, you have come back a man,
With strange new depths underneath your tan.
What was it you saw out there, my lad,
    That set such deeps in your eyes?

"Strange things, and sad, and wonderful—
    Things that I scarce can tell;
I have been in the sweep of the Reaper's scythe,
    With God, and Christ, and hell.

"I have seen Christ doing Christly deeds;
    I have seen the devil at play;
I have gripped to the sod in the hand of God.
    I have seen the godless pray.

"I have seen Death blast out suddenly
    From a clear blue summer sky;
I have slain like Cain with a blazing brain,
    I have heard the wounded cry.

[1] Used by permission of the author.

410

"I have lain alone among the dead,
   With no hope but to die;
I have seen them killing the wounded ones,
   I have seen them crucify.

"I have seen the devil in petticoats
   Wiling the souls of men;
I have seen great sinners do great deeds
   And turn to their sins again.

"I have sped through hells of fiery hail,
   With fell red-fury shod;
I have heard the whisper of a voice,
   I have looked in the face of God."

You've a right to your deep, high look, my lad.
   You have met God in the ways,
And no man looks into His face
   But he feels it all his days.
You've a right to your deep, high look, my lad,
   And we thank Him for His grace.

—*John Oxenham*

The Blue and the Gray

BY the flow of the inland river,
   Whence the fleets of iron have fled,
Where the blades of the grave-grass quiver,
   Asleep are the ranks of the dead:—
      Under the sod and the dew

411

Waiting the Judgment Day:—
Under the one, the Blue;
Under the other, the Gray.

From the silence of sorrowful hours
  The desolate mourners go,
Lovingly laden with flowers,
  Alike for the friend and the foe:—
    Under the sod and the dew
    Waiting the Judgment Day:—
    Under the roses, the Blue;
    Under the lilies, the Gray.

Sadly, but not with upbraiding
  The generous deed was done.
In the storms of the years that are fading
  No braver battle was won:—
    Under the sod and the dew,
    Waiting the Judgment Day:—
    Under the blossoms, the Blue;
    Under the garlands, the Gray.

No more shall the war cry sever,
  Or the winding rivers be red:
They banish our anger forever
  When they laurel the graves of our dead!
    Under the sod and the dew,
    Waiting the Judgment Day:—
    Love and tears for the Blue;
    Tears and love for the Gray.

—Francis Miles Finch

412

In Flanders Fields

IN Flanders fields where poppies grow
  And where the crosses row by row
    Now mark our dead,
Sleeping beneath the silent sod,
A witness both to man and God
    That fear had fled.

The gates of death refuse to hide
The valor of our men who died
    In Freedom's fight;
Out from their graves in Flanders fields
The crimson soil a harvest yields.
    Sweet hope, glad peace and light.

—Adapted from **John D. McCrae.**

Man the Enemy of Man

THE hunting tribes of air and earth
  Respect the brethren of their birth;
Nature, who loves the claim of kind,
Less cruel chase to each assigned.
The falcon, poised on soaring wing,
Watches the wild-duck by the spring;
The slow-hound wakes the fox's lair;
The greyhound presses on the hare;
The eagle pounces on the lamb;
The wolf devours the fleecy dam;
Even tiger fell, and sullen bear,
Their likeness and their lineage spare.
Man, only, mars kind Nature's plan,

413

And turns the fierce pursuit on man;
Plying war's desultory trade,
Incursion, flight, and ambuscade,
Since Nimrod, Cush's mighty son,
At first the bloody game begun.

—Sir Walter Scott

Hohenlinden

ON Linden, when the sun was low,
  All bloodless lay the untrodden snow;
And dark as winter was the flow
  Of Iser, rolling rapidly.

But Linden saw another sight,
When the drum beat at dead of night,
Commanding fires of death to light
  The darkness of her scenery.

By torch and trumpet fast array'd,
Each horseman drew his battle-blade,
And furious every charger neigh'd,
  To join the dreadful revelry.

Then shook the hills, with thunder riven;
Then rushed the steed, to battle driven;
And, louder than the bolts of heaven,
  Far flash'd the red artillery.

But redder yet that light shall glow,
On Linden hills of stained snow;

And bloodier yet the torrent flow
　Of Iser, rolling rapidly.

'Tis morn; but scarce yon level sun,
Can pierce the war-clouds, rolling dun,
Where furious Frank and fiery Hun
　Shout in their sulph'rous canopy.

The combat deepens. On ye brave,
Who rush to glory, or the grave!
Wave, Munich, all thy banners wave,
　And charge with all thy chivalry!

Few, few shall part, where many meet!
The snow shall be their winding-sheet,
And every turf beneath their feet
　Shall be a soldier's sepulchre!

　　　　　　　　　　—Thomas Campbell

Bannockburn

Robert Bruce's Address to His Army

SCOTS, wha hae wi' Wallace bled,
　Scots, wham Bruce has aften led;
Welcome to your gory bed,
　Or to victory!

Now's the day, and now's the hour;
See the front o' battle lower;

See approach proud Edward's pow'r—
Chains and slavery!

Wha will be a traitor knave?
Wha would fill a coward's grave?
Wha sae base as be a slave?
  Let him turn and flee!

Wha for Scotland's King and law
Freedom's sword will strongly draw,
Free-man stand, or free-man fa'?
  Let him on wi' me!

By Oppression's woes and pains!
By your sons in servile chains!
We will drain our dearest veins,
  But they shall be free!

Lay the proud usurpers low!
Tyrants fall in every foe!
Liberty's in every blow!
  Let us do, or die!

—*Robert Burns*

Marco Bozzaris

AT midnight, in his guarded tent,
  The Turk was dreaming of the hour
When Greece, her knee in suppliance bent,
  Should tremble at his power:

416

In dreams through camp and court he bore
The trophies of a conqueror;
  In dreams his song of triumph heard;
Then wore his monarch's signet ring,—
Then pressed that monarch's throne,—a king;
As wild his thoughts, and gay of wing,
  As Eden's garden bird.

At midnight, in the forest shades,
  Bozzaris ranged his Suliote band,
True as the steel of their tried blades,
  Heroes in heart and hand.
There had the Persian thousands stood,
There had the glad earth drunk their blood
  On old Plataea's day;
And now there breathed that haunted air
The sons of sires who conquered there;
With arm to strike, and soul to dare,
  As quick, as far, as they.

An hour passed on,—the Turk awoke;
  That bright dream was his last;
He woke, to hear his sentries shriek—
  "To arms!—they come!—The Greek! the Greek!"
He woke, to die midst flame and smoke,
And shout, and groan, and saber stroke,
  And death shots falling thick and fast
As lightnings from the mountain cloud;
And heard, with voice as trumpet loud,
  Bozzaris cheer his band—
"Strike—till the last armed foe expires!
Strike—for your altars and your fires!

Strike—for the green graves of your sires!
  God, and your native land!"

They fought, like brave men, long and well;
  They piled the ground with Moslem slain;
They conquered; but Bozzaris fell,
  Bleeding at every vein.
His few surviving comrades saw
His smile, when rang their proud hurrah,
  And the red field was won;
Then saw in death his eyelids close
Calmly, as to a night's repose,
  Like flowers at set of sun.

Bozzaris! with the storied brave
  Greece nurtured in her glory's time,
Rest thee: there is no prouder grave,
  Even in her own proud clime.
  We tell thy doom without a sigh;
For thou art Freedom's now, and Fame's—
One of the few, the immortal names,
  That were not born to die!

                    —*Fitz-Greene Halleck*

Sheridan's Ride [1]

UP from the South at break of day,
  Bringing to Winchester fresh dismay,
The affrighted air with a shudder bore,
Like a herald in haste, to the chieftain's door,

[1] Courtesy J. B. Lippincott Company.

The terrible grumble, and rumble, and roar,
Telling the battle was on once more,
And Sheridan twenty miles away.

And wider still those billows of war
Thundered along the horizon's bar;
And louder yet into Winchester rolled
The roar of that red sea uncontrolled,
Making the blood of the listener cold,
As he thought of the stake in that fiery fray,
With Sheridan twenty miles away.

But there is a road from Winchester town,
A good, broad highway leading down;
And there, through the flush of the morning light,
A steed as black as the steeds of night
Was seen to pass, as with eagle flight;
As if he knew the terrible need,
He stretched away with his utmost speed;
Hills rose and fell; but his heart was gay,
With Sheridan fifteen miles away.

Still sprung from those swift hoofs, thundering South,
The dust, like smoke from the cannon's mouth;
Or the trail of a comet, sweeping faster and faster,
Foreboding to traitors the doom of disaster,
The heart of the steed and the heart of the master
Were beating like prisoners assaulting their walls,
Impatient to be where the battlefield calls;
Every nerve of the charger was strained to full play,
With Sheridan only ten miles away.

Under his spurning feet the road
Like an arrowy Alpine river flowed,
And the landscape sped away behind
Like an ocean flying before the wind,
And the steed, like a barque fed with furnace ire,
Swept on, with his wild eye full of fire.
But lo! he is nearing his heart's desire;
He is snuffing the smoke of the roaring fray,
With Sheridan only five miles away.

The first that the general saw were the groups
Of stragglers, and then the retreating troops;
What was done? What to do? A glance told him both,
Then, striking his spurs, with a terrible oath,
He dashed down the line 'mid a storm of huzzas,
And the wave of retreat checked its course there, because
The sight of the master compelled it to pause.
With foam and with dust the black charger was gray;
By the flash of his eye, and the red nostril's play,
He seemed to the whole great army to say,
"I have brought you Sheridan all the way
From Winchester down to save the day!"

Hurrah! Hurrah for Sheridan!
Hurrah! Hurrah for horse and man!
And when their statues are placed on high,
Under the dome of the Union sky,
The American soldier's Temple of Fame;
There with the glorious general's name,
Be it said, in letters both bold and bright,
   "Here is the steed that saved the day,

By carrying Sheridan into the fight,
From Winchester, twenty miles away!"

—*Thomas Buchanan Read*

The Battle of Ivry

NOW glory to the Lord of hosts, from whom all glories
are!
And glory to our Sovereign Liege, King Henry of Navarre!
Now let there be the merry sound of music and of dance,
Through thy corn-fields green, and sunny vines, oh pleas-
ant land of France!
And thou, Rochelle, our own Rochelle, proud city of
the waters,
Again let rapture light the eyes of all thy mourning
daughters.
As thou wert constant in our ills, be joyous in our joy,
For cold, and stiff, and still are they who wrought thy
walls annoy.
Hurrah! hurrah! a single field hath turned the chance of
war,
Hurrah! hurrah! for Ivry, and King Henry of Navarre.

Oh! how our hearts were beating, when at the dawn of
day
We saw the army of the League drawn out in long array;
With all its priest-led citizens, and all its rebel peers,
And Appenzel's stout infantry, and Egmont's Flemish
spears.
There rode the brood of false Lorraine, the curses of our
land!

And dark Mayenne was in the midst, a truncheon in his
hand!
And as we looked on them, we thought of Seine's em-
purpled flood,
And good Coligni's hoary hair all dabbled with his blood;
And we cried unto the living God, who rules the fate of
war,
To fight for His own holy name, and Henry of Navarre.

The King is come to marshal us, in all his armour drest,
And he has bound a snow-white plume upon his gallant
crest.
He looked upon his people, and a tear was in his eye;
He looked upon the traitors, and his glance was stern and
high.
Right graciously he smiled on us, as rolled from wing to
wing,
Down all our line, a deafening shout, "God save our Lord
the King!"
"And if my standard-bearer fall, as fall full well he may,
For never saw I promise yet of such a bloody fray,
Press where ye see my white plume shine, amidst the
ranks of war,
And be your oriflamme to-day the helmet of Navarre."

Hurrah! the foes are moving. Hark to the mingled din
Of fife, and steed, and trump and drum, and roaring
culverin!
The fiery Duke is pricking fast across Saint André's plain,
With all the hireling chivalry of Guelders and Almayne.
Now by the lips of those ye love, fair gentlemen of France,

Charge for the Golden Lilies now—upon them with the lance!

A thousand spurs are striking deep, a thousand spears in rest,

A thousand knights are pressing close behind the snow-white crest;

And in they burst, and on they rushed, while, like a guiding star,

Amidst the thickest carnage blazed the helmet of Navarre.

Now, God be praised, the day is ours! Mayenne hath turned his rein.

D'Aumale hath cried for quarter. The Flemish Count is slain.

Their ranks are breaking like thin clouds before a Biscay gale;

The field is heaped with bleeding steeds, and flags, and cloven mail;

And then, we thought on vengeance, and, all along our van,

"Remember St. Bartholomew," was passed from man to man;

But out spake gentle Henry, "No Frenchman is my foe:

Down, down with every foreigner, but let your brethren go."

Oh! was there ever such a knight, in friendship or in war,

As our Sovereign Lord King Henry, the soldier of Navarre!

Ho! maidens of Vienna! Ho! matrons of Lucerne!

Weep, weep, and rend your hair for those who never shall return.

Ho! Philip, send, for charity, thy Mexican pistoles,
That Antwerp monks may sing a mass for thy poor spear-
men's souls!
Ho! gallant nobles of the League, look that your arms be
bright!
Ho! burghers of Saint Genevieve, keep watch and ward
to-night!
For our God hath crushed the tyrant, our God hath raised
the slave,
And mocked the counsel of the wise, and the valour of
the brave.
Then glory to His holy name, from whom all glories are;
And glory to our Sovereign Lord, King Henry of Navarre.

—*Lord Macaulay*

The Armada

ATTEND, all ye who list to hear our noble England's
praise;
I sing of the thrice famous deeds she wrought in ancient
days,
When that great fleet invincible, against her bore, in vain,
The richest spoils of Mexico, the stoutest hearts in Spain.

It was about the lovely close of a warm summer's day,
There came a gallant merchant ship full sail to Plymouth
bay;
The crew had seen Castile's black fleet, beyond Aurigny's
isle,
At earliest twilight, on the waves, lie heaving many a mile.
At sunrise she escaped their van, by God's especial grace;

And the tall Pinta, till the noon, had held her close in
    chase.
Forthwith a guard, at every gun, was placed along the
    wall;
The beacon blazed upon the roof of Edgecombe's lofty
    hall;
Many a light fishing bark put out, to pry along the coast;
And with loose rein, and bloody spur, rode inland many
    a post.

With his white hair, unbonnetted, the stout old sheriff
    comes,
Behind him march the halberdiers, before him sound the
    drums:
The yeomen, round the market cross, make clear and
    ample space,
For there behooves him to set up the standard of her
    grace:
And haughtily the trumpets peal, and gaily dance the
    bells,
As slow upon the labouring wind the royal blazon swells.
Look how the lion of the sea lifts up his ancient crown,
And underneath his deadly paw treads the gay lilies
    down!
So stalked he when he turned to flight, on that famed
    Picard field,
Bohemia's plume, and Genoa's bow, and Cæsar's eagle
    shield:
So glared he when, at Agincourt, in wrath he turned to
    bay,
And crushed and torn, beneath his claws, the princely
    hunters lay.

Ho! strike the flagstaff deep, sir knight! ho! scatter
  flowers, fair maids!
Ho, gunners! fire a loud salute! ho, gallants! draw your
  blades!
Thou, sun, shine on her joyously! ye breezes, waft her
  wide!
Our glorious *semper eadem!* the banner of our pride!

  The fresh'ning breeze of eve unfurled that banner's
    massy fold—
The parting gleam of sunshine kissed that haughty scroll
  of gold:
Night sunk upon the dusky beach, and on the purple sea;
Such night in England ne'er had been, nor ne'er again
  shall be.
From Eddystone to Berwick bounds, from Lynn to Mil-
  ford bay,
That time of slumber was as bright, as busy as the day;
For swift to east, and swift to west, the warning radiance
  spread—
High on St. Michael's Mount it shone—it shone on
  Beachy Head:
Far o'er the deep the Spaniard saw, along each southern
  shire,
Cape beyond cape, in endless range, those twinkling points
  of fire.
The fisher left his skiff to rock on Tamar's glittering
  waves,
The rugged miners poured to war, from Mendip's sunless
  caves;
O'er Longleat's towers, o'er Cranbourne's oaks, the fiery
  herald flew,

And roused the shepherds of Stonehenge—the rangers of
    Beaulieu.
Right sharp and quick the bells rang out all night from
    Bristol town;
And, ere the day, three hundred horse had met on
    Clifton Down.

The sentinel on Whitehall gate looked forth into the
    night,
And saw, o'erhanging Richmond Hill, that streak of
    blood-red light:
The bugle's note, and cannon's roar, the death-like silence
    broke,
And with one start, and with one cry, the royal city woke;
At once, on all her stately gates, arose the answering
    fires;
At once the wild alarum clashed from all her reeling
    spires;
From all the batteries of the Tower pealed loud the voice
    of fear,
And all the thousand masts of Thames sent back a louder
    cheer:
And from the farthest wards was heard the rush of
    hurrying feet,
And the broad streams of flags and pikes dashed down
    each rousing street:
And broader still became the blaze, and louder still
    the din,
As fast from every village round the horse came spurring
    in;
And eastward straight, for wild Blackheath, the warlike
    errand went;

And roused, in many an ancient hall, the gallant squires
of Kent:

Southward, for Surrey's pleasant hills, flew those bright
coursers forth;

High on black Hampstead's swarthy moor, they started
for the north;

And on, and on, without a pause, untired they bounded
still;

All night from tower to tower they sprang, all night from
hill to hill;

Till the proud peak unfurled the flag o'er Derwent's rocky
dales;

Till, like volcanoes, flared to heaven the stormy hills of
Wales;

Till, twelve fair counties saw the blaze on Malvern's
lonely height;

Till streamed in crimson, on the wind, the Wrekin's crest
of light;

Till, broad and fierce, the star came forth, on Ely's stately
fane,

And town and hamlet rose in arms, o'er all the boundless
plain;

Till Belvoir's lordly towers the sign to Lincoln sent,

And Lincoln sped the message on, o'er the wide vale of
Trent;

Till Skiddaw saw the fire that burnt on Gaunt's embattled
pile,

And the red glare on Skiddaw roused the burghers of
Carlisle.

—Lord Macaulay

The Battle of Blenheim

IT was a summer evening,
  Old Kaspar's work was done;
And he before his cottage door
  Was sitting in the sun,
And by him sported on the green
His little grandchild Wilhelmine.

She saw her brother Peterkin
  Roll something large and round,
That he beside the rivulet,
  In playing there, had found;
He came to ask what he had found,
That was so large, and smooth, and round.

Old Kaspar took it from the boy,
  Who stood expectant by;
And then the old man shook his head,
  And with a natural sigh,
'Tis some poor fellow's skull, said he,
Who fell in the great victory.

I find them in the garden, for
  There's many here about,
And often when I go to plough
  The ploughshare turns them out;
For many thousand men, said he,
Were slain in the great victory.

Now tell us what 'twas all about,
  Young Peterkin he cries,

And little Wilhelmine looks up
    With wonder-waiting eyes;
Now tell us all about the war,
And what they kill'd each other for.

It was the English, Kaspar cried,
    That put the French to rout;
But what they kill'd each other for,
    I could not well make out.
But everybody said, quoth he,
That 'twas a famous victory.

My father lived at Blenheim then,
    Yon little stream hard by;
They burnt his dwelling to the ground,
    And he was forced to fly:
So with his wife and child he fled,
Nor had he where to rest his head.

With fire and sword the country round
    Was wasted far and wide,
And many a childing mother then,
    And new-born infant, died.
But things like that, you know, must be
At every famous victory.

They say it was a shocking sight,
    After the field was won,
For many thousand bodies here
    Lay rotting in the sun;
But things like that, you know, must be
After a famous victory.

Great praise the Duke of Marlbro' won,
  And our good Prince Eugene.—
Why, 'twas a very wicked thing!
  Said little Wilhelmine.—
Nay—nay—my little girl, quoth he,
It was a famous victory.

And everybody praised the Duke
  Who such a fight did win.—
But what good came of it at last?
  Quoth little Peterkin.—
Why that I cannot tell, said he,
But 'twas a famous victory.

                              —*Robert Southey*

The Burial of Sir John Moore

NOT a drum was heard, not a funeral note,
  As his corse to the rampart we hurried;
Not a soldier discharged his farewell shot
  O'er the grave where our hero we buried.

We buried him darkly at dead of night,
  The sods with our bayonets turning;
By struggling moonbeams's misty light,
  And the lantern dimly burning.

No useless coffin enclosed his breast,
  Not in sheet nor in shroud we wound him;
But he lay like a warrior taking his rest,
  With his martial cloak around him.

                       431

Few and short were the prayers we said,
  And we spoke not a word of sorrow;
But we steadfastly gazed on the face that was dead,
  And we bitterly thought of the morrow.

We thought as we hollowed his narrow bed,
  And smoothed down his lonely pillow,
That the foe and the stranger would tread o'er his head,
  And we far away on the billow!

Lightly they'll talk of the spirit that's gone,
  And o'er his cold ashes upbraid him,—
But little he'll reck, if they let him sleep on
  In the grave where a Briton has laid him.

But half our heavy task was done,
  When the clock struck the hour for retiring;
And we heard the distant and random gun
  That the foe was sullenly firing.

Slowly and sadly we laid him down,
  From the field of his fame fresh and gory;
We carved not a line, and we raised not a stone—
  But we left him alone with his glory.

                              —*Rev. Charles Wolfe*

War!

O HEAR ye that foul and fiendish laughter
  Ascending from the depths of hell!
In conclave plot for our disaster

The foulest of the demons fell.
The plot's arranged—the work is done—
Then hie they to their malicious fun:
They stir two nations into strife,
As we might stir two foolish curs;
And while they fight, the demons fife
And cast at them their leering slurs.
They send the evil of contention
To move the spirit of the just,
Nor suffer they the least suspension
Of this blood-thirst of mortal dust;
And often in an angel's guise
They draw a veil o'er Christians' eyes,
Nor suffer to desist.

'Tis strange that generals are called "great,"
And lauded with a hero's fame,
Who win by driving on to fate
A million of our noblest men.
'Tis strange that nations should be termed
"Christian," "civilized" and "learned,"
Whose citizens so barbarous are
As to turn homicides in war,
And on the slightest provocation
Make tiger-like retaliation;
But 'tis true!

—*J. Gilchrist Lawson*

WATER

Famous Toast To Water

John B. Gough, famous and eloquent temperance lecturer, during an address in the Young Men's Christian Association in Boston, seized a tumbler of water from the table and holding it up to the view of all, uttered the following historic toast:

"LOOK at that, ye thirsty ones of earth! Behold it! See its purity! How it glitters as if a mass of liquid gems! It is a beverage brewed by the hands of the Almighty Himself! Not in the simmering still, over smoky fires, choked with poisonous gases, and surrounded by the stench of sickening odors and rank corruptions, doth your Father in heaven prepare the precious essence of life—the pure, cold water—but in the green glade and grassy dell, where the red deer wanders and the child loves to play— there God brews it; and down, down, down in the deepest valleys, where the fountains murmur and rills sing; and high up the tall mountain tops, where the naked granite glitters like gold in the sun, where the storm clouds brood, and the thunderstorms crash; and away far out on the wide sea, where the hurricanes howl music and the waters roar the chorus, sweeping the march of God—there He brews it, that beverage of life, health-giving water! And everywhere it is a thing of beauty, gleaming in the dew-drop; singing in the summer rain; shining in the ice gem till all the trees seem turned to living jewels, spreading a golden veil over the setting sun or a white gauze over the midnight moon; sporting in the cataracts; sleeping in the glaciers; dancing in the hail shower; folding its bright cur-

434

tains softly about the wintry world; and weaving the many colored iris, that seraph's zone of the sky whose warp is the raindrop of earth, whose woof is the sunbeam of heaven, all checkered over with celestial flowers by the mystic hand of refraction—still always it is beautiful, that blessed life-water. No poison bubbles on its brink; its form brings no sadness or murder; no blood stains its limpid glass; broken-hearted wives, pale widows and starving children shed no tears in its depths; no drunkard's shrieking ghost from the grave curses it in the words of eternal despair—beautiful, pure, blessed and glorious, forever the same, sparkling, pure water!"

Beautiful Water

WATER is ever changing; it is the "poetry of motion." It hastens to the sea, but the sea cannot retain it; it floats in the clouds and falls to earth again in refreshing showers. To him that hath eyes and ears it speaks a varied language. It patters on the roof, it bubbles in the spring, it gushes in the streamlet, it splashes in the pool, it sings in the mountain brook, it dances in the cascades, it laughs in the cataract, it ripples in the lake, it weeps in the storm, it surges in the sea and roars in the ocean. It has been the world's music since the dawn of creation, and will be until the end of time on earth.

In the geysers water seethes, boils, hisses, spouts and plays all sorts of whimsical tricks. In the glaciers, icebergs and snowy peaks of the mountains it is wondrously beautiful. It haloes the moon, paints the hues of the rainbow and sunsets and forms the beauties of the mystic cloud land. With the frost crystals it draws fantastic pictures on the window panes, and its frozen dewdrops sparkle like diamonds in the light of the early morning. Aided by the south wind and sunshine, it makes the grass grow, the flowers bloom and the trees to bud and bear fruit. With the north wind it covers the trees with silvery coats of ice, and with the snow crystals it weaves old Mother Earth a new white dress, in which she appears pure and innocent, although she has drunk the blood of many of her sons in battle; and it furnishes skating and sleighing for those who delight in outdoor recreations.

As this beautiful, working force of Nature flows gracefully down the river to the sea it furnishes water power which is utilized in promoting our commercial enterprises; when heated into steam it turns the wheels that move the world along in its rush for supremacy, both in times of war and peace; and it is (of itself) the great broad highway upon which the world's traffic is transported.

Pure, clear, cold, sparkling, crystal water! It relieves pain, it quenches the fevered thirst, it is life-giving, without it nothing could live, it is the emblem of purity, it cleanses the world. Study it to be wise, drink it to be strong, sing its praises to be free from rum's awful curse.

Water is composed of two gases, oxygen and hydrogen. It contains no poison that intoxicates the brain and causes delirium. It never drives women and children homeless and friendless into the streets. Our prisons are not filled with its victims; it doesn't rob the nation of its manhood; it does not "regulate" our elections by fraud; it never cost the American people two thousand million dollars in one year. Water is innocent of all crime. It is one of God's free gifts, found in all zones; the supply is

world-wide. It was "Adam's ale;" let it be our drink,
for the Lord made nothing better.

—George K. Edwards

WOMEN

Women Men's Shadows

FOLLOW a shadow, it still flies you,
    Seem to fly it, it will pursue:
So court a mistress, she denies you;
Let her alone, she will court you.
Say are not women truly, then,
Styled but the shadows of us men.

—Ben Jonson

WORRY

Don't Trouble Trouble

DON'T you trouble trouble till trouble troubles you.
    Don't you look for trouble; let trouble look for you.
Who feareth hath forsaken the heavenly Father's side;
What He hath undertaken He surely will provide.

The very birds reprove thee with all their happy song;
The very flowers teach thee that fretting is a wrong.
"Cheer up," the sparrow chirpeth; "Thy Father feedeth
    me;
Think how much He careth, oh, lonely child, for thee."

437

"Fear not," the flowers whisper; "since thus He hath
    arrayed
The buttercup and daisy, how canst thou be afraid?"
Then don't you trouble trouble till trouble troubles you;
You'll only double trouble, and trouble others too.

—Mark Guy Pearse

The Town of Don't-You-Worry

THERE'S a town called Don't-You-Worry,
    On the banks of River Smile,
Where the Cheer-up and Be Happy
    Blossom sweetly all the while.
Where the Never-Grumble flower
    Blooms beside the fragrant Try,
And the Ne'er-Give-Up and Patience
    Point their faces to the sky.

—Anon.

Index of First Lines

439

442

One step at a time, and that well placed, 196

One sweetly solemn thought, 158

On June 15, 1215, King John met, 193

On Linden, when the sun was low, 414

Others weary of the noise, 246

Po' lil' brack sheep dat strayed away, 144

Precious thought, my Father knoweth, 382

Putting God in the Nation's life, 140

Rest is not quitting the busy career, 332

Ring out, wild bells, to the wild sky, 258

Rocked in the cradle of the deep, 380

Scots, wha hae wi' Wallace bled, 415

Seated one day at the organ, 249

She was not as pretty as women I know, 151

Smile and the world smiles with you, 340

Somebody said that it couldn't be done, 319

Some day, some happy day, 311

Some leaders lead too far ahead, 192

Some one started the whole day wrong,—was it you? 27

Some people think I think I'm good, 52

Somewhat back from the village street, 366

Stand! the ground's your own, my braves! 407

Sunset and evening star, 107

Sure, this world is full of trouble, 29

Sweet hour of prayer! sweet hour of prayer! 330

Sweet Solitude, thou placid queen, 351

Tell me not, in mournful numbers, 194

Thank God for the country; the vast stretch of land, 56

The Assyrian came down like the wolf on the fold, 406

The boneless tongue, so small and weak, 68

The boy stood on the burning deck, 234

The bravest battle that ever was fought, 241

The bread that bringeth strength I want to give, 146

The breaking waves dashed high, 58

The curfew tolls the knell of parting day, 89

The heavens declare the glory of God, 136

The hours I spent with thee, dear heart, 200

The hunting tribes of air and earth, 413

The life that counts must toil and fight, 396

The little cares that fretted me, 251

The Lord had a job for me, but I had so much to do, 120

The Lord's my shepherd; I'll not want, 379

The man who seeks one thing in life, and but one, 356

The melancholy days are come, 1

The night has a thousand eyes, 204

The quality of mercy is not strained, 239

There are hermit souls that live withdrawn, 225

There are lonely hearts to cherish, 172

There are loyal hearts, there are spirits brave, 153

443

445

Index of Titles

446

447

448

451

Index of Authors

453

454

455